RAISING THE BAR AND CLOSING THE GAP

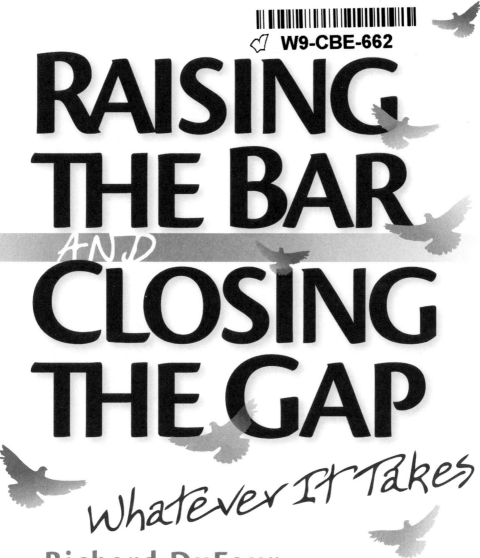

Whatever It Takes

Richard DuFour
Rebecca DuFour
Robert Eaker
Gayle Karhanek

Solution Tree | Press

a division of

Solution Tree

555 North Morton Street
Bloomington, IN 47404

800.733.6786 (toll free) / 812.336.7700
FAX: 812.336.7790

email: info@solution-tree.com
solution-tree.com

Visit **go.solution-tree.com/PLCbooks** to download materials related to this book.

Printed in the United States of America

13 12 11   4 5

Library of Congress Cataloging-in-Publication Data

Raising the bar and closing the gap : whatever it takes / Richard DuFour ... [et al.].

p. cm.

Includes bibliographical references and index.

ISBN 978-1-935249-84-9 (perfect bound) -- ISBN 978-1-935249-85-6 (library binding) -- ISBN 978-1-935249-99-3 (perfect bound institute edition) 1. Effective teaching--United States. 2. School improvement programs--United States. 3. Educational change--United States. 4. Learning. I. DuFour, Richard, 1947-

LB1025.3.R35 2010

371.102--dc22

2009037636

Solution Tree

Jeffrey C. Jones, CEO & President

Solution Tree Press

President: Douglas M. Rife
Publisher: Robert D. Clouse
Vice President of Production: Gretchen Knapp
Managing Production Editor: Caroline Wise
Senior Production Editor: Suzanne Kraszewski
Proofreader: Elisabeth Abrams
Text and Cover Designer: Orlando Angel

I dedicate this book to the heroic educators who persist in their quest to do something that no group of educators, in any country, at any point in history, has been able to do: help all students learn at high levels. In what other enterprise are people called upon to achieve so much with so little? In what other field would people continue to work so hard on behalf of others in a system designed to ensure they will ultimately be labeled failures? I entered this profession forty years ago this year. I have never been more proud to be a member of it than I am today. So I dedicate this book to those who make education their calling as a small token of appreciation for how their own dedication serves as a source of continuing inspiration to me.

—Richard DuFour, 2009

I have been blessed throughout my life to be surrounded by many models of lifelong learners—parents, siblings, extended family, friends, and of course my wonderful husband, Rick. I dedicate this book, however, to my four living paternal aunts: Evelyn, Geraldine, Kathleen, and Helen.

Growing up at a time when fewer than 4 percent of American women had a college degree, each of my father's five sisters graduated from high school, three earned advanced degrees, and two ultimately received master's degrees in education and spent their careers making a positive difference in the lives of thousands of students. These four extraordinary women still maintain the century-old family farm in central Virginia and exemplify raising the bar and doing *whatever it takes* to live life to the fullest. They continue to serve as a source of inspiration to me, to my daughter, Hannah, who is just beginning her career as a school counselor, and to everyone else fortunate enough to know and love them.

—Rebecca DuFour, 2009

For the last three years, the administration, faculty, and staff of the White River School District in Buckley, Washington, have graciously allowed me to become part of the White River family and a constant companion on their journey to becoming a districtwide professional learning community. It has been an exciting experience for me, and I have learned much about reculturing an entire school district. I am appreciative of their support, encouragement, and, most of all, their friendship. My White River experience has convinced me more than ever in the power of the professional learning community concept and has renewed my faith in America's public schools. To everyone in White River, especially Superintendent Tom Lockyer and Deputy Superintendent Janel Keating, I offer my thanks and my sincere appreciation.

—Robert Eaker, 2009

To Nancy and Rich for their ongoing assistance, knowledge, support, and sense of humor; to Iona for her excellent preparation of the manuscript; and to all of the educators across America whose wisdom, dedication, and passion will continue to inspire me to share the intervention journey until every student achieves high school graduation.

—Gayle Karhanek, 2009

ACKNOWLEDGMENTS

We continue to be avid students of the work of the giants in educational reform in North America including Larry Lezotte, Doug Reeves, Rick Stiggins, Bob Marzano, Michael Fullan, Mike Schmoker, Tom Guskey, Dennis Sparks, and Jon Saphier. The friendship they have extended to us and their willingness to share their ideas, counsel, and thinking so freely have deepened our understanding of the elements of effective schooling.

Our team of professional learning community associates has now grown to over sixty exceptional educators throughout North America. The associates include some of the most outstanding educational leaders we have ever known. We are indebted to them not only because they were able to implement the PLC concept in their own schools and districts, but also because their work has deepened, enriched, and improved the concept. We have learned much from them. To find out more about this extraordinary group of educators, go to www.solution-tree.com and visit the PLC at Work professional development page.

Our relationship with Jeff Jones, president of Solution Tree, is entering its second decade. We could not ask for a more ardent or effective proponent of our work. Jeff has turned a once small publishing company into one of the leading providers of quality professional development in North America. In the process, he continues to attract wonderful people to Solution Tree. This book has benefited from the input and interest of Douglas Rife, president of Solution Tree Press and Gretchen Knapp, director of production. Once again, we relied on the skillful editing of Sue Kraszewski to make our ideas more clear and our prose more readable. It is difficult for us to imagine writing a book without her support and guidance. We also remain indebted to Shannon Ritz, the director of professional development for Solution Tree and our envoy and ally for almost a decade.

Finally, and most importantly, we wish to acknowledge the real heroes of this book: the teachers, principals, central office leaders, and superintendents who have joined forces to demonstrate that "learning for all" can be a collective commitment rather than a catch phrase. *Raising the Bar and Closing the Gap* could not have been written without the contributions and insights of Eric Twadell, Janet Gonzalez, Bernice Cobbs, Ray Myrtle, Lyn Rantz, Garrick Peterson, Bonnie Brasic, Tom Many, Sandy Thorstenson, Loring

Davies, Rich Russell, Nancy Bosserman, Marcus Johnson, and Rich Smith. Their passion for their work and their regard, admiration, and affection for their staffs were palpable as they described how their schools and districts are making a difference in the lives of students. We found their stories of collaborative cultures and collective effort to be not only informative but also inspirational. We sincerely hope that sharing their accomplishments will convince others in our profession to heed the words of the Oraibi elders of the Hopi Nation: "The time of the lone wolf is over. Gather yourselves. . . . We are the ones we have been waiting for" (2001, p. 1).

—Richard DuFour, Rebecca DuFour, Robert Eaker, and
Gayle Karhanek, 2009

Visit go.solution-tree.com/PLCbooks to download materials related to this book.

TABLE OF CONTENTS

About the Authors xi

Introduction 1

What Is a Professional Learning Community? 7

The Power of Stories 9

Creating the Conditions for Success 11

1 The Shifting Mission of Public Schooling:
    Establishing the Historical Context 13

From "All Students Can Learn" to "All Students Must Learn" 14

Yet Another Legislative Initiative: Response to Intervention (RTI) 16

The Need for Reform 21

2 Laying the Groundwork for Effective Intervention 23

The Team Learning Process 26

Focusing on the Right Work 33

Concluding Thoughts 35

3 Confronting the Brutal Facts:
    The Traditional Response to Students Who Do Not Learn 37

A Key Shift in Assumptions: Learning as the Constant—
    Time and Support as Variables 39

Providing Time and Support 41

Concluding Thoughts 43

4 Sustaining Excellence: A Return to Adlai Stevenson High School 45

A Look Back 45

Pre-Enrollment Initiatives 46

Coordinated Support for Students 49

Assisting All Students With the Transition to High School 50

Providing Extra Time and Support for Students Who Experience Difficulty 53

Enrichment at Adlai Stevenson High School 56

Raising the Bar Requires Increasing Support 60

Strengthening the Pyramid 61

But Is It Sustainable? 62

An Elegantly Simple Strategy 64

Concluding Thoughts 65

5 Hand in Hand We All Learn: A Return to Boones Mill Elementary School ... 67

A Critical First Step: Building Shared Knowledge of the Current Reality 68

Fostering Adult Learning so Students Can Learn 71

Aligning Resources With Purpose and Priorities 71

Connecting Special and General Education 77

Creating Systems of Communication 79

Boones Mill Today 80

Results 83

Concluding Thoughts 85

6 Embracing Systematic Intervention: Prairie Star Middle School 87

A Proactive Approach to Intervention 87

Laying the Groundwork 88

Intervention and Enrichment at Prairie Star 89

Building Relationships With a Caring Adult 90

Additional Layers of Support 91

The Need to Change Adult Practice 92

Results 96

Concluding Thoughts 98

7 Success and Triumph in a Worthy Endeavor: Lakeridge Junior High School ... 99

Intervention at Lakeridge 100

Making Time for Intervention 102

Reaching the Intentional Nonlearner 103

Building Staff Capacity to Function as a PLC 104

Results 106

Concluding Thoughts 108

8 From State Sanctions to National Recognition: Highland Elementary School 109

Creating the Schedule to Support Intervention 112

Reading Intervention at Highland Elementary School 114

Results 117

Concluding Thoughts 119

9 Building Toward the F.U.T.U.R.E.: Cinco Ranch High School 121

A Focus on Freshmen 121

Laying the Groundwork for Intervention 122

Intervention at Cinco Ranch High School 123

Technology as an Accelerator of the PLC Journey 124

Results   126

Concluding Thoughts   128

10 From Good to Great: Implementation of PLC Concepts
   in Kildeer Countryside Community Consolidated School District 96   129

Systematic Intervention in District 96   132

PACE   135

Attention Is All There Is   136

Results   137

Concluding Thoughts   139

11 Whatever It Takes—Staying the Course: Whittier Union High School District   141

The Whittier Union Journey   141

Dispersing Leadership   143

Promoting Prevention   146

Systematic Intervention at Whittier   147

Results   148

Concluding Thoughts   150

12 Under No Circumstances Blame the Kids: Sanger Unified School District   151

Systems of Interventions in Sanger   153

Developing Principals as Leaders   155

Administrative Retreats   158

Ongoing Support and Focus   159

Results   160

Concluding Thoughts   162

13 "Yah, but . . .": Considering Challenges to Systematic Intervention   163

Pragmatic Concerns   163

Philosophical Concerns   165

Concluding Thoughts   177

14 Finding Common Ground: The Shared Practices
   of Highly Effective Schools and Districts   179

Clarity of Purpose   180

Collaborative Culture   181

Collective Inquiry Into Best Practice and Current Reality   181

Action Orientation   182

Commitment to Continuous Improvement   183

Focus on Results   184

Strong Leaders Who Empower Others
   (Simultaneous Loose and Tight Leadership) 185

Concluding Thoughts 190

**15 Whatever It Takes: How Effective Schools and Districts Overcome
Barriers to Systematic Intervention and Enrichment** 193

Stevenson High School 193

Boones Mill Elementary 196

Prairie Star Middle School 198

Lakeridge Junior High 198

Kildeer Countryside 199

Whittier Union 200

Sanger Unified 200

A Universal Issue: Not Everyone Initially Embraces the PLC Process 201

Concluding Thoughts 206

16 Changing the Culture of Schooling to Embrace Effort-Based Enrichment 207

The Growth Mindset 210

Enrichment in a Professional Learning Community: Beyond Proficiency 212

How Many Schools Would It Take? 215

Concluding Thoughts 220

17 Moving Forward: Planning for Effective Intervention 221

Questions to Guide Planning 221

Building Momentum by Planning for Short-Term Wins 224

From Planning to Doing 226

A Final Analogy 227

Concluding Thoughts 228

Resources 229

References 229

Index 237

ABOUT THE AUTHORS

Richard DuFour, Ed.D., is recognized as a leader in helping school practitioners apply the principles of professional learning communities in their schools. During his tenure as superintendent of Adlai Stevenson High School District 125 in Lincolnshire, Illinois, Stevenson became one of the most recognized and celebrated high schools in America.

Rick received his state's highest award as both a principal and superintendent and was presented the Distinguished Alumni Award of Illinois State University, the Distinguished Scholar Practitioner Award of the University of Illinois, and the Distinguished Service Award from the National Staff Development Council. He has coauthored ten books and more than seventy-five professional articles. He developed the video series on the principalship for the Association for Supervision and Curriculum Development and was a featured columnist for the *Journal of Staff Development* for almost a decade. He is an active consultant with school districts, state departments of education, and professional organizations throughout North America.

Rebecca DuFour, M.Ed., is a former elementary school principal who helped her school earn state and national recognition as a model professional learning community. Becky is one of the featured principals in the Video Journal of Education program *Leadership in the Age of Standards and High Stakes* (2001). She is also the lead consultant and featured principal for the Video Journal of Education production of *Elementary Principals as Leaders of Learning* (2003) and is featured in three other videos on professional learning communities produced by Solution Tree Press. Becky is coauthor of seven books and has written for numerous professional journals. She is an active consultant with school districts, state departments of education, and professional organizations throughout North America.

Robert Eaker, Ed.D., has been associated with Middle Tennessee State University for more than thirty-seven years as a professor, dean of the Department of Education, executive vice president, and provost. He is a former fellow with the National Center for Effective Schools Research and Development. He has written widely on the issues of effective teaching, effective schools, helping teachers use research findings, and high expectations and student achievement. Bob is coauthor of ten books and numerous professional journal articles. Bob is an active consultant with school districts, state departments of education, and professional organizations throughout North America.

Gayle A. Karhanek, M.Ed., M.A., worked as director of student services at Adlai Stevenson High School in Lincolnshire, Illinois, from 1979 to 2004. As architect of the Adlai Stevenson pyramid of interventions, Gayle has worked with educators across the United States to create the foundational structures necessary to ensure that students are guaranteed systematic access to viable interventions that address their academic, behavioral, and social-emotional needs. She is an active consultant whose passion comes from the results she has seen once schools become professional learning communities and are committed to answering the question, what do we do when students don't learn?

INTRODUCTION

I believe we are closer than ever in knowing what must be done to engage all classrooms and schools in continuous reform. Knowing what must be done . . . is not the same as getting it done.
                                                                                    —MICHAEL FULLAN, 2007

We will know we have succeeded when the absence of a "strong professional learning community" in a school is an embarrassment.
                                                                                    —MIKE SCHMOKER, 2004

In our writings on professional learning communities (PLCs) that have spanned more than a decade, we have challenged educators to confront the question, what happens in our school when, despite our best efforts in the classroom, a student does not learn? We have contended that traditionally the response to that question has been left to the discretion of individual teachers, leading to a kind of educational lottery for students. We continue to argue that this individualistic and random approach is neither effective nor equitable. We insist that a school committed to helping all students learn at high levels should provide a multilayered *collective* response that *guarantees* all students who struggle will receive additional time and support for learning. We propose that a school sincerely interested in the learning of each student should actually have a plan for monitoring that learning and a comprehensive pyramid of interventions for responding promptly, consistently, and effectively when some students do not learn. In short, a school that purports to be a PLC should be able to answer in the affirmative to the following questions about its response to students who experience difficulty:

- Is our response based upon **intervention** rather than remediation? Does our plan provide students with additional time and support for learning as soon as they experience difficulty rather than rely on remediation—summer school, retention, remedial courses—when students fail to meet a standard at the conclusion of a course or grade level?

- Is our response **timely**? How quickly are we, as a school, able to identify students who need additional time and support? How often do we ask, "How do we know if our students are not learning?" And how quickly are we able to respond when a student has been identified as in need of additional help?

- Is our response **directive**? Do we *invite* students to seek additional help, or does our systematic plan *require* students to receive the additional assistance and devote the extra time necessary to master the concept? A decade of research into the "things that matter most" in raising student achievement found that schools that improve the most insist students get extra help whenever there is evidence that those students are having difficulty in learning (Bottoms, 1998).

- Is our response **systematic**? Have we created processes that ensure we respond to students according to a schoolwide plan rather than according to the discretion of individual teachers? Are procedures in place to monitor the execution of the plan? Are all staff members aware of the procedures? Do we provide consistent responses if asked to explain the steps our school takes when students have difficulty in learning?

We have raised these same issues in our previous books as we have attempted to:

- Persuade educators to confront the brutal facts regarding how schools have traditionally been organized and how they have responded when students experience difficulty

- Examine the historical antecedents and continuing assumptions behind the way schools are structured

- Make a compelling case that a new conceptual framework, the professional learning community, is needed if schools are to help all students learn

- Provide specific recommendations regarding the conceptual framework and how it can be implemented in schools, tools and resources to assist with implementation, and clear parameters and benchmarks for monitoring progress

- Clarify the new roles, responsibilities, and relationships that educators must embrace if their schools are to operate as PLCs

- Explain how such vital activities as curriculum implementation, assessment, and professional development are addressed in a PLC

- Offer detailed illustrations of how different schools have implemented the PLC concept at the elementary, middle, and high school levels

- Examine arguments that are often made to oppose the PLC concept and offer suggestions for responding to those arguments and building consensus for moving forward

- Alert educators to the shortcuts and compromises that weaken the effectiveness of the PLC concept

- Identify the cultural shifts that are necessary to support this fundamental change in the way schools should operate, and offer advice regarding how to shape school culture

In *Whatever It Takes: How Professional Learning Communities Respond When Kids Don't Learn* (DuFour, DuFour, Eaker, & Karhanek, 2004), we specifically explored the question of what happens when students don't learn. We provided a case study of how four schools dramatically impacted student achievement by designing effective systems of interventions. This book, *Raising the Bar and Closing the Gap*, serves as the sequel to *Whatever It Takes*. In it, we hope to reiterate, reinforce, and expand upon the ideas we have traditionally presented by exploring the following questions:

1 **Is the PLC improvement process sustainable?**

Educational expert Michael Fullan is fond of saying that improvement in individual schools can usually be attributed to serendipity or luck. An effective principal comes to a school with a receptive staff, and the magic that occurs is brief and fleeting. As key leaders depart, the improvement initiative grinds to a halt, and the school returns to business as usual.

In *Whatever It Takes* we told the story of four schools that had used the professional learning community concept to bring about dramatic improvement in student learning. Each of the four has undergone significant changes in leadership since we wrote about them in 2004, but each has sustained and improved upon its record of extraordinary student achievement. After experimenting with a coprincipalship for a few years, Los Peñasquitos in the Poway, California, school district appointed a new principal, yet its Academic Performance Index continues to improve every year, and it remains in the top 10 percent of elementary schools in California. Clara Sale-Davis is no longer the principal of Freeport Intermediate in Brazosport, Texas, yet the school continues as a model of a high-poverty, high-minority school that has eliminated the achievement gap. With 70 percent minority and 77 percent of its students living in poverty, the school continues to outperform the state in every subject and every grade level. In 2008, Freeport Intermediate earned Recognized status from the Texas Department of Education and was presented with the state's Gold Performance

Acknowledgement Award for student achievement in reading, language arts, writing, and social studies.

In this book, we return to two of the schools we featured in *Whatever It Takes* to examine once again the intervention and enrichment processes they put in place and to consider how those processes have impacted student achievement since 2004. Adlai Stevenson High School in suburban Chicago has had three different principals and two different superintendents since 2004, yet it remains one of the premier high schools in the United States. Boones Mill Elementary School in Franklin County, Virginia has also had three different principals and two different superintendents since 2004, and yet it continues to win state and national recognition. In brief, we posit that the achievement of these schools cannot be attributed to luck or the charisma of a single leader, but must be attributed to systematic processes that have been implemented and *sustained* in those schools. Like Fullan, we will argue that it is not changes in leadership, but changes in direction that interfere with sustained improvement. We offer specific advice regarding how schools and districts can develop the capacity of staff to make continuous improvement a fundamental part of the culture of their organizations.

2   Is this improvement process transferable?

It is becoming more difficult for educators to deny the power of the PLC concept by dismissing the success of other schools with the explanation, "But that school is not like ours." While every school is unique to some extent, schools of all kinds throughout North America, representing very different communities and diverse student populations, have demonstrated the benefits of a commitment to high levels of learning for all students, the collaborative culture and collective effort vital to that learning, and the ongoing monitoring of learning essential to improving professional practice and responding to students who experience difficulty. In this book we explore the practices of schools at different grade levels, from different parts of the country, serving very different student populations to consider how they have transferred the research base on best practice and the experience of other schools to become some of the best schools in North America.

There are now over 150 schools recognized as model PLCs at www.allthingsplc.info that we could have highlighted in this book. We have been particularly inspired by the extraordinary achievement of elementary schools like Victoria Elementary in Costa Mesa, California; Westview Elementary and Graham Road Elementary in Fairfax County, Virginia; Elizabeth Vaughan Elementary in Prince

William County, Virginia; R.H. Dana Elementary in Dana Point, California; Chaparral Elementary in Ladera Ranch, Calfornia; Virgina Murray Elementary in Albemarle County, Virginia; and William Velasquez Elementary in Richmond, Texas. These schools serve as models of what middle schools can be: Margaret Mead Middle School in Schaumburg, Illinois; Eisenhower Junior High School in Hoffman Estates, Illinois; and Overland Trail Middle School in Overland Park, Kansas. Riverside-Brookfield High School in Riverside, Illinois; Granby High School in Granby, Connecticut; Papillion-LaVista South High School in Papillion, Nebraska; Francis Howell High School in St. Charles, Missouri; Chardon High School in Chardon, Ohio, and Eastview High School in Apple Valley, Minnesota demonstrate that high schools can function as high-performing PLCs. We would have been pleased to tell the story of each of these schools if space permitted, and we offer them as examples of what educators can accomplish.

3   What is the role of the central office in promoting the professional learning community concept throughout a district?

Most of our early work focused exclusively on how individual schools apply the professional learning community concept. In recent years, we have become much more aware of the critical role the central office can play in building the capacity of staff in schools throughout the district to function as PLCs. In this book we devote three chapters to case studies that examine how three different school districts have created the expectation that all the schools in their districts would operate as professional learning communities.

One of the most gratifying aspects of writing this book was the number of districts we could have featured. We focus on schools from districts in Montgomery County, Maryland; Blue Valley, Kansas; Orem, Utah; and Katy, Texas; but we could have easily focused on the entire district rather than a single school. We could have chosen to feature Schaumburg District 54 in suburban Chicago, Fairfax County Public Schools in Virginia, Brevard County Public Schools in Florida, Albemarle County Public Schools in Virginia, Fort Leavenworth School District in Kansas, the White River School District in Washington, or Granby Public Schools in Connecticut—all of which have experienced gains in student achievement after embracing and implementing the PLC concept. If that concept is to become the norm in all schools of a district rather than part of the feel-good story of the occasional isolated school, central office leaders must play a major role in the transition.

4   **How should we enrich and extend the learning of students who are proficient?**

In *Whatever It Takes* we focused intensively on students who experienced academic difficulty. We stressed the importance of three critical questions that educators must work collaboratively to address: 1) exactly what is it we want all students to learn, 2) how will we know when each student has acquired the essential knowledge and skills, and 3) what happens in our school when a student does not learn? We argued that attention to ensuring all students learn would benefit all students and that more students would achieve at the highest levels. Our work with districts convinced us, however, that we were not sufficiently attentive to the issue of how schools might systematically extend and enrich the learning of students who were already proficient. We address this fourth question in this book and illustrate how the effective implementation of the PLC concept not only closes the gap for students who have historically struggled in our schools but also raises the achievement bar for *all* students.

5   **What prerequisite framework must be put in place for schools to create effective intervention and enrichment systems?**

Creating effective intervention and enrichment systems must be part of a larger cultural transformation of a school. Our experience with school improvement has demonstrated that educators often fail to fully appreciate the comprehensive change that must occur. Those who regard creating a system of interventions and enrichment as a task to accomplish or as a mere addendum to their existing practices will not have significant impact on student achievement. Furthermore, if educators merely focus on creating systems of interventions without also addressing strategies to improve the professional practice of teachers individually and collectively, it is unlikely that the system of interventions will have the desired effect on student achievement. No system of interventions can compensate for weak and ineffective teaching. In this book we attempt to be very explicit about the prerequisite work a school must address and the structures that must be in place as part of the process of creating powerful interventions and enrichment.

6   **How have the changes in national educational policy impacted the premise that schools should have a systematic plan for responding to the learning needs of students?**

We have addressed No Child Left Behind (NCLB) in the books we have written since its passage. Although there was a great deal in the legislation that troubled us initially, we enthusiastically supported the legislation's underlying premise that educators should be committed to ensuring the learning of all students. As we write this book, the Obama administration has taken office and the future of NCLB is somewhat cloudy. We are hopeful that the onerous parts of the legislation will be modified, and the focus on learning for all students sustained. We contend, however, that the commitment to help all students learn is a moral imperative, not a legal one, and that educators must embrace that commitment regardless of whether they are legally bound to do so.

Another significant legislative initiative speaks directly to the premise we have articulated regarding a well-designed plan to provide a collective and systematic response to students who experience difficulty. The Individuals with Disabilities Education Improvement Act (IDEIA) legislation of 2004 has dramatically altered how schools are to respond when students do not learn. The response to intervention (RTI) component of that legislation not only aligns with, but actually mirrors, the call for a pyramid of interventions that we have advocated in our work. We will address the connection between RTI and the professional learning community concept in this book. For those seeking a fuller examination of the regulation and its relationship to the principles of PLCs, we highly recommend the outstanding book *Pyramid Response to Intervention* authored by our friends and colleagues Austin Buffum, Mike Mattos, and Chris Weber (2009).

What Is a Professional Learning Community?

In his research on high-performing organizations, Jim Collins (2001) found that great organizations "simplify a complex world into a single organizing idea, a basic principle, or concept that unifies and guides everything" (p. 91). Noel Tichy (1997) came to a similar conclusion, arguing that effective organizations establish a few "big ideas" or overriding principles that unite people in the pursuit of a shared purpose, common goals, and clear direction. In our recent work we have attempted to simplify the complexities of the PLC concept into three big ideas.

The first (and biggest) of the big ideas that drives the work of schools and districts that operate as PLCs is straightforward: the fundamental purpose of the school is to ensure that all students *learn* rather than to see to it that all students are *taught*—an enormous distinction. This emphasis on learning leads those within the school and district to concentrate their effort and energy on four critical questions:

1 What is it we want all students to learn—by grade level, by course, and by unit of instruction?

2 How will we know when each student has *learned*—that is, has acquired the knowledge, skills, and dispositions deemed essential?

3 How will we respond when students experience initial difficulty in their learning?

4 How will we enrich and extend the learning for students who are already proficient?

The intense focus on these questions helps educators develop a shared sense of the school they hope to create to better fulfill the purpose of learning for all. Educators, then, move the school toward that shared vision by articulating the collective commitments they will make to each other and to their students in order to create their ideal school. They establish specific, measurable goals to serve as targets and timelines that monitor their progress on their journey. They align the practices and procedures of their schools with the fundamental purpose of learning for all students. This shared purpose (or mission), clear direction (or vision), collective commitments (or values), and specific indicators of progress (or goals) bind the members of a PLC together in a common cause. They represent the very foundation of a PLC.

The second big idea guiding a PLC is that helping all students learn requires a collaborative culture and a collective effort. Therefore, educators will be organized into collaborative teams in which members work interdependently to achieve a common goal for which they hold themselves mutually accountable: learning for all students. Teachers must work together rather than in isolation to address the four critical questions.

The third big idea is that schools will be unable to monitor their effectiveness in helping all students learn unless they create a results orientation. In a PLC educators are constantly gathering evidence of student learning to inform and improve their professional practice. They use common assessments and make results from those assessments easily accessible and openly shared among members of the team in order to build on individual and team strengths and to identify and address areas of concern. And, very importantly, they use results to identify students who are experiencing difficulty and need additional time and support for learning as well as students who are highly proficient and require enrichment and extension. In his fifteen-year study of over 800 meta-analyses relating to student achievement, two of John

Hattie's (2009) most emphatic conclusions were that teacher reflection about the impact of instruction must be done *collaboratively* and that it must be based on *evidence* of the impact of their teaching on student learning.

Leading educational researchers and the professional organizations serving educators recognize the power of the PLC concept to transform schools and help educators meet the unprecedented demands confronting them. (Visit www.allthingsplc.info to review the consensus recognizing the PLC concept as the most promising strategy for sustained, substantive school improvement.)

If educators based their programs, policies, and decisions on evidence of best practice or the recommendations of their professional organizations, these big ideas would be deeply embedded in every school and district. Unfortunately, schools that operate according to these principles remain the exception rather than the rule. It is not a lack of evidence that interferes with their adoption, but rather the fact that these ideas run counter to the traditional stories educators have told themselves about the nature of their work.

The Power of Stories

Richard Axelrod (2002) wrote, "Universities come to know about things through studies, organizations come to know about things through reports, and people come to know about things through stories. . . . Storytelling is an ancient form of passing wisdom, the most ancient form of knowing" (p. 112). While we certainly concur with his position that stories have represented a powerful tool for shaping individual thinking and behavior in all cultures throughout history, we also contend that stories have a major impact on organizations and the people within them.

All organizations have stories—typically unexamined assumptions, beliefs, and interpretations of experience that help members create a vision of perceived reality, explain how things "ought" to be, and specify "the way we do things around here." Organizational change thus becomes the process of shifting the story the people in the organization accept as true (Gardner & Laskin, 1996; Senge, Kleiner, Roberts, Ross, & Smith, 1994). This shift, however, is extremely difficult, "even when the stories we use to understand reality are not just obsolete but destructive" (James, 2008). As the founder of Leadership Now explains:

> We develop patterns of thought or mental models that shape what we "see" or "perceive" and thus what we think and how we will choose to think about

> new information that comes our way. We persist in or hold on to thinking that connects with the mental pictures or mental models we have already formed in our mind. . . . Call it a persistence of thought. We see what makes sense to us. We form a picture of ourselves and develop beliefs and opinions around what is consistent with what is already there in our heads. Anything that is inconsistent with that image or contrary to our current ideas or thinking, seems to go unnoticed or is consciously ignored. (McKinney, 2005)

Implementing the big ideas of a PLC will require educators to engage in the difficult work of revising their stories. The premise that the purpose of the school is to ensure all students learn means abandoning the historical origins of schooling in this country. Public schools were not created to help all students learn at high levels, but were specifically intended to sort and select students according to their innate ability and presumed vocations. If educators are to help all students achieve at high levels, they will need to replace the mantra of "it is our job to teach, but it is their job to learn" with a commitment to do "whatever it takes."

If schools are to create collaborative cultures where people work interdependently to achieve goals for which members are mutually accountable, educators will need to break down the walls of isolation they have created in their institutions. They will need to place a higher value on equity, effectiveness, and mutual accountability for the success of all students than they do on their personal autonomy.

If schools are to be results-oriented, educators must stop considering the primary purpose of assessment as assigning grades to assist in the sorting and selecting process and must begin using assessment to inform and improve their practice and respond to the needs of their students. In brief, in order to make the changes that are necessary to meet the extraordinary challenges schools are facing, educators at all levels will need to change both their traditional practices and the assumptions that drive those practices.

As Jennifer James (2008) cautions, "It becomes very hard to adapt, to tell new stories, the ones you need to fit into the new world, if you cannot take apart the old stories." Therefore, we have attempted to examine some of the old stories that must be addressed if schools are to meet the unprecedented challenges of the twenty-first century. Furthermore, we have provided illustrations of important distinctions between traditional schools and PLCs through the vehicle of new stories about schools, districts, and the practices of educators that we hope will resonate with school practitioners.

We remain convinced that the professional learning community concept offers the best strategy for connecting educators to the moral imperative of their work. It is our hope that this book and the inspirational stories that it presents will encourage educators throughout North America to align the practices of their own schools and districts with this powerful concept so they might better fulfill the moral imperative of making a positive difference in the lives of the students they serve.

Creating the Conditions for Success

Diane Ravitch (2007), the former United States Under Secretary of Education, concluded that the task confronting contemporary American educators is not merely difficult; it is impossible. As she points out, no nation or state has ever achieved 100 percent proficiency for all of its students, and to create a system that will eventually label every school a "failure" that is unable to achieve the unattainable is likely to breed resignation and a sense of hopelessness on the part of educators. Rosabeth Moss Kanter (2004) describes these twin elements of despair—resignation and lack of self-efficacy—as the primary pathologies that prevent people and organizations from solving problems and improving their situations. As she wrote, "When people become resigned to their fate, nothing ever changes. When people are surrounded by the feeling that they are the victims of uncontrollable forces around them—they drag others down with them, finding the worst in everything, or resisting other people's ideas but offering none of their own" (p. 256).

We have witnessed this resignation in some of the schools in which we have worked. When faced with ever-higher standards and no additional support for achieving those standards, students who have struggled in school are not inevitably disposed to redouble their efforts. They are, in fact, more inclined to conclude school does not offer them a place to find a sense of accomplishment or self-worth. When educators working in isolation conclude it is impossible to meet either the incredibly diverse needs of their students or the goals imposed upon them by others, they are less likely to demonstrate the confidence, persistence, and resilience essential to sustained improvement.

The antidote to such despair is hope, which Snyder (1991) defines as "believing you have the will and the way to accomplish your goals, whatever they might be" (p. 579). But instilling hope requires more than pleasant affirmations and a sunny disposition. Furthermore, while hope is an important personal attribute, it is not an effective organizational strategy. Organizations can, however, foster hope, optimism, and collective self-efficacy when they create systems that put people in the position to achieve success. As Pfeffer and Sutton (2006) observed, "Wide-ranging research . . . shows it is impossible for even the most talented people to do competent, let alone brilliant, work in a flawed system. Yet a well-designed system filled with ordinary—but well-trained—people can consistently achieve stunning performance levels" (p. 96). We are convinced that the problems of education are not caused by uncaring or incompetent educators, but rather by the ineffective system in which they work. In the coming chapters we examine an alternative system—the professional learning community—and expose some of the stunning results educators who work within that system are achieving.

> **Visit go.solution-tree.com/PLCbooks to download materials related to this book.**

THE SHIFTING MISSION OF PUBLIC SCHOOLING: ESTABLISHING THE HISTORICAL CONTEXT

> Think about every problem, every challenge we face. The solution to each starts with education. For the sake of the future—of our children and the nation—we must reform America's schools.
>
> —GEORGE H. W. BUSH, 1991

> Many groups fall prey to what is known as "collective conservatism": the tendency of groups to stick to established patterns even as new needs arise.
>
> —RICHARD THALER & CASS SUNSTEIN, 2008

Contemporary American educators are not only being asked to do something that their predecessors never considered—ensuring all students learn at high levels—but they are also attempting to meet this challenge in institutions that were specifically designed to achieve a fundamentally different purpose. The United States was the first nation to embrace the idea of free universal public education for all of its children; however, historically those children have been guaranteed only the right to attend school, not the right to learn. In fact, the prevalent assumption that has driven public education throughout most of the history of the United States is that few students are capable of high levels of learning.

The idea that a student's education should reflect his or her innate ability and socioeconomic status went largely unchallenged for almost all of American history. Researchers provided evidence to support the conventional wisdom that differences in student achievement were not a function of the quality of schooling students received, but instead merely reflected their aptitude and environment. A report published in 1966 titled "Equality in Educational Opportunity" concluded that schools had little influence on a child's achievement that was independent of the background and social context of that student (Coleman et al., 1966). Six years later another study reported that a student's achievement was primarily a function of his or her background, that schools did little to lessen the gap between more and less able students, and that there was little evidence to suggest school reform had any impact on student achievement (Jenks et al., 1972).

In the last quarter of the twentieth century, however, researchers began to establish that what happens in schools can have a major impact on student achievement. Ron Edmonds (1982), Larry Lezotte (2004), Michael Rutter (1979), and Wilbur Brookover (1979) were among the researchers who provided evidence that achievement among students from similar backgrounds varied significantly based on the practices of their schools. In his analysis of research conducted over thirty-five years, Robert Marzano (2003) concluded not only that schools have a significant impact upon student achievement, but also that "schools that are highly effective produce results that almost entirely overcome the effects of student backgrounds" (p. 7).

The effective schools research challenged the long-standing belief that only those who had won the genetic lottery were capable of high levels of learning. Compelling evidence was presented to support two bold new premises: first, "all students can learn," and second, "schools control the factors necessary to assure student mastery of the core curriculum" (Lezotte, 2004, p. 1).

The assertion that all students can learn became the rallying cry for schools throughout North America. Because the research had identified a clear and focused mission as one of the correlates of effective schools, schools and districts throughout the continent labored over the development and word-smithing of their own mission statements. Although created in thousands of different school communities across the continent, these statements came to sound very much alike because they all reflected the premise that all children can learn. Yet even as educators were congratulating themselves on their enlightened mission statements promising to help all students achieve at high levels, they often continued with traditional policies, programs, and practices that virtually guaranteed all students would not learn. The long-standing belief that high levels of learning were reserved for the few, and the structures that had been put in place to support that belief, were not to be overcome simply by drafting a new mission statement.

From "All Students Can Learn" to "All Students Must Learn"

As we wrote in *Revisiting Professional Learning Communities at Work* (DuFour, DuFour, & Eaker, 2008), the history of public education in the United States is basically the history of repeated attempts to transform schooling in this country as "Americans have translated their cultural anxieties and hopes into dramatic demands for educational reform" (Tyack & Cuban, 1995, p. 1). In the past fifty years the notion that the nation's system is broken and needs to be fixed has been a recurring political theme; the launching of Sputnik, the publication of *A Nation at Risk* (National Commission on Excellence in Education, 1983), and the Governors' Summit that created Goals 2000 are just some of the events that fueled the call for the overhauling of American schools.

When George W. Bush came to office in 2001, the reform of education was once again brought to the forefront as he made it the first item on his domestic agenda. His reform initiative, commonly referred to as No Child Left Behind (NCLB), passed Congress with strong bipartisan support. The law ramped up testing requirements, mandating annual assessments in reading and mathematics in grades 3 through 8 and once in high school; called for reporting student test results separately by race, ethnicity, and other key demographic groups; and required schools to demonstrate adequate yearly progress (AYP) on state tests for each group of students. If schools could not demonstrate AYP, they faced interventions followed by increasingly severe sanctions. The law also stipulated that students could transfer to schools that performed better or receive tutoring if their schools did not demonstrate sufficient progress, required states to ensure that every teacher was "highly qualified," and mandated detailed reports to parents on school performance and teacher quality. Finally, the law designated annual increases in the percentage of students achieving proficiency on the state assessment until 2014, when the poor performance of a single student would designate the entire school as "failing."

The law was clearly the most ambitious educational initiative in American history. As one report concluded, "NCLB has affected families, classrooms and school districts throughout the country. Virtually every aspect of schooling—from what is taught in elementary, middle and high school classes, to how teachers are hired, to how money is allocated—has been affected by the statute" (Commission on No Child Left Behind, 2007, p. 14).

The NCLB legislation certainly added a new dimension to the discussion about what happens when students do not learn. The legislation threatened schools and their educators with escalating sanctions if they failed to meet newly imposed standards. The rationale behind this approach suggests that educators have always known how to help all kids learn but have been too disinterested in the welfare of their students or too lazy to put forth the necessary effort. Fear is needed to provide the necessary motivation—either perform or risk closing your school and/or losing your job.

We believe this premise is fundamentally flawed. First, we believe that educators, in general, have the best interests of their students at heart and are willing to work very, very hard in the effort to help all students be successful. In fact, we contend that there are few, if any, occupations in which people work harder than educators. Second, the idea that people can be threatened or coerced into higher performance runs contrary to what is universally recognized as best practice for leading organizations. Fear may produce some short-term efforts, but it is ineffective at generating the sustained motivation necessary to transform a school into a PLC. As Fullan (2006) contends, reforms based on sanctions and external pressure and control may help a school move from awful to adequate, but they work on only a small part of the problem, violate everything known about change processes that lead to sustainable reform, cause the best teachers to abandon a "failing" school, and actually create conditions that guarantee the improvements will not be sustained. The NCLB threat to continue the beatings until morale improves seems unlikely to create the energy and enthusiasm for the difficult work at hand.

The motivation behind NCLB legislation has been widely debated. Proponents portray the initiative as a sincere attempt to guarantee that every child, particularly poor and minority students, receives an education that leads to high levels of learning. Opponents contend the legislation is unrealistic and/or simplistic at best or a thinly veiled attempt to dismantle the public system of education at worst. We offer a detailed analysis of NCLB and the arguments for and against the legislation in *Revisiting Professional Learning Communities at Work* (DuFour, DuFour, & Eaker, 2008).

As President Barack Obama took office, the future of NCLB was much in doubt. By mid-2007, nearly two-thirds of American adults preferred the law be rewritten or abolished. The more familiar people were with the law, the more likely they were to oppose it (Hargrove & Stempel, 2007). Although President Obama has been critical of some of the specific applications of NCLB and the way in which it has been funded, he has repeatedly said the goals of the legislation are correct and that the nation's commitment to helping all students learn at high levels must not be diminished. It appears that contemporary American educators will continue to be called upon to achieve a standard that goes far beyond the goals of any previous generation—high levels of learning for all students.

Yet Another Legislative Initiative: Response to Intervention (RTI)

The idea that schools should respond when students are not learning is certainly not new. In fact, the legislation that established special education was enacted, in part, to meet the needs of students who were not learning. In 1975, the Education for All Handicapped Children Act (Public Law 94-142) made it illegal to exclude students with disabilities from public schools and required schools to serve those students in "the least restrictive environment." The initial intent of the legislation was to "move children with disabilities from institutions into classrooms, from the outskirts of society to the center of class instruction. . . [to give] children who were once ignored. . . unprecedented access to a free appropriate public education" (President's Commission on Excellence in Special Education, 2002, p. 3).

Twenty-five years later, however, only 10 percent of special education students in the United States fall into the categories of sensory impaired (such as visually or hearing impaired) or physically and neurologically disabled (such as orthopedic impairment or traumatic brain injury). The remaining 90 percent of students in special education can be categorized as having developmental disabilities such as specific learning disabilities (SLD), speech and language impairment, emotional disturbance, or developmental delay. Almost half of the students identified as eligible for special education fall into the category of specific learning disability, and the number of students with that designation has grown by more than 300 percent in the past quarter century. Eighty percent of those students were identified as having specific learning disabilities "simply because they *haven't learned how to read*" (President's Commission on Excellence in Special Education, 2002, p. 3).

A commission convened by President George W. Bush to assess the status of special education in the United States offered a stinging critique. Some of its findings are as follows:

- **A culture of compliance**—The commission concluded that fear of litigation over the morass of complex special education rules and regulations had created a culture that "placed process above results, and bureaucratic compliance above student achievement, excellence and outcomes" (p. 7). It criticized the excessive paperwork and inordinate administrative demands of special education regulations that diverted both energy and attention from the mission of ensuring students actually learn.

- **Reliance upon a discrepancy model**—The commission was particularly critical of what it described as the "antiquated discrepancy model" that waited for children to fail before providing services instead of a model based on prevention and intervention. This "wait to fail" model required schools to demonstrate a discrepancy between the student's actual achievement and his or her ability as determined by a formal administration of measures of intelligence, typically an IQ test. The commission blasted the reliance on IQ discrepancy, contending "there is little justification for the ubiquitous use of IQ tests . . . given their cost and the lack of evidence that IQ tests are related meaningfully to intervention outcomes" (p. 25). It called for driving "a stake through the heart of the discrepancy model for determining the kinds of students who need service" (p. 25) and replacing that model with a focus on early identification of and immediate support for students who were experiencing difficulty.

- **Overidentification of students with specific learning disabilities (SLD)**—The commission was also critical of the highly subjective, ambiguous criteria being used to identify students with specific learning disabilities. As it concluded, "The lack of consistently applied diagnostic criteria for SLD makes it possible to diagnose almost any low- or under-achieving child as SLD" (p. 24). The commission also expressed concern that the federal funding for special education students provided financial incentives for districts to identify students as eligible for special education and to isolate them from the general program. It was convinced that many students placed in special education were "essentially instructional casualties and not students with disabilities" (p. 26).

- **The separation of special education and general education**—The commission lamented the fact that educators tended to regard special education and general education as separate worlds rather than pooling their efforts and resources to support the learning of all students. In too many cases, the commission found classroom teachers and administrators absolved themselves from responsibility for student learning and assumed that the task of addressing the needs of unsuccessful students fell to the special education program.

- **Lack of results**—Finally, the commission cited the lack of evidence that students were benefitting from special education as the most compelling argument for reform. It argued that too often special education had been a dead end for students rather than a gateway to better instruction and effective intervention. It presented statistics showing that special education students were far more likely to leave school without a diploma and to be unemployed or underemployed than students in the general education program.

The commission presented three general recommendations for reforming special education in the United States. First, it called for a focus on results rather than process—to shift the emphasis of special education from compliance with regulations to a commitment to discover and utilize the best practices for helping all students to learn. Second, it stressed the need to replace the discrepancy model of waiting for students to fail before identifying them for services with early identification and swift intervention in order to prevent failure. Third, it called for a unified effort of general education and special education educators and greater flexibility in the use of funds, including those provided through the Individuals with Disabilities Education Act (IDEA), so that the comprehensive resources of the school could be utilized to meet the needs of all students.

The recommendations of the President's Commission on Excellence in Special Education were ultimately enacted into law with the passage of the Individuals with Disabilities Education Improvement Act (IDEIA) in December of 2004. Schools are now called upon to implement a systematic response to intervention (RTI) to meet the needs of all students. The National Center on Response to Intervention (2006) defines RTI as "an organizational framework for instructional and curricular decisions and practices based upon students' responses . . . [a process to] integrate assessment and intervention within a multi-level prevention system to maximize student achievement and to reduce behavior problems" (pp. 7, 8).

The National Center explains that a school's response to intervention should include three levels. In the first tier, all students have access to high-quality, research-based instruction in the core academic curriculum specified by the state or district, and the learning of each student is monitored on a frequent and timely basis. This monitoring occurs through a process of universal screening to review each student's performance through both formal and informal assessments to determine the student's progress in relation to benchmarks and learning standards. In the second tier, students who are not being successful are given additional time and support, such as small-group tutoring. The third tier is reserved for those few students who need the most intense intervention, such as individualized instruction more tailored to their specific needs. The RTI model also specifically calls for this tiered approach to resolve not only the academic difficulties of students, but their behavioral issues as well. As a result, students would typically not be considered for special education until there was evidence that the RTI tiers had not resolved their issues.

The best analysis of RTI and its implications for schools that we have seen is *Pyramid Response to Intervention* (Buffum, Mattos, & Weber, 2009). As the authors explain:

> Response to intervention (RTI) is a new movement that shifts the responsibility for helping all students become successful from the special education teachers and curriculum to the entire staff.... Simply put, under RTI, schools will consider most students for special education services only after the students have not responded to a series of timely, systematic, increasingly focused, and intensive research-based interventions, which are the responsibility of the regular education program. (pp. 2–3)

For readers of our earlier work, this will all sound familiar. The idea that an entire staff has a collective responsibility to ensure all students acquire agreed-upon essential knowledge, skills, and dispositions; that student learning must be monitored on a timely, ongoing basis using common methods of assessment; and that a school must have a plan for providing struggling students with additional time and support for learning on a timely, directive, and systematic basis has been at the heart of our work for a decade. As Buffum, Mattos, and Weber (2009) conclude, RTI mirrors both the basic premise and the specific practices of the pyramid of interventions we introduced in *Whatever It Takes* (DuFour, DuFour, Eaker, & Karhanek, 2004).

It should come as no surprise, then, that we are enthusiastic proponents of RTI. We agree with David Tilly (2006), who wrote, "RTI is likely the best opportunity we have to improve education for students with disabilities—*and students without them* [our emphasis]—that has occurred since the passage of the Education of the Handicapped Act in 1975" (p. 1).

Our enthusiasm is tempered, however, by several significant caveats. RTI will *not* have a positive impact on student achievement if educators:

- View it as a *program* to be added to the existing traditional structure and culture of their schools
- Regard it as a special education issue
- Approach it with a sense of compliance rather than a spirit of commitment
- Cling to the assumption it is their job to teach and the students' job to learn
- Continue to regard the primary purpose of assessment as assigning grades to assist in the sorting of and selecting of students into achievers and nonachievers

On the other hand, RTI has the potential to help transform schools if the educators within them embrace the following three big ideas of a professional learning community:

1   **A commitment to high levels of learning for all students**

The fundamental purpose of our school is to ensure all students learn at high levels, and the future success of students depends on how effective we are in achieving that fundamental purpose. There must be no ambiguity or hedging regarding our commitment to learning, and we align all practices, procedures, and policies in light of that fundamental purpose. We recognize that a commitment to the learning of each student means we must work together to clarify exactly what each student must learn, monitor each student's learning on a timely basis, provide systematic interventions that ensure a student receives additional time and support for learning when he or she struggles, and extend and enrich learning when a student has already mastered the intended outcomes. We also recognize that if all students are to learn at high levels, we must also be continually learning. Therefore, we must create structures to ensure all staff members engage in job-embedded learning as part of our routine work practices.

2   **A commitment to a collaborative culture**

We cannot achieve our fundamental purpose of learning for all if we work in isolation. Therefore, we must build a collaborative culture in which we work together interdependently and assume collective responsibility for the learning of all students.

3   **A commitment to using results to foster continuous improvement**

We will not know whether or not all students are learning unless we are hungry for evidence that students are acquiring the knowledge, skills, and dispositions most essential to their success. We must systematically monitor each student's learning on an ongoing basis and use evidence of that learning to respond immediately to students who experience difficulty, to inform our individual and collective professional practice, and to fuel continuous improvement.

In other words, we concur with Buffum, Mattos, and Weber (2009), who conclude that RTI will not impact student learning unless it is part of a larger effort to build the capacity of educators to shape the cultures and structures of their schools so that they can function as members of a professional learning community.

The Need for Reform

It could be argued that there is much to celebrate when looking at the contemporary educational landscape. A greater percentage of high school graduates are pursuing postsecondary education, more students are taking rigorous college-level courses in high school than ever before, public approval for the quality of their local schools has risen almost 20 percent since the publication of *A Nation at Risk* (National Commission on Excellence in Education, 1983), and that approval is at one of its highest points in four decades (Rose & Gallup, 2006). How is it that the victims of an educational system that has been so deficient for half a century have continued to accomplish so much? Why is it that schools represent the fundamental problem in bad times but apparently contribute so little to the good? We concur with the assessment of educational historians David Tyack and Larry Cuban (1995), who concluded, "The public schools, for all their faults, remain one of our most stable and effective public institutions—indeed, given the increase in social pathologies in the society, educators have done far better in the last generation than might be expected" (p. 38).

Even if, however, much of the popular criticism of schools has been unfair and unfounded, we contend that educators have both a professional and moral responsibility to constantly seek better ways of meeting the needs of their students. We want to stress that, while we are sympathetic to the difficult conditions in which educators find themselves, we are not apologists for the status quo. The assumptions, expectations, beliefs, behaviors, and structures that have guided educational practice throughout the history of this country and others are inadequate to meet the present challenges. Educators can help more students succeed at higher levels than ever before *if* they are willing to change many of their assumptions and practices, most of which draw their origins from earlier times when education was intended to serve a far different purpose. Educators *must* escape the burdens of their history and make substantive changes in the structure and culture of their schools and districts. In the next chapter we present some of the preliminary work that must be done as educators examine the issue of how they can better respond to the needs of their students.

2
LAYING THE GROUNDWORK FOR EFFECTIVE INTERVENTION

[Highly effective schools] succeed where other schools fail because they ruthlessly organize themselves around one thing: helping students learn a great deal. This seems too simple an explanation, really. But, by focusing on student learning and then creating structures that support learning, these schools have drastically departed from the traditional organizational patterns of American schools.

—KARIN CHENOWETH, 2009

Quality teaching requires strong professional learning communities. Collegial interchange, not isolation, must become the norm for teachers. Communities of learning can no longer be considered utopian; they must become the building blocks that establish a new foundation for America's schools.

—NATIONAL COMMISSION ON TEACHING AND AMERICA'S FUTURE, 2003

We hope the remaining chapters of this book persuade educators to work collaboratively to meet the needs of students by establishing timely, directive, and systematic interventions and enrichment. It is imperative, however, that educators understand certain fundamental prerequisites *must* be in place if a system of interventions is to be effective in improving student learning. Those who approach the task as if it were simply a program to add to the existing practices of the school will miss a basic premise of this book. Addressing the question of how will we respond when students do not learn is not a *program*: it must be part of a broader *process* to transform the culture of a school.

Intervention will have a powerful impact on student achievement when the educators in a school:

- Acknowledge a collective responsibility to ensure that students learn rather than that they are taught

- Are organized into collaborative teams whose members work interdependently to achieve common, results-oriented goals for which members accept mutual accountability

- Work together collaboratively to establish the *essential* knowledge, skills, and dispositions all students must learn in each unit of instruction

- Create pacing guides or curriculum maps each teacher will follow to clarify when the essential skills will be taught

- Develop frequent *common formative assessments* to monitor the learning of each student, and provide teachers with relevant feedback

- Clarify the common standard of proficiency each student must demonstrate in order to be deemed proficient and/or the agreed-upon criteria the members of the team will use to assess the quality of each student's work

- Have access to timely and accurate information regarding student learning in order to identify students who need support, students who need enrichment, and the instructional strategies that appear to be most effective in helping all students learn

When these elements are in place, systematic intervention is powerful: if they are not in place, systematic intervention is impossible for the reasons noted in table 2.1.

In *Learning by Doing* (DuFour, DuFour, Eaker, & Many, 2006) and again in *Revisiting Professional Learning Communities at Work* (DuFour, DuFour, & Eaker, 2008) we examined how schools build the capacity of teachers to work as members of collaborative teams. We have provided specific guidelines and strategies for organizing teachers into meaningful teams; providing them with time for collaboration; helping team members clarify the work they must accomplish; establishing clear expectations among team members regarding how they will work together; setting goals that are strategic, specific, measurable, attainable, results-oriented, and timebound (or SMART goals); monitoring the work of teams; providing teams with relevant data to inform and improve their practice; improving the effectiveness and productivity of teams; building consensus for decisions; persuading skeptics; and responding to resisters. We recommend those books to readers interested in a deep exploration of how schools address those topics to support the learning of adults in the organization.

This book tells the stories of schools and districts that have developed schoolwide plans to ensure their students receive additional time and support for learning without being removed from new direct instruction. The attention these schools and districts devoted to intervention and enrichment did not, however, occur in a vacuum. The educators in these schools also worked together collaboratively to clarify what students were to learn, how they would monitor their learning, and the specific standards students were to achieve to demonstrate proficiency. It was this work that established the foundation for their systems of support. So, before turning to our schools and their stories, let's briefly examine the process used by collaborative teams to build this foundation for powerful intervention and enrichment.

Table 2.1: Prerequisites for Systematic Intervention and Consequences When Collaborative Teams Fail to Meet the Requirements

Necessary Prerequisites for Systematic Intervention	Likely Consequences of Missing the Prerequisite
Acknowledging a collective responsibility to ensure all students learn	Teachers may regard the system of interventions as absolving them of responsibility for student learning rather than ensuring it.
Clarifying the *essential* knowledge, skills, and dispositions all students must learn	Teachers may have very different interpretations regarding the meaning and significance of the many standards they are asked to teach.
Creating common pacing guides and curriculum maps each teacher commits to follow that clarify when essential skills will be taught	Some teachers may spend weeks on a standard that other teachers ignore. Effective intervention and enrichment require clarity regarding what students must learn and when they will be expected to demonstrate their learning.
Developing *common formative assessments* to monitor each student's acquisition of the essential knowledge, skills, and dispositions	Without *common* assessments, teachers will have no basis of comparison to inform them of the strengths and weaknesses of their teaching. Without *formative* assessments teachers may continue to regard assessment as a tool for assigning grades rather than promoting learning.
Establishing the common standard of proficiency each student must demonstrate in order to be deemed proficient (for example, 80 out of 100 points or 3 out of 5 on the team's rubric for performance-based assessment)	Without agreement regarding how students will demonstrate proficiency, teachers may use very different criteria for monitoring the quality of student learning and accept very different levels of performance as proficient.
Designating a block of time for intervention/enrichment that will not require students to miss new direct instruction	Without time dedicated to intervention/enrichment, it will continue to fall to individual teachers to determine how, and if, that time will be provided.

The Team Learning Process

Educators in a professional learning community understand that in order for a comprehensive system of student support to be effective, it is incumbent upon every team within the PLC to identify each student who needs assistance on a timely basis, use consistent standards and processes in identifying those students, and pinpoint the specific skill in which each student is having difficulty. Teaching teams in a PLC meet these challenges by engaging in the six steps of the team learning process, which are outlined in the following pages.

Step 1: Identify Essential Outcomes All Students Must Learn in Each Content Area at Each Grade Level During This School Year and During Each Unit of Instruction

Teams begin the process of clarifying essential outcomes (knowledge, skills, and dispositions) by collectively studying local, state, provincial, and national resources such as:

- Standards documents
- Curriculum guides
- "Wish lists" of critical skills identified by teachers at the next course or grade level
- Assessment frameworks describing how students will be assessed
- Data generated in recent years from those assessments
- Examples of current student work
- Criteria by which the quality of that work will be judged
- Standards-based report cards
- Textbooks
- Teacher-made units of instruction from previous years

As team members study these resources together to build shared knowledge, they begin to arrive at similar conclusions regarding the content of these resources, develop common understandings, and clarify misconceptions or ambiguity regarding the meaning of certain standards. This collective inquiry, or *learning together*, ultimately allows the team to produce a list of the *most essential outcomes* in each course or subject that members are committed to helping all students learn. The list typically includes eight to ten outcomes per course per semester. To separate the *essential outcomes* from the peripheral outcomes, teams can apply the three criteria espoused by Reeves (2002) to each standard:

1 **Endurance**—Are students expected to retain the skills or knowledge long after the test is completed?

2 **Leverage**—Is this skill or knowledge applicable to many academic disciplines?

3 **Readiness for the next level of learning**—Is this skill or knowledge preparing the student for success in the next grade/course?

While the essential outcomes are being clarified for each course and subject at each grade level, teams also engage in *vertical articulation*, working with the teams above and below theirs to identify and close any gaps and avoid curriculum overlaps from one year to the next. At the conclusion of the process, each team should be able to identify the specific knowledge, skills, and dispositions their students must acquire and also articulate those essential outcomes to students, parents, support staff, and volunteers—everyone engaged in the learning process.

Different schools may use different terminology to describe what all students must learn—essential outcomes, power standards, guaranteed curriculum, learning targets, clear and focused academic goals, course objectives, or critical standards. We have witnessed faculties wage great debates over which terms to use. We contend that the specific term they choose is not particularly important. What *is* important is that every teacher acknowledges that if the purpose of the school is to ensure high levels of learning for all students, then those who teach must clarify exactly what each student is expected to learn.

Step 2: Create Common Pacing Guides and Curriculum Maps Each Teacher Will Follow

As they clarify and agree upon essential outcomes, teams also engage in dialogue regarding the best way to sequence and pace the content of the curriculum to ensure all students acquire the essential outcomes. Common pacing guides or curriculum maps are developed as a result of this dialogue so the members of each team can establish some consistency in the amount of time devoted to the initial instruction for those essential outcomes. Although we are not advocates for lock-step, day-by-day pacing from classroom to classroom (for example, every teacher must teach the exact same lesson, in the exact same way, on the exact same day, during the same class period), we do advocate that all the teachers of the same course or grade level agree upon the window of time during which they will teach each essential outcome. We also promote individual teacher autonomy regarding how to teach the essential outcomes, with the understanding that each teacher will strive to use the instructional strategies and resources he or she believes will help students learn the essential outcomes at high levels.

Step 3: Develop Multiple Common Formative Assessments

Clarifying common outcomes and establishing common sequencing and pacing of curriculum are prerequisites for developing common formative assessments. Three decades of research have established that frequent monitoring of each student's learning is an essential element of good instruction and a characteristic of an effective, continuously improving school. In such schools, teachers are clear on the criteria they will use to assess the quality of students' learning and know how well each student is doing in meeting the criteria (Hattie, 2009). We know that good teachers assess student learning in their classrooms each day using a variety of informal and formal assessment tools and strategies. The addition of team-developed common formative assessments to each teacher's assessment arsenal is a powerful weapon not only for monitoring student learning in a consistent and equitable way, but also for providing each teacher with vital information regarding the effectiveness of his or her instructional strategies. Because common formative assessments represent the lynchpin of the collaborative team process in a PLC, we want to clarify what we mean by that term.

Common Formative Assessment

In a PLC, teams create *common* assessments. They agree on what students must learn and create instruments or processes to monitor the learning of each student in the same way while honoring the adaptations and modifications stipulated in the individualized education plan of special education students.

Most of the assessments used by teams are also *formative*. Educators today are typically attuned to the distinction between *summative* and *formative* assessments. They understand a summative assessment is an assessment *of* learning, a tool to answer whether a student learned by the deadline. The answers are limited to yes or no, pass or fail, proficient or not proficient (Stiggins, 2007). They have learned a formative assessment is an assessment *for* learning, a tool used to inform both the teacher and student about the student's current level of achievement, guide the teacher's instructional practice, help the student understand what steps he or she must take to further his or her learning, and motivate the student to take those steps (Wiliam & Thompson, 2007). They have been told that while a summative assessment is designed for accountability, a formative assessment supports learning (Stiggins, 2007) because the evidence from the assessment is used to adapt teaching strategies to meet student needs (Black & Wiliam, 1998). Doug Reeves' (2000) vivid analogy—a formative test is to a summative test as a physical examination is to an autopsy—has helped educators sharpen the distinction between these two very different types of assessments.

Many educators, however, operate under the delusion that while high-stakes annual state and provincial tests are summative, assessments created by the individual classroom teacher are formative. They are not. It is not who administers the assessment, when the assessment is administered, or even the content of the assessment that determine if it is formative. The essential element of a formative assessment is determined by what happens *after* students are assessed. In order to be *formative*:

- The assessment is used to identify students who are experiencing difficulty in their learning.

- Students who are experiencing difficulty are required to utilize a coordinated intervention process that provides them with additional time and support for learning in a way that does not remove them from new direct instruction.

- Students are given additional opportunities to demonstrate their learning.

Those interested in a deeper exploration of common formative assessments and the rationale and research supporting this powerful tool for school improvement should read the two chapters on assessment (chapters 8 and 9) from *Revisiting Professional Learning Communities at Work* (DuFour, DuFour, & Eaker, 2008).

The Process for Creating Common Formative Assessments

Before a team develops a common formative assessment, members must once again build shared knowledge by studying best practices in assessment in an attempt to determine the most equitable, valid, and authentic ways to monitor each student's mastery of each essential outcome. Teams become students of the district, state, provincial, and national assessments that their students will take. In addition, they become students of the knowledge base most relevant to them as they collectively answer the critical question, how will we know if each student is learning each essential outcome? The following are examples of the research and resources a collaborative team may study:

- Recommendations from assessment experts including Rick Stiggins, Doug Reeves, Larry Ainsworth, W. James Popham, and Dylan Wiliam

- Released items from district, state, provincial, and national assessments (ACT, SAT, ITBS, NAEP, and so on)

- Websites such as www.nces.ed.gov/nationsreportcard, which provides released sets of assessment items and prompts for each subject area taken from the National Assessment of Educational Progress, identifies the levels of difficulty of questions, explains the nature of the mistake when students choose an incorrect response, and specifies the percent of students who were able to answer correctly on the national exam

- Data from past indicators of achievement

- Methods of alternative assessments

- Examples of rubrics

- Examples of the assessments that individual members of the team have created and administered over the years

As a result of engaging in collective inquiry into this shared knowledge base, each team, over time, creates a variety of common formative assessments to be administered to all the students in their course or grade level following an initial period of instruction that corresponds to the team's pacing guide. Some of the common assessments will likely be traditional multiple choice, true/false, fill-in-the-blank, or short-answer tests. In order to achieve a balanced approach to assessment, however, others will certainly be performance-based assessments, in which the team agrees to use such instruments as portfolios, writing prompts, projects, independent reading inventories, and oral presentations with supporting rubrics or checklists established by the team.

Teams must address two significant challenges if they hope to draw valid conclusions regarding student achievement from performance-based assessments. First, all members of the team must agree on the criteria by which they judge the quality of student work. All teachers should be so clear on the team's definitions of what excellent, above average, good, below average, and poor student work look like on their common assessments that they can describe the criteria with precision to each other, their students, and parents. Second, all members of the same team must apply those criteria consistently. In other words, they must establish inter-rater reliability.

To address these challenges, team members practice applying their agreed-upon criteria to random, anonymous samples of student work. As long as the variation in scoring is no more than one point on a five-point scale, for example, the team is demonstrating inter-rater reliability. If, however, any two members of the same team vary more than one point, the team should stop, discuss the ratings and the criteria they have established, and work together until they can agree on the application of the criteria.

Teams often find they also need consistency in the administration of assessments. For example, when using oral assessments, the members of the team must agree on guidelines for administration—the setting, allowable "wait time" before the student would be expected to respond, whether prompting is appropriate, and so on.

Step 4: Establish a Target Score All Students Must Achieve to Demonstrate Proficiency in Each Skill on Each Common Formative Assessment

As a common assessment is developed, the team sets a benchmark score that each student is required to attain to demonstrate proficiency. The score is intended to be fair, yet challenging. For example, a team may establish 80 percent on a test or three on a five-point rubric as the score students must achieve in order to be deemed proficient on a particular skill. The proficiency target is the same for all students—even those struggling to learn the skills and concepts being taught. Teams operate with the assumption that with appropriate levels of time and support, *every* student will demonstrate proficiency on the essential outcomes.

Step 5: Administer the Common Assessments and Analyze Results

Each team agrees to administer its common assessment according to the timetable established in the team's pacing guide. Group assessments are typically administered at the same time and on the same day in order to promote consistent assessment conditions. Individual assessments, such as independent reading inventories or oral presentations, are completed during an agreed-upon window of time established by the team.

After the assessments are administered to all students in each course or grade level, individual teachers submit results to the designated person in the school (for example, team leader, department chair, principal, data coach, or other appropriate individual) who compiles the data for the course or grade-level team and promptly forwards the results to the team members for joint analysis. Each team then works together to analyze the results for all students—skill by skill (and sometimes item by item)—and identify areas of celebration and concern.

Initially teachers may be reluctant to share their results with their colleagues. For that reason, some schools provide each teacher with his or her own data compared to the total group rather than providing each teacher's results to all members of the team. This practice allows teachers to begin sharing results at their discretion when they are comfortable, as opposed to having results exposed by the administration.

Teachers may also feel anxious that the results will be used against them in the teacher evaluation process. We recommend that the results of common formative assessments be used to help teachers identify their individual strengths and weaknesses, allow teams to identify areas of concern in student achievement in that course or grade level, and identify students who need either additional time and support or enrichment. We do not believe common formative assessments are an effective tool for rating and ranking teachers. When a four-member team administers an assessment, someone on the team will have the best results and another will have the worst, regardless of the quality of the individual teachers, the team, or the school. The purpose of common formative assessments should not be to rank or rate teachers but rather to provide them with the information they need to improve continuously, both individually and collectively. We have found that when teachers have acknowledged certain outcomes are essential, helped to create assessments they agree are valid tools for monitoring student proficiency, and then discovered irrefutable evidence that their students are not learning as well as students taught by a colleague, they are motivated to improve without the necessity of rankings or ratings.

Step 6: Celebrate Strengths and Identify and Implement Improvement Strategies

The data from the common assessments make it possible for all teams to identify and celebrate program strengths—skills and concepts in which all or almost all students achieve the team's target. At the same time, however, each team and each member of the team can identify at least one area for improvement. Individual teachers are able to identify problem areas in their teaching, and then call upon teammates for help in addressing those areas. If the entire team is experiencing difficulty in teaching a specific concept, that team should have access to school or district support to receive the professional development members need to address the difficulty. This process enhances the effectiveness of both the team and its individual members. As Mike Schmoker (2003) writes, "Instructional improvement depends on such simple, data-driven formats—teams identifying and addressing areas of difficulty and then developing, critiquing, testing, and upgrading efforts in light of ongoing results" (p. 24).

Very importantly, this team learning process identifies any student who has not yet achieved the target proficiency score on each skill or concept being assessed. This information is of little use, however, unless the school is able to develop an effective system of providing these students with additional time and support for learning. Creating procedures for identifying students who need help is a critical step, but two crucial questions remain: Now that we know which students have not achieved the intended standards, how do we intend to respond? How will we enrich and enhance the learning for the students who have met or exceeded our proficiency target?

Focusing on the Right Work

One of the most common mistakes we have seen educators make as they attempt to implement the PLC concept is to regard collaboration as the end itself, rather than as a means to an end. Collaboration will impact student achievement in a positive way only if the "co-laboring" and collective inquiry focus on the *right* work. Planning field trips, debating the provisions of student dress codes, or commiserating about student apathy will not help students or teachers learn at higher levels. Once again, effective collaboration will engage teams in continually deeper dialogue on the following four critical questions that drive the work of PLCs:

- **Question 1—What is it we want our students to learn?** Ask almost any teacher in North America if he or she believes all kids can learn, and it is almost guaranteed the teacher will answer in the affirmative. But ask that teacher if he or she believes all students can master calculus by the end of their freshman year of high school, and the answer will be an emphatic "No." Saying we believe all kids can learn is a pleasant affirmation, but it is only when teachers can articulate exactly what each student is expected to know and be able to do that the "learning for all" mission becomes meaningful.

  The critical importance of teacher clarity regarding the intended outcomes of instruction has been repeatedly cited in the research. In his comprehensive synthesis of research on factors impacting student achievement, John Hattie (2009) concluded that one of the six indicators of excellence in education was that teachers "*know the learning intentions* and success criteria" of what they are teaching (p. 239). Larry Lezotte (2004) found that in effective schools "each of the teachers in the school has a clear understanding of what the essential learner objectives are, grade by grade and subject by subject" (p. 7). Robert Marzano (2003) referred to this clarity of focus as a "guaranteed and viable curriculum." Regardless of the terminology, the premise of learning for all demands that each teacher be clear on the specific knowledge, skills, and dispositions each student must acquire as a result of the course, grade level, and unit of instruction. This clarity requires more than distributing state standards or district curriculum guides to teachers. It demands teachers accept shared responsibility for the learning of all the students assigned to their course or grade level and that they work together to clarify exactly what each student must learn.

- **Question 2—How will we know if each student is learning each of the skills, concepts, and dispositions we have deemed essential?** If a school were truly committed to ensuring that every student mastered the intended outcomes of the core curriculum, each educator within the school would participate in a vigilant collective effort to assess each student's learning on a timely, ongoing basis. Too often, schools and districts leave this question to the discretion of each teacher throughout the year and the high-stakes end-of-year state or provincial assessments that occur late in the year. In one instance, we worked in a district that devoted considerable energy to administering district assessments several times each year, but no one at the school level was able to explain how, or if, the results of the assessments were used at any level in the organization. We endorse the call for *balanced* assessment processes, which acknowledges the significant role state, district, team, and individual teacher assessments can play in the educational process; recognizes that different assessments serve different purposes; and requires multiple and varied assessment strategies and tools to monitor student learning (Stiggins & DuFour, 2009). We argue that frequent team-developed common formative assessments are one of the most powerful weapons in the assessment arsenal, and that effective teams will focus their collaborative efforts on creating high-quality assessments, agreeing on the criteria they will use in monitoring the quality of students' work, and using the results of assessments to inform and improve the professional practice of both individual members and the team at large.

- **Question 3—What happens in our school when a student does not learn?** Marzano (2003) has described three different levels of curriculum. The first is the *intended curriculum*—what we intend for each student to learn. The second is the *implemented curriculum*—what is actually taught. The third is the *attained curriculum*—what students actually learn. Effective collaboration addresses all three, ensuring that every teacher is clear on what students are to learn, that procedures are in place to guarantee that every student has access to that intended learning in his or her classroom, that each student's learning is carefully monitored, and that students who are experiencing difficulty are provided with additional time and support for learning in a timely, directive, and systematic way that will not remove the student from new instruction.

- **Question 4—What happens in our school when students already know it?** Bob Eaker is fond of saying that he has found it is much easier to teach when students already know the material. Every veteran teacher has experienced students who demonstrate they are already proficient in the essential skills and concepts of the course, grade level, or unit. How can a school enrich and extend the learning for these students? What structures are in place to advance their learning and ensure that attention to students who are struggling does not come at the expense of the learning of proficient students?

While a single team of teachers at a grade level or course could address the first two critical questions regarding intended learning and strategies for monitoring learning, the questions about how we respond when students struggle and how we are able to extend the learning for students who are proficient require a coordinated, schoolwide response. Attention to these two questions is a crucial step on the journey to becoming a PLC. As later chapters will demonstrate, a coordinated effort to address these questions tremendously benefits students and teachers alike.

Concluding Thoughts

We worked with a middle school faculty that embraced the idea a school should provide additional time and support for students who are not learning but rejected the idea that teachers should work in teams, develop a guaranteed curriculum, establish common sequencing and pacing of content, use common assessments, or designate a specific time in the day for intervention and enrichment. They believed that such coordination would infringe on their academic freedom, something they valued a great deal.

The district agreed to invest considerable resources in the school's attempt to create a system of interventions, and the school was able to hire three certified teachers to serve as full-time tutors. Each tutor was assigned a room and developed a sign-in sheet so teachers could schedule students for individual tutoring in twenty-minute blocks. In order to arrange for this support, a teacher first had to establish when a tutor was available. Often, the only time a tutor might have to assist a student with mathematics was when the student was scheduled for language arts. Thus, tutoring often came at the expense of the students' attendance during new direct instruction. Teachers resented having students removed from their class to get help with another class.

Because each teacher was free to establish the sequencing and pacing of the content of his or her curriculum, tutors soon discovered that they needed more precise information regarding the difficulties students were experiencing. Knowing that a student was failing language arts was of no use to the tutor if that tutor had no idea which skills a particular teacher might be focusing on at any given time or how the skills were being assessed. Therefore, tutors began to ask teachers to complete a review sheet to clarify the specific skills causing the student difficulty, sections of the textbook the tutor should use, supplementary materials that might be useful, and recommendations for assessing the skills. Teachers began to see this additional paperwork as an imposition.

Finally, the tutors discovered that often a student's failure was not the result of a lack of proficiency, but an unwillingness to complete homework. Sending those students to the tutor for academic support did nothing to prevent them from failing if they persisted in their refusal to do homework.

As time went on, teachers began to use the tutors less and less. By the end of the year there was no evidence that the tutors had impacted student achievement, and this very expensive program was dropped.

Throughout this book, we assert that creating systems of interventions and enrichment will not require a windfall of new resources; however, it will require a coordinated and collective effort that is part of a larger endeavor to shape the structure and culture of a school. The schools and districts we feature in this book—schools and districts that have been highly successful in creating systems of interventions and enrichment—did not have the infusion of financial support of the middle school described above. Their faculties realized, however, that a system of interventions is more effective when it supports *collaborative teams* of teachers who have agreed on what students must learn, when they will learn, and how they will demonstrate their learning—as opposed to attempting to support *individual classroom kingdoms* in which each teacher has his or her own interpretation of what students should learn, appropriate curricular calendars, and methods and standards of assessment. In short, they recognized that if they were to help all students learn, they needed to place a higher value on systems, coordination, and cooperation than individual autonomy and adult convenience.

In the next chapter, we turn our attention to how schools have traditionally responded when students do not learn.

3

CONFRONTING THE BRUTAL FACTS: THE TRADITIONAL RESPONSE TO STUDENTS WHO DO NOT LEARN

> There is always a huge difference between individual capability and collective capability and individual learning and collective learning. But schools are designed and structured in a way that reinforces the idea that my job as teacher is an individual teaching my kids. Our unit of innovation has usually been the individual teacher, the individual classroom, or a new curriculum to be implemented individually by teachers.
>
> —PETER SENGE (O'NEIL, 1995)

> We are misled by certainty which causes us to ignore a massive amount of contradictory evidence. . . . The only way to counteract this bias for certainty is to create inner dissonance. We must force ourselves to think about the information we don't want to think about, to pay attention to the data that disturbs our entrenched beliefs.
>
> —JONAH LEHRER, 2009

Before exploring how schools *should* respond when students experience difficulty, it would be helpful to examine how schools have traditionally responded. Often in our workshops we show the video *Through New Eyes: Examining the Culture of Your School* (DuFour, 2002), which shows the experience of the same student, Johnny Jones, as he attends two very different schools. Johnny is apathetic, irresponsible, and unorganized. He frequently fails to complete his assignments. In his first school, Johnny's algebra teacher concludes that he is not algebra-capable and advises his mother that Johnny should transfer from algebra to pre-algebra. His history teacher advises his mother that while it is his job to teach, it is Johnny's job to learn, and it is time for Johnny to accept responsibility for himself. If Johnny does not complete his work on time, he must suffer the consequences because, in life, failure to meet deadlines carries consequences. Johnny's English teacher concludes Johnny suffers from low self-esteem and advises his mother that she intends to focus on building his self-esteem and will deal with his academic problems later. At the end of the semester Johnny fails all three classes and is recommended for placement in special education.

The participants who view the video are typically very critical of how the school responds to Johnny. When we ask them to describe the school's response, they invariably say things like, "They lowered their expectations for Johnny," or "They put all the responsibility on him and none on themselves," or "No one tried to get to know Johnny." We then ask them to consider this possibility: if the question is, how did the school respond to Johnny, the most accurate answer is that the *school* never responded to Johnny. What we see are three very different responses from three different teachers who are left to their own devices to determine an appropriate course of action. One teacher removes Johnny from the course, another allows him to suffer the consequences of being irresponsible, while a third decides his academic needs should be subordinated to the image issues that she perceives as the cause of his problems. There is never any coordinated or collective response to Johnny.

Every time we show this video and have this discussion, the audience, without exception, agrees that the response to Johnny's problems was left to the discretion of individual teachers who were free to respond in very different ways. When we ask viewers how they would characterize the video (satirical comedy, fantasy, or reality television) if they were writing a review for *TV Guide*, without exception, the group agrees that Johnny's experience in the video reflects reality and represents the norm for many students who struggle.

As we delve further into this issue, participants acknowledge that in their own school, students who experience difficulty in learning will be subject to very different responses based upon the beliefs and practices of the individual teachers to whom they are assigned. Some teachers are far more likely to fail a student, recommend retention, or refer for special education than others. Some will provide help to students before and after school, and some won't. Some will accept late work, and some won't. Some will allow students to retake tests, and some won't. Some will demand students revise their work until it meets standards, and some won't. Furthermore, this blatant disparity is common knowledge. Parents realize it, older students realize it, and most damningly, educators realize it as well. McLaughlin and Talbert (2001) characterize this phenomenon as an "instructional lottery" in which the experiences and opportunities for learning for students in the same school will "depend heavily on the teachers they draw, from class to class and from year to year" (p. 64).

We have presented the video and engaged in this dialogue with literally tens of thousands of educators. The two most striking aspects of this exercise over the years have been the virtually universal agreement regarding the disparity that exists when students experience difficulty and the complete absence of any outrage over that disparity. Educators readily acknowledge that the fate of a student who is not learning will depend on the random- ness of the teacher to whom he or she is assigned rather than any collective, coherent, systematic plan for meeting the needs of all students. But those same educators—professionals who almost universally express their desire for consistent treatment from administrators and who frequently press for contractual language assuring they are entitled to such consistency—seem strangely unaffected by the obvious randomness and incoherence of their organization's response to students. How can well-intentioned people who clearly care for the well-being of their students and who demonstrate their deeply held belief in equity seem so oblivious to such an inherently inequi- table situation? We suggest that the answer to this question is found in the traditional story that has driven the work of educators for over a century. The educators are impervious to the situation because the haphazard way in which their schools currently intervene is exactly how the schools they attended reacted when they were students.

We contend that it is time for educators to embrace a new story. A school truly committed to the concept of learning for each student will stop sub- jecting students to a random, de facto educational lottery program when they struggle academically. It will stop leaving the critical question of how we will respond when a student is not learning to the discretion of each teacher. It will instead develop consistent, systematic procedures that ensure each student is guaranteed additional time and support when needed. In fact, until the staff of a school begins to respond to students communally rather than as individuals, the school will never become a professional learning community.

A Key Shift in Assumptions: Learning as the Constant—Time and Support as Variables

Here is a scenario that plays out daily in traditional schools. A teacher cre- ates a unit to assist her students in acquiring an important skill or concept, determines she can devote three weeks to the unit, and then teaches that unit to the best of her ability each day during the fifty minutes available for the class. At its conclusion, she assesses each student's learning. The results make it evident that while some students have not yet become proficient, others have mastered the content. On one hand, the teacher would like to take the time to help those students who are struggling. On the other hand, she feels compelled to move forward with students who have mastered the content, particularly in light of the vast amount of curriculum she is expected to cover during the course of the year. If the teacher uses instructional time to assist those who have not learned, the needs of students who have mastered the content are not being met; if the teacher pushes on with new concepts, struggling students are likely to fall further behind.

There are inherent problems in this scenario. First, each student receives the exact same amount of time to learn: fifty minutes a day for three weeks. Time for learning is a constant for the students in her class. Second, given the number of students she must teach and the amount of material she is expected to cover over the course of the year, the teacher cannot provide individual students with a great deal of additional attention and support during the class period. She will teach to the group and move on when the *group* seems to be ready. Most importantly, she is left to her own devices to resolve the issue of moving forward with those who are proficient or taking additional time to address the needs of students who are struggling at the risk of boring those who have learned.

There is a tendency to make light of these problems by advising the teacher to differentiate instruction in order to meet the varied needs of students who are highly proficient and require more challenging curriculum, students who are becoming proficient and require additional practice and feedback, and those who are lost. We fully support the idea of differentiated instruction and recognize that master teachers are constantly expanding their skills to meet the different interests, learning styles, and needs of all of their students. We endorse the idea that teachers should receive training and support in acquiring the skills of differentiated instruction. We also contend, however, that instead of relying solely on how to help individual teachers be effective in a poorly designed system, schools and districts should examine how to improve the system to increase the likelihood that well-intentioned, diligent people can be more successful in their work.

When time and support for learning are regarded as constants, learning will always be the variable. Some students, probably most students, will learn, and some will not. Educators regret that fact, but they assume that is how schools operate.

A professional learning community operates from a very different premise. Each teacher in a PLC begins the unit by advising students of an *essential* outcome, an outcome so important, so significant, that every student *must* achieve it. Learning will be the constant. In this situation, it is imperative that time and support become variables. Some students require more time to learn, and so the school develops strategies to provide those students with additional time during the school day. Some students require more support for learning. They may never learn the concept in the classroom setting, and so the school develops systems to provide them with small group or one-on-one tutorials until they have achieved mastery. Rather than placing responsibility for student learning solely on the backs of overburdened classroom teachers, the school develops a *collective* response to assist classroom teachers by giving students extra time and extra support. Educators must recognize that there are inherent limitations in what an individual teacher working in an isolated classroom can do to intervene for students who need support and simultaneously enrich and extend the learning for students who have demonstrated mastery. The most effective intervention strategies to help all students learn at high levels require the cooperation and coordination of the school as a whole.

Providing Time and Support

The rest of this book illustrates how this system of time and support for students can work in the real world of schools; however, a few caveats are in order. First, many of the examples we provide come from schools that have been building their system of response for a number of years. The examples are comprehensive, but it is important that readers understand these systems did not suddenly emerge fully formed. The process was messy and nonlinear. The schools learned through trial and error what worked and what did not work. Many of the steps in the system of response were developed only when earlier steps failed to accomplish all that was hoped for when they were implemented.

Second, the examples are offered as illustrations of what schools can accomplish when staff members work together to consider the questions, what happens in our school when students do not learn, and how can we enrich and extend the learning for students who are proficient? They are not intended to serve as models for other schools to transplant. *Each staff must develop its own plan for meeting the needs of students in its unique school.* Not every program presented in the following chapters will be desirable or even possible for every school in every state or province. Avoid the temptation to simply dismiss the example with a cursory, "We can't do that here." Instead, accept the challenge of working with colleagues to identify alternatives that *can* work in your setting.

Third, the idea that schools can provide students with additional time and support relies more on determination and will than on additional resources.

We understand the budgetary constraints schools are facing and recognize the futility of offering ideas for improvement that demand significant additional expenditures. We are convinced that support systems can be provided within existing resources because we have done it. Some of the schools and districts we feature are from states with the lowest per-pupil expenditures in the nation. They all spend considerably less in per-pupil expenditures than many other schools in their state that are far less effective. It is not imperative to have a windfall of additional funding to implement these ideas, but it is imperative that staff members demonstrate a willingness to change some traditional assumptions, practices, roles, and responsibilities.

Fourth, readers must not fall in love with a tree: they must embrace the forest. The stories we present are filled with examples of creative and innovative programs—advisories, flex schedules, peer tutoring, buddy programs. Many of the specific programs are good ideas; however, none of the programs, in isolation, will bring about the changes in the assumptions, beliefs, expectations, and habits that constitute the culture of a school. We have seen highly ineffective schools with advisory programs and wonderfully effective schools that do not offer advisories. An advisory program *may* be beneficial, but it is not a school-transforming idea. The big idea, the idea that can help transform the culture of a school, is this:

> In this school, whenever a student experiences academic difficulty or demonstrates a need for enrichment, we will ensure the student receives additional time and support for learning in a timely, directive, and systematic way.

This idea, when embraced and successfully implemented in a school, will transform a school's culture. It will no longer be the same place with a new program added as an appendage to old assumptions: it will be a fundamentally different place.

Finally, we cannot overstate this fact: *no system of interventions will ever compensate for bad teaching.* A school that focuses exclusively on responding to students who are having difficulty without also developing the capacity of every administrator and teacher to become more effective will fail to become a professional learning community. The most important resource in every school is the professionals within it. Implementing procedures to monitor each student's learning on a timely basis and creating systems of interventions and enrichment to assist students who need additional time and support are necessary steps in becoming a PLC, but they are not sufficient. The professionals within the school will also be called upon to build a collaborative culture, engage in collective inquiry regarding matters that impact student learning, participate in action research, create continuous improvement processes, and help each other monitor and improve upon results. They will do more than voice the belief that all students can learn; they will act on that belief.

Most of our other books and videos focus primarily on providing educators with the time, support, and strategies to enhance their professional practice. This book focuses primarily on providing time, support, and strategies to assist students; however, the importance of building the capacity of a staff to function as a PLC cannot be overemphasized and must not be overlooked. As Roland Barth (2001) states:

> Ultimately there are two kinds of schools: learning-enriched schools and learning-impoverished schools. I've yet to see a school where the learning curves of the youngsters are off the chart upward while the learning curves of the adults are off the chart downward, or a school where the learning curves of the adults were steep upward and those of the students were not. Teachers and students go hand in hand as learners—or they don't go at all. (p. 23)

Concluding Thoughts

In schools throughout North America, teachers begin the year with the sincere hope that they will be able to help all of their students learn the most essential knowledge and skills of their grade levels or courses. They work very, very hard to achieve this goal of learning for all. Yet, by the third or fourth week of school, it becomes evident that some students are not learning. This finding never comes as a surprise. Although it happens each year, schools that proclaim their mission is to ensure learning for all typically have no plan or strategy for responding to the inevitable moment when a student is not learning.

As we wrote in *Revisiting Professional Learning Communities at Work*:

> This lack of a coordinated response when some students do not learn ranks near the top of the list of the many illogical and incomprehensible practices that occur in schooling. If certain conditions are absolutely essential to the ability of an enterprise to fulfill its fundamental purpose, people would expect the enterprise to monitor those conditions and to have a plan in place to ensure a timely response if they were compromised. We expect Starbucks to have a plan for monitoring coffee levels and for responding when coffee runs low. We expect Burger King to have a plan in place to ensure customers could purchase a burger or that Red Lobster could, in fact, provide lobster to a hungry diner. We would find it odd indeed if those companies could not provide a basic service so essential to their fundamental purpose. We expect

those running a nuclear power plant to monitor the conditions that allow it to provide safe nuclear power and to know what they will do if those conditions are compromised. If they failed to do so we would certainly charge negligence and threaten punitive damage. We expect an organization created for the specific purpose of responding to emergencies to have a coordinated plan for dealing with natural disasters in a timely manner, and we are outraged when we discover they do not. Yet, educators, who claim the fundamental purpose of their schools is to ensure all students learn, seem not only unconcerned, but also unaware of the fact that their schools have no coordinated plan for addressing students who are not learning. Does this not seem odd? Where is the outrage at what could be argued is educational negligence? It is time for educators to confront some brutal facts and align their practices with their stated missions. (DuFour, DuFour, & Eaker, 2008, pp. 245–246)

One of the key messages of this book is that a professional learning community acknowledges the incongruity between a proposed commitment to learning for all and the absence of a coordinated strategy to respond when students do not learn or require advanced learning. The staff addresses this discrepancy by designing systems and processes to ensure such students receive additional time and support for their learning—regardless of who their teacher might be. Our investigation of how those systems and processes might operate begins in the next chapter.

4

SUSTAINING EXCELLENCE: A RETURN TO ADLAI STEVENSON HIGH SCHOOL

Adlai Stevenson High School is widely recognized as a standard bearer of excellence among high schools. . . . The vision and beliefs that have made Stevenson what it is today are deeply embedded in the daily practices of its teachers, counselors, and administrators.

—JOAN RICHARDSON, 2004

Stevenson's results are a tribute to the power of vision, focus, organized intelligence, persistence—and courage. There is much to learn here.

—MIKE SCHMOKER, 2001

Adlai Stevenson High School in Lincolnshire, Illinois, is one of the only high schools in the nation to receive the United States Department of Education's Blue Ribbon Award on four separate occasions—an accomplishment that means the school was deemed excellent, *and then continuously increased student achievement for more than two decades.* In this chapter, we review the elements of Stevenson's system of interventions and enrichment that we first presented in *Whatever It Takes* (DuFour, DuFour, Eaker, & Karhanek, 2004), examine how that system has evolved in the years since that book was published, and consider evidence to determine if the school has been able to sustain its tradition of academic excellence.

A Look Back

In the early 1980s, Adlai Stevenson High School seemed to have several advantages. The suburban Chicago community it served consisted of primarily middle- and upper-middle-class families with very few families living in poverty. The faculty demonstrated an exceptional work ethic. Nevertheless, despite the hard work of the staff, many students were not finding success at the school. More than 25 percent of the student body had been relegated to remedial curricular tracks, and at the end of each semester, teachers were recommending that hundreds of students be transferred to a lower track. The percentage of students receiving grades of D or F topped 35 percent, and the annual number of out-of-school suspensions as a percentage of the student body had risen to over 75 percent.

Residents seemed disenchanted with Stevenson. In the early 1980s, they defeated a referendum to resolve the severe overcrowding the school was experiencing. Parents in Lincolnshire, one of the villages whose residents sent their children to the school, began a petition drive to detach from the school district and annex to a neighboring district to avoid sending their children to Stevenson. In a series of neighborhood coffees attended by members of the board of education and administration to build support for the school, parents expressed a consistent concern: Stevenson lets students fall through the cracks. They criticized the school both for its inability to identify students who were having difficulty until it was too late and for its tendency to seek a solution by moving students to lower tracks. One tearful mother recounted that she had sent her son to Stevenson with high hopes for his success, but week after week went by with no feedback from the school. Finally, in the eleventh week of the semester, she received his report card and found that he had received three grades of D. As she explained it:

> Doesn't anyone at Stevenson understand the implications of your failure to keep parents informed about the progress of our children? My son will never be admitted to the leading public university in our state because 50 percent of his grade in three of his classes in his first semester of high school is locked in as a D. He no longer has access to a number of opportunities and options that are available to successful students. Yet no one in the school had the courtesy to let me know he was having difficulty. How do you expect parents to be partners in the education of their children if you keep us in the dark until it is too late?

If the purpose of school is simply to give students the *opportunity* to learn, Stevenson was fulfilling its purpose in the early 1980s. Many of its students were achieving at very high levels, and the school could point to them as evidence that the problem was not with the school, but with the inability or unwillingness of some students to put forth the effort to learn. To the enduring credit of Stevenson's wonderful faculty, they did not settle for giving students the chance to learn. Instead, they began a systematic effort to better meet the needs of all students so that the school's promise of "success for all" might be a reality rather than a slogan.

Pre-Enrollment Initiatives

When the Stevenson staff took time to analyze the current reality of the school, it became evident that the school needed to become more proactive in identifying students who would need additional support in order to be successful in high school. As a result of that finding, the school initiated several new programs and procedures.

Counselor Watch Program

Student failure is often more a function of lack of motivation, alienation, or emotional issues than difficulty in understanding key skills and concepts. The Counselor Watch program was created to address the needs of those students through both prevention and intervention.

Every January, Stevenson counselors ask the principal of each of the middle schools that send their graduates to Stevenson to complete a Counselor Watch Referral Sheet for any student who meets the criteria for the program—poor academic progress, personal or family problems, poor attendance, peer relationship issues, or chronic underachievement. In effect, Stevenson asks the staff of each middle school, which of your students will be most in need of our help?

In April, Stevenson counselors visit every middle school to review the referral sheets with the middle school principal, counselor, social worker, and nurse. These meetings not only clarify and elaborate upon the concerns the middle school staff may have expressed regarding a student, but also identify the interventions and support the student will require when entering high school. Students are identified for specific programs and services months *before* they ever enter the high school. Rather than waiting for the student to experience frustration and failure before responding to the situation, the school assumes a proactive stance that provides students with support services designed to promote their immediate success in high school.

Proactive Student Registration

Each February, Stevenson counselors travel to the middle schools to meet with individual eighth-grade students and their parents to register students for their freshman classes. Counselors use this opportunity to foster an expectation of achievement and participation. All students are asked to identify three goals they hope to achieve during their freshman year, as well as three cocurricular activities they may wish to join. These conversations reveal a great deal about student dispositions toward their upcoming high school experience and begin the personal connection between counselors and students.

Survival Skills for High School Summer Course

Stevenson created a special summer school course, Survival Skills for High School, to teach students how to take notes, annotate their reading, use a planner to organize their time and materials, read for comprehension, set goals, and communicate effectively. Parents of any student who received two or more grades of D in middle school are contacted by Stevenson counselors and urged to enroll their son or daughter in this summer program. The course is taught by a Stevenson teacher who has both a talent and interest in working with students who have a history of achieving below their academic potential. The course runs for four hours each day for four weeks each summer, and students who complete the course receive one elective credit.

Although the staff had high hopes for this new course, it initially failed to generate much student interest due to two major obstacles. First, like all of the summer school courses offered by Stevenson, it was scheduled at the same time as many of the athletic camps being offered at the high school. Students were forced to make a choice between a summer school course or football, basketball, volleyball, and soccer camps—and summer school was losing that competition. So the decision was made to stop forcing students to make that choice. Coaches were told that athletic camps could not be offered while summer school was in session. Because classes were scheduled from 8:00 a.m. until noon for eight weeks, most coaches simply moved their camps to the afternoon to give students the opportunity to take advantage of both programs.

The second obstacle was more problematic. North American students have been conditioned to regard summer school as punitive. For years they have heard, "You had better improve your grades, or we will force you to go to summer school." So when parents suggested the Survival Skills for High School course to their sons and daughters, most students were adamantly opposed to enrolling. They wanted nothing to do with the program because of the perceived social stigma of attending summer school.

Stevenson attacked this problem by expanding its summer school options in every department and beginning a concentrated effort to convince parents that every incoming freshman would benefit from enrolling in a summer school course. At every meeting with parents of eighth graders, the principal and counselors pointed out how much more comfortable students would be on the first day of high school if they had already learned their way around the building, met students from other middle schools, discovered what the homework load was like in a high school class, and earned a credit because of enrolling in a summer school course. When counselors met with parents to register students for their freshman courses, they also brought registration materials for the summer program. Because the district had a policy that summer school had to be revenue neutral, tuition was charged for all summer programs; however, a community foundation was established to pay the tuition of any student who needed financial assistance. Busing was provided for any interested student. Attending summer school lost its stigma, and today at Stevenson, over 80 percent of every entering freshman class enrolls in a summer school course.

Coordinated Support for Students

The pre-enrollment initiatives just described enabled Stevenson to be more proactive in addressing the needs of incoming students. The staff also recognized, however, that the school should have a program to monitor and support at-risk students as soon as they arrived on campus. Elements of that program are described in the following sections.

The Good Friend Program

Prior to the first day of school, counselors review the information on incoming students who were identified as needing additional support through the Counselor Watch program. Based on this analysis of the needs and interests of the student, counselors recruit a Good Friend staff member to provide additional encouragement, support, and attention to students who are at risk of experiencing problems that might impact their school performance. The Good Friend, who may be a teacher, administrator, coach, or club sponsor, is asked to make a concerted effort to connect with the student, discover the student's concerns and interests, establish a positive personal relationship, monitor the student's well-being, and advise the counselor regarding the best ways to assist the student. Students are unaware that they have been identified for the program or that they are the beneficiaries of this extra effort to assist them.

Counselor Check-In Program

Students identified for the Counselor Check-In program during the Counselor Watch discussions are scheduled to meet individually with their counselors on a weekly basis for at least the first six weeks of the school year. During these private conversations, the counselor monitors the academic progress and emotional well-being of the student and attempts to help the student find solutions to any problems he or she may be experiencing.

Assisting All Students With the Transition to High School

Another initiative identified by the Stevenson staff fell into the broad category of providing greater support for all incoming students as they make the transition into high school. The staff was able to develop a comprehensive support system by collectively considering the questions, what can we do to promote the academic success of every entering student, and what steps can we take to help each student feel personally connected to people and programs in our schools?

Freshman Orientation Day

When staff members asked juniors and seniors to reflect on the most difficult aspect of the first day of high school, they consistently pointed to how self-conscious they felt trying to find their way around the building in the presence of older students. They explained it was difficult to be "cool" when they were obviously lost, much to the amusement of other students.

Stevenson addressed this problem by scheduling freshmen to attend school one day earlier than the rest of the student body. A portion of Freshman Orientation Day is spent in a general orientation to the school that includes tours of the building. Students also follow an abbreviated schedule that allows them to find their way from class to class and gives them a chance to meet their teachers. The day ends with a pep rally and welcome party sponsored by the Parent Association. The Student Council takes the lead in Freshman Orientation Day, and selected juniors and seniors lead tours, assist students, and answer questions. When the rest of the student body arrives the next day, the inevitable anxiety that freshmen feel as they begin high school has diminished considerably.

Freshman Advisory Program

The daily schedule for freshmen is designed so that all freshmen meet with their faculty advisor four days each week for twenty-five minutes. The advisor is not responsible for providing instruction but, instead, is asked to create an environment in which students can relax, get to know one another, and have their questions answered. The advisor is also responsible for monitoring the academic achievement of each student and counseling individual students regarding any difficulties they are experiencing.

Because all of the students assigned to an advisor have the same counselor, the counselor attends the advisory one day each week to check in on each student. This weekly visit serves a variety of purposes. Counselors are able to build relationships with their new students as they come to know each one as an individual. Conversations go beyond academic progress to include the student's interests, hobbies, and involvement in cocurricular activities, as well as his or her goals for high school. Counselors are able to share the most pertinent information with small groups of freshmen in a setting that encourages students to ask questions and seek clarification. Counselors are assured weekly contact with each of their freshmen and can schedule a more private meeting with any student who might need extra help. Thus, the Freshman Advisory Program gives each incoming student sustained contact and a personal relationship with two caring adults—an advisor and a counselor—for the entire school year.

Freshman Mentor Program

Assisting each faculty advisor are five upperclassmen who serve as mentors and meet with their freshmen each day during the advisory period. The upperclassmen divide the twenty-five students among themselves, with each assuming responsibility for five freshmen. The mentor's job is to do whatever is necessary to help his or her five students become successful at Stevenson. Within the first week of school, all freshmen are required to pass a test on the school rulebook, so mentors tutor them on the rules until each freshman is able to pass. By the fourth week of school, all freshmen are required to solidify their academic, social, and participation goals for their four years of high school, so their mentor guides them through that process. Most importantly, every freshman knows that he or she has a "big brother" or "big sister" to turn to each day for help with questions that can range from "How do I ask a girl to Homecoming?" to "What is the best way to study for final exams?"

Participation in Cocurricular Programs

Stevenson offers a wide array of cocurricular programs to its students— athletics, clubs, fine arts, community service, intramurals—but surveys of students revealed that many were electing not to participate. When staff reviewed research that demonstrated students who become involved in school activities experience greater satisfaction with school and higher academic achievement than those who do not, they concluded that Stevenson should do a better job of engaging incoming students in the cocurricular program.

A *Cocurricular Handbook* was created to describe each activity and any requirements for participation. A Cocurricular Fair gives eighth graders information on every program and answers any questions the students or parents might have about that program. Students who indicate an interest in a particular program receive a letter from the sponsor urging them to join and advising them of procedures for doing so. Finally, when counselors meet with incoming freshmen and parents to register students for courses, they also register the students for a cocurricular activity.

The school schedule was adjusted to provide one activity period during the school day each month. Club sponsors can use that period to schedule meetings with members. A student who is intent on finding a cocurricular program that makes no demands on his or her time outside of the school day can join a program that only meets during the activity period, but few choose that option. The school creates the expectation that every student needs to belong to something—a team, a cast, an ensemble, or a club—and that no one will remain on the periphery throughout their high school years.

Frequent Monitoring of Student Progress

When the Stevenson staff compared the practices of its school to research findings on the characteristics of highly effective schools, it became evident that procedures used for reporting student progress were problematic. Although the research called for frequent monitoring of student learning and strong partnerships with parents, Stevenson grading practices made it impossible for either the school or parents to get an overview of a student's academic performance until the eleventh week of the semester. The school could not respond to students on a timely basis, and parents were being kept in the dark.

Stevenson addressed this discrepancy by creating a faculty task force and presenting its members with the charge to develop academic reporting procedures that were more aligned with the school's mission of success for all. After examining the research, looking at the practices of other schools, and investigating the potential of technology to assist with more frequent progress reporting, the task force recommended that the school change from two nine-week grading periods per semester to three six-week grading periods. It also recommended that all students receive a progress report at the midpoint of each six-week period. The effect of this change meant that each student, designated Stevenson staff, and parents would have a report of that student's learning, in every course, every three weeks.

In recent years, Stevenson has made electronic gradebooks available to teachers. Parents are able to go online to monitor homework completion and grades for their students. Thus, the school has gone from advising parents of student progress every eleven weeks, to every three weeks, to real-time progress reporting. Armed with that information, parents are in a much better position to be partners in the education of their children, and the school is in a much better position to respond to students who need support or enrichment.

Providing Extra Time and Support for Students Who Experience Difficulty

There was great hope among the staff that these initiatives—a more proactive support system and a comprehensive plan to assist students in making the transition to high school—would lead to success for every student. Regrettably, they did not.

It soon became evident that some students continued to flounder—notwithstanding all of the hard work of classroom teachers and despite the collective effort of the staff to create a school climate that supported learning. It also became evident that the commitment to monitor each student's learning on a more timely basis would accomplish little unless the school was prepared to respond when it discovered that a student was experiencing difficulty. Ultimately, in spite of all they had done to support students, the teachers and administrators of Stevenson could not escape the question, what are we prepared to do when a student does not learn? The collective response to that question became known as the Stevenson Pyramid of Interventions. The elements of the pyramid are explained in the following sections.

Student Support Teams

Any system of interventions for students is only as effective as the process that is in place to monitor student learning and respond when students experience difficulty. Stevenson organized its Student Services Department into Student Support Teams (SSTs). The effectiveness of the school's pyramid of interventions continues to depend upon the work of these teams.

The SSTs were originally comprised of a counselor, a social worker, and the dean of students. Together they shared responsibility for the same group of students. More recently, a school psychologist has become an integral member of the team. Student Support Teams meet each week to review reports and computer printouts that offer insights into a student's academic progress, attendance, and behavior, as well as anecdotal accounts regarding concern for the well-being of a student. It is the team's responsibility to initiate the appropriate assistance whenever these indicators suggest a student is experiencing difficulty.

Conferencing and Optional Tutoring

When progress reports issued at the end of the first three weeks of the grading period indicate students are in danger of failing, students face a cadre of adults expressing concern. The classroom teacher meets with the student, suggests strategies to improve the situation, and offers the student passes from a supervised study hall to the tutoring center. Advisors receive a copy of the progress report from every course for all of their students and meet with each student to review the reports. The advisor will counsel the student, suggest the student take advantage of additional support in the tutoring center, and assign the upperclassman mentor to assist the student with homework each day. The counselor, who is also armed with a copy of the progress report, will stop in on the advisory during the week. The counselor will also meet with each student, express concern, and ask the student what steps he or she has taken to improve the situation. The parents receive a copy of the progress report and are urged to address the matter with their child. At this point, students begin to get the impression that they are being quadruple-teamed from people harassing them about their unacceptable academic performance. When confronted with this level of support (or perhaps scrutiny from the perspective of the student), most students recognize that they will not be allowed to slack off and decide to put forth sufficient effort to improve the situation—if only to ease the pressure and attention from school personnel and parents.

Mandatory Tutoring Program

If, despite all of this attention, students earn a grade of D or F at the end of the six-week grading period, the SST will assign those students to mandatory tutoring. Students are no longer *invited* to get extra help from tutors; they are *required* to do so. Students are assigned to the tutoring center rather than supervised study hall for two days each week. Course-specific teams of teachers provide tutors with materials, assignment sheets, and upcoming dates for tests and projects, and tutors work with students to meet the standards established in each of their classrooms. The progress of students assigned to mandatory tutoring is monitored on a weekly basis. When students fail to demonstrate improvement, the SST considers moving them to the next level of intervention, the Guided Study Program.

Guided Study Program

Most of the study halls at Stevenson have between eighty and a hundred students assigned to them each period. The Guided Study Program has no more than ten students in a given period. Whereas students in traditional study halls are required only to maintain an atmosphere conducive to study, in Guided Study they are required to complete their work under the direct supervision of the Guided Study teacher. Prior to assigning students to Guided Study, the SST meets with students and their parents to clarify expectations and develop a contract specifying what all parties pledge to do to help the student be successful. Students and parents, alike, are expected to make and observe commitments regarding the changes they intend to initiate to help the student experience academic success. Students and parents also attempt to clarify any personal or family issues that are contributing to the student's difficulty.

The goal of the Guided Study Program is to provide students with the skills, disposition, and direct supervision to ensure they complete their work and begin to experience academic success. The Guided Study teacher works with students on such study skills as using an assignment notebook, creating a schedule to ensure the timely completion and submission of homework, and developing strategies to prepare for tests. He or she also contacts the classroom teachers of assigned students and asks to be kept informed regarding the classroom behavior, grades, pending projects, tests, and homework of each student. Most importantly, the Guided Study teacher insists students complete their work under his or her intense supervision. The teacher becomes a liaison not only between students and teachers, but also between parents and the school staff. He or she contacts the parents of all students assigned to Guided Study on a weekly basis to review the progress students are making.

The Mentor Program

The Guided Study Program has been extremely effective in raising the achievement levels of students placed in the program, but a small percentage of students fail to respond to this support. When that occurs, the SST and the Guided Study teacher convene to determine if the student should be moved to the next step in this systematic approach to intervention: the Mentor Program. This program provides two periods of support each day in a small-group setting of ten students to one teacher. Participants in the program earn one credit toward graduation each semester. The first hour of the program operates in a similar manner to the Guided Study Program, with the mentor teacher ensuring that students complete all homework and assignments. He or she insists on reviewing all of a student's work before it is turned in to the classroom teacher.

The second hour of the program is quasitherapeutic, as the mentor teacher attempts to help students and parents identify the reasons a child is choosing to fail. The teacher works in close alliance with a social worker, and one day each week is devoted to the social worker leading group processes. Students with specific problems that are interfering with academic success—substance abuse, anger management issues, grief, and so on—are also enrolled in a series of student support groups that meet each week to help students address their issues. The mentor and social worker also set aside one evening each month to meet with parents to help them acquire the skills that will make them effective partners in the effort to help their students be successful in high school.

The key to both the Guided Study Program and the Mentor Program is the ability of the teachers to develop a connection with students who have typically been alienated from school. These teachers have a special interest in working with academically at-risk students and a commitment to persevere in the face of student indifference. They monitor students closely, insist upon the completion of homework and assignments, and celebrate with students each time one of them is able to improve a grade.

The pyramid of interventions presented in figure 4.1 is the graphic depiction of Stevenson's effort to create a foundational level of support for all students and increasingly more directed and intensive support for students who are not being successful.

Enrichment at Adlai Stevenson High School

Prior to launching its pyramid of interventions, Stevenson's basic structure reflected the traditional selecting and sorting mentality upon which high schools were created. Throughout their four years of high school, students were assigned into five different ability groups that reflected the bell-shaped curve. Initial placement was based solely on a student's performance on a single nationally normed test administered to them in eighth grade. A local percentile ranking was established for each member of the incoming class, and students were then assigned into one of the high school's five curricular tracks on the basis of their ranking. Placement adhered to rigid caps and quotas. Only 10 percent of the incoming students could qualify for the most rigorous track (the honors program) while 25 percent were automatically relegated to the two remedial tracks (the modified and basic programs).

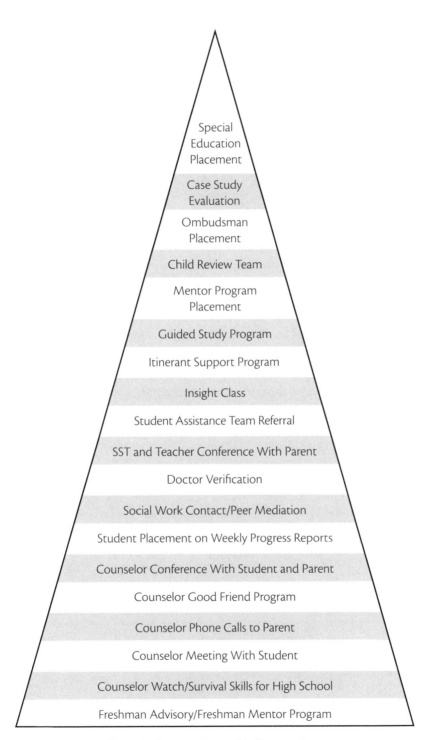

Figure 4.1: Stevenson's pyramid of interventions.

Because placement was based on how a student ranked in the incoming class rather than on demonstrated proficiency, the same score that qualified a student for the college preparatory curriculum one year could relegate a different student to the remedial program the next year.

This placement process had several adverse effects. It restricted the number of students who could have access to rigorous curriculum. It automatically designated one-fourth of every entering class into a substandard remedial curriculum. It provided an easy but ineffective solution to both students and teachers when a student was not being successful in a particular class. From the teacher's perspective, a student who was not putting forth enough effort to be successful could be moved into a less-rigorous curriculum. A student failing algebra could be moved to modified algebra. If the student continued to fail, he or she could be moved to general math. From the student's perspective, there was always an easy way out of class because the school would inevitably offer a less-challenging program. The less a student did, the less he or she was required to do—because the school was perfectly willing to lower the bar. Finally, and perhaps most unfortunately, the entire structure of the school conveyed the message to students, "You will be highly successful here only if you are smart, and very few of you are capable of meeting that standard."

As the staff began to grapple with the question, how will we respond when kids don't learn, the incongruity between the school's mission statement that promised success for every student and a school structure designed to sort and select students according to the bell curve became apparent. Working in partnership with teachers from the six middle schools, they began the exploration of the first critical question of a professional learning community: what is it we want all students to learn? Within a few months teachers were able to clarify what every student leaving eighth grade was expected to know and be able to do in the areas of reading, writing, mathematics, and foreign languages.

The high school and middle school teachers then turned their attention to the second critical question: how will we know if each student has achieved the intended outcomes by the end of eighth grade? Neither state standards nor state assessments had yet been developed, so the middle school and the high school teachers worked together to develop criterion-referenced proficiency tests to answer that question. These proficiency tests became the basis for placing students into Stevenson's newly designed program.

The five different ability levels were collapsed into three. One standard proficiency score was established based on the recommendation of the teachers who had developed the tests, and students were advised that all those who reached that standard in a given area of the test would be invited into the honors program—a program specifically designed to help students earn college credits while still in high school. No longer would that program be reserved for the top 10 percent of an entering class. A second proficiency score was established as the qualifying standard for entry into the college-preparatory program—a program designed to provide students with a solid, rigorous curriculum that would prepare them for success in higher education. Placement was by area rather than by track; that is, a student who qualified for honors mathematics might be recommended for the college preparatory English program based on his or her proficiency score in language arts.

Students who were unable to achieve the prerequisite score for either the honors or college preparatory curriculum were recommended for the modified program. This program, however, was designed to be far different than the remedial programs that preceded it. Students assigned to those earlier programs would languish there for four years. There was virtually no opportunity for upward mobility into higher-level curriculum. The new structure, however, limited modified courses to the freshman and sophomore years. Juniors and seniors would have only two levels available to them— college preparatory and honors. This change redefined the entire purpose of the modified program. No longer was it a four-year holding pen; now it was a two-year launching pad that accelerated student learning so that all students would have access to rigorous college preparatory curricula in their final two years of high school. Juniors and seniors who pursued technical or vocational programs were now expected to complete the same English, math, science, and social studies courses as their college-bound classmates.

The proficiency tests were not used as a barrier to student aspirations. If students or parents were disappointed with the recommended placement, students were given multiple opportunities to demonstrate proficiency on different forms of the placement test during the second semester of eighth grade. A summer program was offered for students who sought tutoring in order to improve their placement. And, in the final analysis, if the student or parent persisted in seeking the higher placement despite the school's recommendation, the student would be enrolled in the more advanced course and given six weeks to demonstrate that he or she was capable of meeting its standards.

Raising the Bar Requires Increasing Support

Stevenson's new structure called upon students to reach for higher levels of achievement. Students who in the past could have sought the comfort and low expectations of the remedial program were now called upon to be successful in the college preparatory program. Students who in the past would have been excluded from rigor of the college-level honors program were now a part of the program. The school was raising the bar, but raising the bar without provisions both for extra support and for strengthening the instructional practice of teachers is likely to lead to more failure rather than higher levels of learning. Therefore, the changes in placement and structure were accompanied by a commitment to provide students with levels of intervention and to provide teachers with the time and support essential to effective collaborative teams.

The pyramid of interventions was available to students at all levels. A student struggling in a calculus class had just as much access to tutorial support during the school day as a student experiencing difficulty in a pre-algebra class. As students began to experience the benefits of tutoring, demand for the service grew. Certified teachers in different subject areas who enjoyed working with students but did not want the responsibility of being classroom teachers were hired to support the tutoring center. Members of the National Honor Society were asked to tutor in the center as a way of fulfilling the service requirement for membership. The center expanded its hours into the evening at the end of each grading period.

Teachers began making changes in their practice as well. The entire math program restructured its classes so students could support one another in their learning by working together in collaborative teams. As teachers of advanced placement courses opened their programs to a growing percentage of the student body, they began creating voluntary study and tutoring sessions for their programs. The message of the school began to change from, "You can achieve at high levels if you are smart" to "You can achieve at high levels if you work hard."

This restructuring and reculturing of Adlai Stevenson High School benefited students of all levels and helped the school become what the United States Department of Education has described as one of the most recognized and celebrated schools in America. It was the first comprehensive high school to be named by the United States Department of Education as a "New American School," a model of successful school reform, and it has been cited repeatedly in the popular press and professional literature as one of the nation's best schools. And yet, the school continues to improve.

Strengthening the Pyramid

Stevenson has taken significant steps to improve the effectiveness of its pyramid of interventions since we featured it in *Whatever It Takes* (DuFour, DuFour, Eaker, & Karhanek, 2004). With the passage of response to intervention legislation, the school redesigned the structure of its Student Support Teams to give social workers and school psychologists a larger role in early intervention. Under the former structure, some psychologists and social workers were assigned to work specifically with special education students, a structure that devoted half of those personnel in the school to fewer than 10 percent of its students. The new structure eliminated the separation of those positions into special education and general education tracks and made all staff responsible for all of the school's students. School psychologists now coordinate the work of the SSTs and focus more on early intervention and less on testing for special education placement. The restructuring was cost neutral. It did not require new money, but it did require psychologists, social workers, and counselors to redefine their roles and responsibilities.

In the face of growing research that 1) socially and emotionally competent students do better in school, engage in more prosocial behaviors, and are more likely to experience career success, and 2) social and emotional competencies can be explicitly taught as an enhancement to rather than a detractor from the curriculum, Stevenson has also taken steps to teach those competencies and monitor their presence in all of its students. A schoolwide task force has taken the lead in developing a common vocabulary, identifying the most vital competencies, and providing information to all staff regarding how those competencies can be explicitly and implicitly taught in both the curricular and cocurricular programs.

Stevenson has also worked with the middle and elementary schools to create and administer surveys designed as social-emotional screeners to students in all grades as a means of plotting the development of these competencies in students over time. The goal is to identify students who have concerns about their own interpersonal, intrapersonal, stress management, and adaptability skills, and then have Student Support Teams implement specific interventions to assist those students.

In this area, once again, we see the PLC process at work. The school has used research on best practices to extend its focus on how it might serve *all* students. Staff members have engaged in clarifying exactly what they want for students (that is, the vital social and emotional behaviors), worked collaboratively to determine the best way to teach those behaviors, developed a strategy to monitor the progress of each student, and designed systems of interventions for the students who need support. Furthermore, the process remains fluid as the school continues to find ways to improve.

But Is It Sustainable?

Stevenson has undergone significant changes in personnel since we featured it in *Whatever It Takes*. Two different superintendents and three different principals have led the district and school, respectively. An early retirement incentive by the state of Illinois has resulted in huge turnover among teachers, and the majority of the leadership team that was in place in 2004 is no longer at the school.

In the face of these significant changes, Stevenson has not merely sustained the extraordinary commitment to student success and the resulting high levels of student achievement that we described in *Whatever It Takes*—it has improved in all areas. Consider the following.

Grade Distribution

The grade distribution at Stevenson approximated the bell curve in the early 1980s, with fewer than 30 percent of assigned grades reported as A/B and more than 35 percent of the grades designated as D/F. The cumulative grade point average for the student body was less than 2.0 on a 4.0 scale. When we reported on the school in 2004, the grade distribution had improved to 78 percent A/B and 4.5 percent D/F, with a student body grade point average of 3.3. By 2008 the school had improved upon that extraordinary grade distribution with 80 percent A/B and 4 percent D/F for a student body grade point average of 3.4. Only 1 percent of the almost 25,000 grades assigned at the end of each semester of the 2007–2008 school year was failing grades.

State Assessment

Stevenson continues to score in the top 1 percent of all high schools in Illinois on every section of the state exam. The exceptionally high student scores we reported in 2004 improved in all areas by 2009. The school ranks sixth in the state and third among comprehensive public high schools in Illinois on the state assessment. There has been no regression toward the mean on the state assessment.

ACT Exam

All high school juniors in Illinois must take the ACT exam, even if they have no plans to attend postsecondary education. Stevenson scores, already among the best in the state in 2004, have increased on each of the subject areas of the exam, and the composite score has increased from 24.9 to 25.7. In other words, the composite score for this school, where all students *must* take the exam, is dramatically better than the national composite score of 21.1—even though the national composite is based almost exclusively on college-bound students . . . and the scores continue to improve.

Advanced Placement Exams

In 1985, 88 Stevenson students wrote a total of 133 advanced placement (AP) exams. Only 7 percent of that graduating class earned honor grades. By 2004, 1,286 Stevenson students wrote 2,503 AP exams, and the percentage of the graduating class that earned honor grades on these college-level assessments had grown to 65 percent. In 2009, the number of students writing exams had increased to 1,537 and the number of exams to 3,489, making Stevenson one of the top comprehensive high schools in the world in advanced placement participation. Despite this increase of almost 1,000 exams in five years, the percentage of honor grades actually increased from 85 percent to 88 percent, and the mean score remained at 3.8, compared to the national average of 2.8. Of Stevenson graduates in 2008, almost 80 percent had earned college credit through the advanced placement program or dual enrollment, compared to approximately 15 percent of the nation's graduates.

Credits Earned

Stevenson awards one credit for every course a student completes success-fully each semester. Students must earn a total of forty-five credits in order to graduate. From 2004 to 2009, 96 percent of the school's graduates have exceeded that total, and more than 70 percent have earned fifty-one or more credits—the equivalent of an additional semester of high school.

An Elegantly Simple Strategy

Stevenson's shift from a focus on sorting and selecting students based on perceptions of their ability to a focus on ensuring high levels of learning for *all* students has proven beneficial to students in all programs and grade levels. By implementing a plan to monitor each student's learning on a timely basis and to intervene with additional time and support in a directive and systematic way, the school has almost eliminated student failure. At the same time, its strategy for raising the bar is remarkably simple: give more students access to a more rigorous curriculum, and provide them with the additional time and support to succeed in that curriculum. The results provide clear evidence of the effectiveness of that approach.

Stevenson's attention to ensuring the success of all students has not come at the expense of its highest-performing students. The mode score of Stevenson students on advanced placement exams each year is five, the highest possible score. The national mode is three. The College Board designates AP Scholar Awards for students who have excelled on the rigorous advanced placement exams. Stevenson has produced more Advanced Placement Scholars than any school in Illinois. The College Board also presents an award to the top male and top female student in each state every year. Once again, Stevenson has produced more state winners than any school in Illinois. The National Merit Scholarship Program recognizes the top-scoring students in the nation on the Preliminary Scholarship Aptitude Test/National Merit Scholarship Qualifying Test. From 2004 to 2009, 101 Stevenson students have been recognized as National Merit finalists, 203 have been recognized as Commended Scholars, and the combined total of honorees has increased for four consecutive years.

Finally, it is important to remember that this record of continuous improvement has occurred despite ongoing challenges. The student enrollment, which was 1,600 students when Stevenson began this journey twenty-five years ago, has grown to over 4,400 students on one campus, and yet its system of interventions is so effective that the school can monitor the academic success and well-being of each of those students on an ongoing basis. When the initiative began, there were no English language learners in the school. Today one of every four students does not use English as the primary language in the home. In addition, the majority of the administrative and teaching staff has been replaced over the past quarter century. Yet the school gets better each year. Perhaps that is why approximately 3,000 educators will again visit Stevenson this year to study its programs, its practices, and most importantly, its culture. Those who question whether school improvement can be sustained can look to this school, which has improved results in virtually every indicator each year for a quarter of a century despite explosions in enrollment, a changing student population, and the turnover of almost the entire staff since the improvement process began. When continuous improvement becomes deeply rooted in the culture of a school, helping students learn at higher levels can be sustained over time.

Concluding Thoughts

There is nothing random or left to chance when it comes to how Stevenson High School interacts with its students. *Every* student who enrolls at Stevenson High School is *guaranteed* a foundational level of support. Students know with certainty that as freshmen they will attend an advisory period four times each week with their faculty advisor, whose sole responsibility is to ensure they have a successful first year of high school. They know an upper-classman mentor will function as their big brother or big sister throughout the year. They know their counselor will visit their advisory period each week to check on their progress. They know their teachers have created the same guaranteed and viable curriculum for each course and that their learning will be closely monitored through daily checks for understanding and frequent common assessments. They know their teachers will provide either a progress report or report card to their parents, advisor, and counselor every three weeks. They know if they are not passing their classes they will be required to participate in an increasingly directive system of interventions, including mandatory study halls, tutoring centers, guided study to monitor their completion of homework, study skills classes, and support groups. They know the school has created a schedule that ensures they have time during their day to receive additional support for learning. They know that passing their courses means they will be given greater privileges and increased autonomy as they advance through school, but keeping those privileges requires them to maintain passing grades. In brief, they know that their learning is not left to chance because their school has created a pyramid of interventions, a plan to monitor their learning on a regular and timely basis and to respond at the first sign they are experiencing difficulty.

In her study of the school, Joan Richardson (2004) reported Stevenson "was widely recognized as a standard bearer of excellence"; however, she also pointed out that at one time it had been considered "an also-ran among suburban high schools" (p. 115). She attributed the change to the fact that "nothing today at Stevenson is haphazard. Structures have been put into place and supported until they have taken root and become part of the body of the school" (p. 115). The pyramid of interventions was one of the most significant of those structures, but structural change alone will not improve a school. Ultimately the educators within a school must create a new culture—new assumptions, beliefs, expectations, values, and habits that constitute the norm for that school. They must learn to tell a new story.

> Visit www.d125.org/ for more information about Adlai Stevenson High School.
>
> For tools and templates from Stevenson that you may find useful, visit go.solution-tree.com/PLCbooks.

5

HAND IN HAND WE ALL LEARN: A RETURN TO BOONES MILL ELEMENTARY SCHOOL

No matter how good school goals are, they cannot be met if the school isn't organized to accomplish them. The school operates as a learning community that uses its own experience and knowledge, and that of others, to improve the performance of students and teachers alike. . . . A culture of shared responsibility is established, and everybody learns from one another.
—NATIONAL ASSOCIATION OF ELEMENTARY SCHOOL PRINCIPALS, 2002

Every school must create systems to monitor student learning that are doable, teacher friendly, and provide teachers and teams with the timely information vital to improved instruction and intervention.
—BERNICE COBBS, PRINCIPAL OF BOONES MILL ELEMENTARY SCHOOL

Boones Mill Elementary School, one of fifteen schools in Franklin County, Virginia, could be considered the antithesis of Stevenson High School in many ways, including size, resources, and the students and community it serves. Boones Mill draws its 465 pre-K through grade 5 students from a rural area of south-central Virginia that has been hit hard by the loss of jobs in local textile and manufacturing industries. The number of students qualifying for free and reduced-cost lunch has increased in recent years, the student mobility rate has increased, and the per-pupil expenditure of the Franklin County school division remains in the bottom 10 percent of the Commonwealth of Virginia. Yet Boones Mill students face the same rigorous assessment challenges as schools in much more affluent areas of the state.

Virginia offers a prototypical model of a state that has embraced high-stakes testing. In 1995, the Virginia Department of Education issued the revised K–12 standards of learning (SOLs) to all schools throughout the Commonwealth, standards that identified rigorous student outcomes by grade level in the areas of English (reading, writing, listening, speaking, research), mathematics, science, and social studies. State assessments were developed for certain grade levels and courses, and schools were informed that if at least 70 percent of their students did not meet the minimum proficiency score on the assessments within a few years, the school would receive sanctions up to and including loss of state accreditation. The first time the tests were administered, only 2 percent of the schools across the Commonwealth met the 70 percent target.

Few could have predicted that Boones Mill, this relatively small school in rural Virginia with very few resources, would become one of the most successful in the Commonwealth in helping students meet the new standards. This achievement is even more dramatic in light of the fact that since the first year of its professional learning community journey, the school includes all of its students in the state assessment program rather than utilizing the option of excluding some students with special needs. Furthermore, every indicator that the school uses to monitor student learning—at the building, district, state, and national levels—has been on a steady climb upward since implementing the PLC model of continuous school improvement, in spite of the fact that five different principals have served Boones Mill during the ten years the school has been on its PLC journey. Equally striking, approximately 50 percent of the current staff is new to the school since the initial implementation of the PLC concept. Nevertheless, the focus on learning, the commitment to working collaboratively, and the use of results to drive continuous improvement are stronger today than ever before. Let us revisit the early steps of the journey at Boones Mill, and then examine the current practices and culture of this school.

A Critical First Step: Building Shared Knowledge of the Current Reality

When Boones Mill began its PLC journey in 2000, like most schools, it was staffed with hardworking, dedicated educators who sincerely wanted to help all students achieve at high levels. Ultimately, the staff recognized that working hard was not enough and concluded that the best hope of achieving the goal of learning for all students was to embrace the concepts of a PLC. That decision led the entire staff to grapple with the third and fourth critical questions: How will we respond, as a school, when it becomes evident that some students are not learning what is being taught despite our best efforts in the classroom? And, how will we respond, as a school, to the students who have already demonstrated proficiency of the essential knowledge and skills?

The staff began their exploration of these questions by building shared knowledge about the current reality in their school. They generated a comprehensive list of practices already in place to address the needs of struggling learners. Like other elementary schools in the district, Boones Mill offered a four-week remedial summer school program for recommended students in grades K through 5. Participation in the program, however, was not required. Other options for additional time and support included an optional after-school remediation program, retention at grade level, promotion to the next grade level with the hope that the difficulty was simply developmental, or referral for special education testing and services.

Outside of those limited options, the issue of whether or how to intervene for struggling students was left to the discretion of each individual teacher. Traditionally, a few teachers offered tutorial sessions before and/or after school. Student attendance at the sessions, however, was by invitation, and the students who were most in need of extra support were typically the least likely to stay to receive it. Family transportation issues, conflicts with cocurricular activities, or lack of parental insistence on their children's participation allowed students to opt out of the sessions.

Many teachers were not in a position to offer extra time and support beyond the student day because of competing professional, personal, and family obligations. Several of those teachers attempted to create opportunities for interventions during the school day; however, they faced the questions of when and how they could offer assistance. Some grade-level teams decided to use student recess time for intervention, with certain teachers assigned to supervise the students in free play while one teacher volunteered to work with struggling learners. This strategy, however well intentioned, did not please some parents and most students. Struggling learners were often denied a much-needed break and ultimately came to view the additional help as punishment.

A few teachers used their own duty-free lunch periods to provide a working lunch for students who needed more time, but again the students were not required to attend. Most students, especially those in the upper elementary grades, chose to eat lunch with their peers in the cafeteria rather than work with their teachers.

In the late 1990s, as state accountability sanctions grew closer, specials classes (such as art, music, physical education, computer skills, library skills, and guidance) were suspended, and the specials class teachers were required to tutor students in the core curriculum for the grade levels facing state assessments. Although this strategy for improving results on the state assessments was clearly misaligned with the school's mission to promote growth in each area of child development, it seemed justified because desperate times called for desperate measures.

Referring students for special education services also became an attractive option for providing additional time and support. Students with an individualized education plan (IEP) were guaranteed extra academic assistance and were typically exempted from some of the consequences faced by general education students when they failed to meet the proficiency standards of district or state testing, such as summer school, loss of elective classes in middle school, after-school remediation the following school year, Saturday school, and so on.

This collective study of, and dialogue about, the current reality of the school helped staff members to come to consensus on the following conclusions:

- Individual teachers responded to students who were not learning in very different ways.

- The only students getting extra support in the core academic areas from adults beyond the classroom teacher during the school day were those eligible for special education services and a few primary grade students who received assistance in phonemic awareness skills from a part-time paraprofessional tutor.

- An after-school program of tutorial support that depended on the willingness and/or ability of students to attend was insufficient to ensure that all students who experienced difficulty would receive extra time and support for learning.

- The school had no human resources other than classroom teachers to provide additional time and support for struggling learners.

- Even though the school had several reliable volunteers, a solid, systematic process of interventions could not be dependent on volunteers.

- An honest assessment of the collective response of the school to students who were not learning could only lead to the conclusion that the response was limited, untimely, and random rather than systematic.

As the staff confronted this reality, they agreed purposeful change was imperative if the school were to achieve the goal of high levels of learning for all students. That conclusion resulted in the staff's willingness to initiate the team learning process.

Fostering Adult Learning so Students Can Learn

The staff agreed that in order for a comprehensive system of student support to be effective, it was incumbent upon every team to identify each student who needed assistance on a timely basis, use consistent standards and processes in identifying those students, and pinpoint the specific skill each student was having difficulty in mastering. Teaching teams of all the teachers of a grade level and the special education teacher who served that grade level were able to meet these challenges by engaging in the team learning process described in chapter 2.

The teams began the process by focusing on mathematics, which seemed less susceptible to a variety of interpretations than other subject areas. Once the members of the team identified the essential outcomes for math, each team turned its attention to the essential outcomes for reading. By the end of the first semester, each team had agreed on the essential outcomes for these two critical areas of the curriculum and were creating and administering common formative assessments aligned to each essential outcome. By the end of the second year of PLC implementation, each team had also engaged in this process for science and social studies.

The resulting clarity regarding what students should know and be able to do and the frequent analysis of evidence of their learning from the team-developed common assessments allowed both teams and individual teachers to identify their own professional development needs. Most importantly, however, this team learning process identified students meeting, exceeding, and falling below the target proficiency score on each skill or concept being assessed. Such information is of little use, however, unless a school is able to develop an effective system of providing students with additional time and support to become proficient. The staff of Boones Mill had developed effective procedures for identifying students who needed intervention or enrichment, but the question they still had to address was, how do we intend to respond?

Aligning Resources With Purpose and Priorities

As the staff began to brainstorm possibilities for providing students with additional time and support for learning during the school day, the principal proposed shifting state remedial funds, which traditionally had been allocated to summer remedial and after-school tutorial programs, to support the hiring of a part-time floating tutor to assist each grade-level team when a student was not learning. The faculty enthusiastically endorsed the proposal and worked together to create a job description for the position.

The availability of a tutor, however, led to a significant logistical challenge: when could the tutor have access to students who needed additional time and support? The principal gave teams latitude in answering that question, provided the solution met the following four parameters:

1   Each grade-level team had to make its students accessible to the tutor for a minimum of thirty minutes per day.

2   The tutorial time identified had to be consistent and constant among all classrooms in the grade level. By making all the students of a grade level available at the same time, the tutor could work with six grade-level units rather than twenty independent classrooms.

3   The designated time could not conflict with any direct instructional blocks (such as language arts, math, science, social studies, and specials classes).

4   The tutorial time could not interfere with the students' recess or other fun activities. The extra time and support could not be presented or perceived as punishment.

A sample grade-level schedule is presented in figure 5.1. The shading in figure 5.1 indicates the time devoted to the different subjects/activities each day and the transition from one subject/activity to the next. The darker shading on Thursday indicates the collaborative team meeting for third grade held from 8:50–9:55 while students are in back-to-back specials classes.

The Floating Tutor

The person hired to fill the part-time floating tutor position was a district-certified substitute teacher who had worked extensively at Boones Mill, had proven to be effective in classrooms at all grade levels, and related well with students, staff, and the parent community. Under the team's direction, the tutor could fulfill the following needs:

● Provide supplementary instruction or intervention for individuals or small groups of no more than eight students on specific activities designed by the grade-level team.

● Review, model, and practice test-taking skills and strategies with students, helping them to feel more confident in responding to a variety of assessment tasks and instruments.

● Supervise classroom activities during the grade level's designated tutorial time to allow the certified teachers to work with identified students on essential skills and concepts.

	Monday	Tuesday	Wednesday	Thursday	Friday
8:00–8:15	Teacher Work Day Begins				
8:15–8:40	Students Arrive: Breakfast, Morning Work, Take-In Procedures				
8:40–8:50	Tardy Bell, Morning Announcements, Instructional Day Begins				

SPECIALS (8:50–9:55)

	Monday					Tuesday				Wednesday					Thursday						Friday				
SPECIALS	LIB	COM	GUI	MUS	PE	LIB	COM	GUI	PE	LIB	COM	GUI	MUS	PE	LIB	COM	GUI	MUS	ART	PE	LIB	COM	GUI	ART	PE
8:50–9:20		3D		3J	3F	3J	3F		3D			3F	3D	3J		3J		3F		3D	3D		3J		3F
9:25–9:55			3D								3F				3F	3D				3J			3J		

	Monday–Friday
9:55–11:45	Language Arts/Social Studies
11:45–12:15	Intervention/Enrichment
12:20–1:15	Lunch and Recess
1:15–2:15	Math
2:15–3:00	Science
3:00–3:10	Afternoon Announcements; K and Grade 1 Car Riders and Loading Buses; 3:05 Dismissal for Grades 2–5; Buses Depart at 3:10
3:10–3:30	Instructional Staff Planning

Figure 5.1: Third-grade master schedule for instruction.

Each grade-level team decided how to group their students during this daily block of time so that all students, not just the students needing intervention, could benefit. This protected block allowed teams to differentiate instruction across each grade level, not just within individual classrooms, and to meet the needs of all learners in unprecedented ways. For example, the kindergarten and first-grade teams created grade-level learning centers by moving learning centers from their individual classrooms to a common area outside their classrooms. Teachers then contributed their best activities from their individual classrooms to each center and aligned those activities with the team pacing guides for each content area.

Second- through fifth-grade teams elected to engage students who had mastered the essential skills in individual and group activities, including computer-based learning and exploration, silent sustained reading, Junior Great Books reading circles, and teacher read-alouds, while their classmates received intervention. In these grade levels, the floating tutor often supervised the enrichment activities while one or more of the teachers on the team provided the small group intervention. Typically, the teacher whose students were most successful on a particular skill on the common assessments would take the lead in working with students who had experienced difficulty with that skill. Thus, students at every grade level had access to the most effective teacher on the team, skill by skill, any time they were unable to achieve the intended standard. After a period of intervention deemed appropriate by each team, the students were given another opportunity to demonstrate their learning. Based on the new data, the team then determined the appropriate next steps.

Within two months, the floating tutorial program was so successful that the faculty decided to shift site-based funds that had been designated for the purchase of instructional materials to hiring a second floating tutor. Thus, by the beginning of second semester, Boones Mill had a team of two floating tutors working in tandem each day according to the schedule outlined in table 5.1.

Team Communication

One serendipitous benefit of creating this designated time for daily intervention and enrichment activities was that the school's volunteer program became much more effective in providing support for learning. Volunteers knew that they would be able to work directly with individual students—listening to them read aloud, reading to them, monitoring their learning center work, drilling them on math facts, and so on. A school-based volunteer committee, jointly run by parents and teachers, worked together to solicit and assign volunteers throughout the school according to requests from individual classrooms and teams. Over time, many parents, grandparents, business partners, senior citizens, college students, and high-school interns considering education as a career option were scheduled into the grade-level tutorial times to assist students and provide more one-on-one support.

Table 5.1: Floating Tutor Schedule

8:20–8:50	Fifth grade
8:50–9:20	Fourth grade
9:30–10:30	First-grade centers
10:30–11:30	Kindergarten centers
11:40–12:15	Third grade
12:15–1:00	Duty-free lunch/planning
1:00–1:30	Second grade
1:30–2:00	Additional time K–5 (by request)
2:00–2:30	Fifth grade
2:30–2:50	Record keeping

The floating tutorial system served as the foundation for the Boones Mill program for providing students with enrichment and intervention. It ensured that every student was guaranteed to receive timely, directive, systematic intervention during the school day whenever that student struggled with initial learning. Nevertheless, the wonderful staff of the school continued to explore new ways that they could support higher levels of learning for all students. Some of the resulting programs are presented next.

Grade-Level Parent Workshops

The staff concluded that parents could become a powerful source to support learning for their children *if* they were armed with the right tools and guidelines. Therefore, within the first four weeks of each new semester, grade-level teams conducted workshops for all parents who had students in their grade level. These workshops were advertised in advance to parents through both school and grade-level publications and were coordinated on the school's calendar so that no other school event conflicted with any workshop.

The grade-level parent workshops were structured to provide parents with a program overview of the key concepts of the curriculum, instructional strategies, purpose and format of assessments, and special events their children would experience during the coming months. Most importantly, the teams provided parents with practice/tutorial packets aligned with the essential outcomes in language arts and math. Teachers then guided parents through the content of the packets so parents could use the materials at home with their children to reinforce essential skills. Parents who attended the workshops left with a good understanding of the expectations the team had for students at that grade level. They also understood that their child was part of a clearly defined program of studies that was not solely dependent on the classroom teacher to whom he or she had been assigned, but was, instead, guided by the experience and expertise of all members of the collaborative team.

Parents who were unable to attend the workshops were sent the packet of materials with a cover letter from the team explaining the contents. A few days later the homeroom teacher contacted those parents to discuss the packet and answer any questions they might have.

Peer Tutoring/Buddy Programs

Another successful layer of time and support for students in all grades was the focused attention on peer tutoring and buddy programs. Teams found there were frequent opportunities for peer tutoring within individual classrooms and between classes in any particular grade. Because all classes at each grade had a common schedule, which included designated times for instruction in each content area, special subject instruction, lunch, recess, planning, and so on, teachers could easily structure flexible groups based on skills, partnerships, cooperative learning teams, and study groups without disrupting routine.

In addition to peer tutoring within grade levels, the faculty also established intergrade partnerships (buddy programs) in which older students served as tutors, reading buddies, mentors, and role models for the younger students. For example, during the first year of the PLC, the principal structured a kindergarten and fifth-grade buddy program that not only provided time for the students at these two grade levels to come together and learn from each other every week, but also gave the kindergarten and fifth-grade teaching teams time to collaborate.

Save One Student Program

Another support program created by the Boones Mill staff was the Save One Student, or SOS program, which called upon each adult in the building who volunteered to do so to take a personal interest in a student who was at risk academically. Classroom teachers identified students who would benefit from regular contact with another friendly, caring adult at school because, for whatever reason, the children lacked an academic support system at home.

Staff members who agreed to participate in the SOS program made a commitment to make two or three contacts per week with their assigned student at times that were mutually convenient for the student and the staff member. The contacts were never made during direct instruction times, but usually occurred when the sponsoring adult and SOS student had a common connection in their schedules. A teacher task force wrote a description of the program and established guidelines for implementation. All forty-two of the adults who worked at Boones Mill in the initial year of implementing the PLC process volunteered for the SOS program and gave their assigned student the gift of attention and support.

Connecting Special and General Education

Prior to implementing the PLC model of school improvement, Boones Mill used one of its two special education teachers to assist all students with learning disabilities assigned to mainstream classes. This resource teacher typically used a "pullout" program to provide services to all students in kindergarten through fifth grade. This presented a tremendous scheduling challenge for the lone teacher as she struggled to help each identified student attain IEP goals and objectives in language arts and math by taking them out of twenty different classrooms, each with its own daily schedule, curriculum pacing guides, instructional strategies, and resources. This arrangement also required regular classroom teachers to keep track of make-up assignments for students pulled away from their instruction in order to receive special education support. Students with the greatest academic needs were either completely missing essential instruction and assignments in one content area in order to receive services in another or were being held accountable for completing assignments at home, during recess, or during specials classes with little or no direct instruction in the relevant skills and concepts.

The second special education teacher managed a kindergarten through fifth grade self-contained special education classroom. The students assigned to this classroom tended to have more profound special education needs—severe developmental delays, behavioral or emotional disabilities, or other handicapping conditions. Traditionally, these students were kept separate from their general education peers for most or all of the day. The variety of learning levels and needs in this classroom, combined with the fact that there was only one teacher and a teacher assistant assigned to these students, meant the primary focus of the program was often managing behavior rather than teaching and learning. There were few opportunities for either the students or adults in these separate programs to interact with their general education counterparts.

As the staff began to work together on implementing PLC concepts, the walls that separated special and general education programs began to crumble. The special education program was redesigned to better meet the needs of both students and adults. The two special education teachers were reassigned to curriculum-level teams—one teacher to the primary teams and the other to upper elementary. Both teachers worked with their grade-level colleagues to clarify the essential outcomes for each grade level, write common assessments, establish the target score, plan and deliver instruction in the essential skills, administer the common assessment to their students according to the accommodations in the IEPs, analyze the results, and identify improvement strategies. Classroom teachers helped their special education colleagues develop greater clarity regarding essential outcomes and the standards students were expected to achieve. The special education teachers advised their teammates regarding effective instructional strategies, supplementary materials, and alternative assessments for special education students. This new sense of shared responsibility for students with special needs between general and special education teachers helped special education students experience a much more connected curriculum and achieve higher levels of learning than ever before.

Prior to the PLC journey at Boones Mill, referral for special education testing was often the first structured attempt to support struggling learners. With the implementation of an intense focus on timely, directive, and systematic learning support, special education became the last resort rather than the first response. As a result, the Child Study Team changed its role from the gatekeeper for initiating special education services to a clearinghouse for intervention strategies to help all students find success in the general education program. In effect, the Child Study Team moved from the top of the pyramid of interventions to play a significant role much earlier in the process.

Creating Systems of Communication

Once the staff completed the team learning process described in chapter 2, each grade-level team faced the challenge of creating effective two-way systems of communication with all the adults who served their children, including the other teams, specialist teachers, tutors, and support staff. Following are some of the communications regarding student learning that flowed between and among teachers and support services:

- **Weekly feedback sheets**—Feedback sheets from team meetings were distributed to the principal and ad-hoc team members to keep them informed of the team's current focus, questions, celebrations, and concerns.

- **Weekly/biweekly grade-level newsletters**—These communications were sent to parents and given to the principal and support services staff so that everyone was informed of essential skills, student celebrations, calendar events, and so on.

- **Monthly vertical team meetings**—Meetings were scheduled during student assemblies so that each team could address a skill or topic with the grade level below and the grade level above it. All six teams also met frequently to review how a concept was developed from kindergarten through fifth grade.

- **Monthly faculty meetings**—These meetings were established with protected time at each meeting for teams to share what they were learning with the entire staff.

- **Monthly "scoop sheets"**—Information was sent from each team to all specialists and support staff listing specific content and skills to be taught at that grade level in the coming month. This helped specialists reinforce key grade-level outcomes in their program.

- **The contract time**—The time immediately after student dismissal at the end of each school day was protected from disruption to afford opportunities for classroom teachers, specialists, and support staff to engage in dialogue or schedule meetings as needed to discuss curriculum and student learning needs.

The ongoing dialogue throughout the school and the coordination within and among teams enabled the entire staff to make meaningful and timely curriculum connections for students. The specials teachers were able to connect their area of expertise and passion with classroom instruction at the different grade levels because of the frequent communication flowing to and from grade-level teams. The full-time specialists assigned to Boones Mill also elected to join one grade-level team each year in completing a year-long action research project that culminated in curriculum and assessment products tied to the team's SMART goal.

For example, the librarian joined the second-grade team, and they worked throughout the year to create multiple units of instruction based on high-interest fiction and nonfiction children's literature. She assisted in developing teacher guides, creating student lessons and activities, and developing assessment tools to enrich the reading program in second grade. The guidance counselor joined the fifth-grade team in its effort to improve the social skills, study habits, and test-taking strategies of fifth graders and to assist those students (and their parents) in a smoother transition to the middle school. The music teacher wrote and produced annual musicals related to the social studies content of certain grade levels. Specialists took pride in the contributions they made to each grade-level team and in helping the students acquire the knowledge, skills, and dispositions necessary for success. And at the completion of the action research, every member of the team, including specialists, was awarded professional development credit, state recertification points, and credit toward the supervision and evaluation requirements of the district.

The open communication and synchronization of schedules and services benefited the staff in other ways as well. Each grade level had the benefit of an intervention team—floating tutors, special education teachers and/or teacher assistants, the part-time state-funded phonemic awareness tutor, the part-time gifted and talented resource teacher, volunteers, and mentors—to assist them in differentiating instruction to better meet the needs of all learners in a timely, systematic, and directive way. Furthermore, the coordination of services among and between grade-level teams provided each classroom teacher with large blocks of protected instructional time and few interruptions to individual classrooms throughout the day.

Boones Mill Today

The willingness of the Boones Mill staff members to align their practices with a mission of high levels of learning for all students has made the school one of the most recognized and celebrated in Virginia; nevertheless, the staff remains committed to improving their collective capacity to enhance their ability to achieve that mission. Bernice Cobbs, one of the key teachers on the staff when the PLC process was initiated in 2000, served as the principal of the school from 2007 to 2009 and now serves as director of elementary education for the district. As she reflects upon the journey, she is able to identify several ways in which the faculty has enhanced its effectiveness in the process since we first told the Boones Mill story in 2004.

The undeniable success of the school's system of interventions and the resulting staff commitment to that system have led it to divert even more site-based resources to floating tutors, doubling the number of part-time staff in that role from two to four. Cobbs also asked each grade level to develop a plan for utilizing a part-time aide assigned specifically to their grade level to assist with tutoring and then hired an aide from January to March for each team. As she put it, "The majority of our budget was spent on human resources, but I think it was worth every penny. We would rather have more people helping the children directly than the latest textbook or newest materials. Whenever we detected an area of weakness, we immediately devoted additional human resources to support that subject or grade level."

Even though the Franklin County School Division has begun to administer benchmark assessments to all schools throughout the county, teachers have become so convinced of the benefits of their own team-developed common assessments they have increased the frequency of their use from once every six to nine weeks to once every week or two. Grade-level teams now complete data collection sheets after each assessment, and these have helped them become more precise in reporting the results. They no longer simply advise the principal that 88 percent of the students were proficient on a skill: they list the four who are not proficient by name and specify the steps they are taking to support those students. The data collection sheet can also alert a team to a colleague who may be having difficulty or an entire team that is struggling to help students master a specific skill or concept.

Another improvement is that teams have added preassessments to their assessment arsenal. The use of common preassessments prior to beginning new units allows teams to differentiate initial new direct instruction by creating flexible learning groups based on the preassessment data. Through collaborative data analysis, teams identify students who may need intervention on the necessary prerequisite skills, those students who already have the necessary prerequisites, and those who have already mastered the skills and concepts of the new unit. Teachers are then able to cluster students for enrichment and intervention in their individual classrooms throughout the day and across the grade level during their team's designated tutorial time.

Principal Cobbs reported that a natural byproduct of the improved student achievement across the school was that the staff became more purposeful in advancing the learning for students who are proficient. A part-time gifted and talented resource teacher assigned to work at Boones Mill has created a menu of enrichment activities in the areas of reading and math for all grade levels. Any student who has demonstrated proficiency of an essential skill, not just those identified as gifted students, can participate in the challenging activities from the menu, either individually or in peer clusters. When present in the school, the gifted and talented resource teacher meets with groups of enrichment students during each grade level's designated block of time. On days that teacher is not assigned to Boones Mill, either the floating tutors or teachers from each grade level supervise the students engaged in enrichment activities.

One thing that has not changed at Boones Mill is the staff's willingness to confront the brutal facts and work collectively to resolve problems. Although the school had continued to excel on state and national assessments, the writing results in fifth grade took a discernible drop in 2008. In March of each year, every fifth-grade student across Virginia writes to a common prompt, and the essays are sent to a central location to be scored by two different people who have been trained to apply the state writing rubric. In 2005, the state discontinued administering a writing assessment at the third-grade level, making fifth grade the only year an elementary student is required by the state to demonstrate proficiency in writing. When the state dropped its assessment of writing until fifth grade, the district also stopped its practice of collecting and scoring writing samples.

When the staff looked at the disappointing writing results on the 2008 state assessment, teachers did not blame the students or criticize the assessment. Instead, they confronted (and acknowledged) a brutal fact: teachers at every grade level were paying far less attention to writing than they had in the past. They also admitted they no longer had a common language for writing instruction from grade to grade, or even class to class, and that they struggled to teach students with learning disabilities how to write.

The staff immediately resolved to attack the problem. The members of the school improvement committee wrote a grant proposal requesting ongoing training, coaching, and support for teaching writing through the T-TAC Learning Center at Virginia Polytechnic Institute and State University. During the 2008–2009 school year, every grade-level team received that training; each team administered multiple common writing prompts throughout the year; the members of each team collaboratively scored student writing samples using a grade-level rubric; and teachers provided feedback and support to students to help them progress as writers. The results should reinforce this staff's strong sense of collective efficacy. In 2009 the percentage of the school's fifth graders demonstrating proficiency on the state writing assessment jumped eleven points—from 81 to 92 percent—while writing scores in the state actually declined. In one year, Boones Mill had gone from 6 percent below the state average to 6 percent above the state average.

Results

When we featured Boones Mill in *Whatever It Takes* (DuFour, DuFour, Eaker, & Karhanek, 2004), it had been recognized for extraordinary student achievement; nevertheless, it has continued to improve. The school has received the Virginia Governor's Award for Educational Excellence every year since it began its professional learning community journey. In 2007, the state also created the VIP Excellence Award for schools that "are soaring far beyond the minimum requirements of the Standards of Learning and No Child Left Behind" (Kaine, 2008). Boones Mill was one of a small number of schools in the state to win the award both years it has been offered. It has been featured in two videos showcasing highly effective elementary schools from throughout the nation. It became one of the first schools in Virginia to receive the No Child Left Behind Blue Ribbon Award from the United States Department of Education.

Tables 5.2 through 5.4 (pages 83–84) indicate that the improvement the school experienced as a result of its PLC process has been sustained and advanced. We present data from 1999–2000, which is the year prior to the PLC initiative at Boones Mill; from 2000–2001 to show the dramatic gains in one year; and from 2005–2008 to show the continuing improvement since we featured the school in *Whatever It Takes*. Virginia did not begin to administer its own state assessment to fourth graders until the 2005–2006 school year. Tables 5.2 through 5.4 present the scores for Boones Mill in comparison to the state scores for that grade level and subject area.

Table 5.2: Percentages of Third-Grade Students Scoring Proficient or Above on State Assessments (Boones Mill/VA)

	Virginia Standards of Learning Assessments				
	1999–2000*	2000–2001	2005–2006	2006–2007	2007–2008
English	85/61	91/65	95/84	98/81	97/84
Math	87/71	97/77	98/90	100/89	100/89
Science	91/73	92/74	100/90	95/88	99/88
Social Studies	79/65	95/72	95/NA	98/93	99/73
*Note: First year of PLC implementation was 2000–2001.					

Table 5.3: Percentages of Fourth-Grade Students Passing State Assessments (Boones Mill/Virginia)

	Virginia Standards of Learning Assessments		
	2005–2006	2006–2007	2007–2008
Reading	94/86	97/87	97/88
Math	95/77	96/81	100/84

*Note: First year of PLC implementation was 2000–2001.

Table 5.4: Percentages of Fifth-Grade Students Scoring Proficient or Above on State Assessments (Boones Mill/VA)

	Virginia Standards of Learning Assessments				
	1999–2000*	2000–2001	2005–2006	2006–2007	2007–2008
English	80/68	85/73	99/87	90/87	92/89
Writing	87/81	88/84	90/89	92/89	81/87
Math	82/63	82/67	97/83	100/86	100/88
Science	78/64	94/75	92/85	88/88	95/88
History	NA/51	72/63	91/NA	84/92	95/90

*Note: First year of PLC implementation was 2000–2001.

Two facts emerge from these charts. First, the implementation of the PLC process at Boones Mill in the 2000–2001 school year led to significant gains in student achievement. Second, those gains have been sustained and, in most cases, improved upon in recent years.

Tables 5.5 though 5.7 reveal the percentage of Boones Mill students who have achieved at the highest level, "advanced proficient," on their state assessment since *Whatever It Takes* was published.

Table 5.5: Percentages of Third-Grade Students Scoring Advanced Proficient on State Assessments (Boones Mill/VA)

	2004–2005	2005–2006	2006–2007	2007–2008
English	23/19	56/39	61/37	62/39
Math	79/52	73/52	60/48	79/51
Science	68/42	58/40	67/39	77/39
Social Studies	68/51	64/57	71/64	88/66

Table 5.6: Percentages of Fourth-Grade Students Scoring Advanced Proficient on State Assessments (Boones Mill/VA)

	2005–2006*	2006–2007	2007–2008
Reading	56/42	48/47	65/47
Math	58/34	55/37	75/42
*There was no state assessment in 2004–2005.			

Table 5.7: Percentages of Fifth-Grade Students Scoring Advanced Proficient on State Assessments (Boones Mill/VA)

	2004–2005	2005–2006	2006–2007	2007–2008
English	31/30	45/42	40/36	54/42
Writing	34/30	38/32	20/26	18/23
Math	35/25	60/45	70/48	59/53
Science	19/15	22/23	15/25	22/24
History	51/44	32/45	36/39	57/39

In 2004, Boones Mill had a higher percentage of its students achieving advanced proficient on every subject area of the state assessment than the state at large, despite the fact that it ranked near the bottom of the state in per pupil expenditures. Although it continues to lag behind the state in spending, it has *increased* the percentage of students who are achieving at the highest standard on the state assessment in seven of the nine areas assessed and maintained its exceptional achievement in an eighth—third-grade math—where its percentage of students scoring advanced proficient is 28 percent higher than the state. In many instances, the percentage increase has been dramatic. The biggest gains that have occurred at Boones Mill in recent years have not been in moving students who were achieving below standard to proficient, but in moving previously proficient students to advanced status.

Concluding Thoughts

For almost a decade, the intensive focus on the learning of each student, the collaborative and coordinated effort among staff members, and the systematic schoolwide plan for intervention have made Boones Mill a great place for students and staff. Every staff member has the benefit of a collaborative team—colleagues to turn to and talk to when looking for better ways to meet student needs. Every student knows that the school will respond promptly with additional time and support if he or she experiences difficulty in learning. Every parent knows there will be a coordinated effort among the members of the team to provide students with a high-quality program and that a system is in place to assist their children when they need additional support.

The Boones Mill motto, "Hand in Hand We All Learn," captures the very essence of the PLC concept. At Boones Mill, the motto represents not merely words on school documents, but a powerful commitment to meeting the needs of students and adults that is carried out every day.

In the next four chapters we turn our attention away from examining the progress made by schools featured in *Whatever It Takes* to tell the inspirational stories of four new schools—a middle school, a junior high school, an elementary school, and a high school.

Visit http://bmill.frco.k12.va.us/ for more information on Boones Mill Elementary.

For tools and templates from Boones Mill that you may find useful, visit go.solution-tree.com/PLCbooks.

6

EMBRACING SYSTEMATIC INTERVENTION: PRAIRIE STAR MIDDLE SCHOOL

High-performing middle schools establish norms, structures, and organizational arrangements to support and sustain their trajectory toward excellence. They have a sense of purpose that drives every facet of practice and decision-making.

—Schools to Watch, 2004

Every student is deserving of our collective best, not just the best that each individual teacher has to offer.

—Lyn Rantz, Principal of Prairie Star Middle School

The concept of the middle school is of relatively recent origin in North America. While public elementary schools can trace their roots to the eighteenth century, and the comprehensive high school was considered innovative in the late nineteenth century, the middle school is a much more recent phenomenon. One might assume that the absence of historical baggage might have made the middle school fertile ground for sowing the seeds of contemporary professional learning community concepts, and in many ways, the middle school model fits comfortably with PLC premises. For example, middle schools have typically been structured to support teachers working together rather than in isolation. The middle school has come under attack by some, however, who charge that the model is inattentive to academic achievement and unaccountable for results. This chapter tells the story of a wonderful middle school that counters that charge and serves as an excellent example of PLC concepts at work.

A Proactive Approach to Intervention

Blue Valley School District, a growing district in northeastern Kansas that serves over twenty thousand students in its thirty-one schools, has implemented the PLC concept on a districtwide basis with spectacular success. The district's mission statement is succinct: "We will ensure unprecedented academic success and unparalleled personal growth for every student." To achieve that mission, the district has articulated two very public commitments: "We will make a continuous effort to reallocate resources, adopt innovative programs, and critically evaluate current practices to assure academic excellence, and we are committed to professional learning communities as the means for continuous school improvement."

The success of the board of education, administration, and teachers in fulfilling those commitments has made Blue Valley one of the highest-performing districts in Kansas. They have raised the percentage of students demonstrating proficiency on the Kansas state test every year from 2004 to 2009—from 83 percent to 96 percent in reading and from 81 percent to 95 percent in math. Each of the thirty-one schools in the district has demonstrated adequate yearly progress throughout those five years. It was selected as a national model for a benchmarking project of effective implementation of PLC concepts conducted by the American Productivity and Quality Center and the General Electric Foundation. Many of Blue Valley's schools illustrate the power of the PLC concept, but in this chapter we focus on one of its middle schools.

Prairie Star Middle School in Leawood, Kansas, serves 603 students in grades 6, 7, and 8. Despite a relatively homogenous middle-class population with less than 5 percent of its students eligible for free and reduced-cost lunch, in 2004–2005, Prairie Star was one of the lower-performing schools in the district. Since 2006–2007, however, it has won the Governor's Achievement Award for academic excellence each year. Principal Lyn Rantz attributes the turnaround to the staff's collective focus on the four critical questions of a PLC: what do we want students to learn, how do we know if they are learning, how will we respond when they are not learning, and how will we respond when they are already proficient?

Laying the Groundwork

Prairie Star made structural changes to support the staff's work around these four critical questions. Every teacher was assigned to both a horizontal interdisciplinary team that meets daily for forty-five minutes and a vertical content team that meets monthly or bimonthly for either 60 or 120 minutes. Each team was asked to address specific issues, complete designated tasks, and generate products that reflected its collective inquiry and collaborative decisions. A "weekly wheel" was established, designating certain days of the week for each team to address one or more of the four critical questions. Software was provided to assist teachers in monitoring student learning and keep parents more informed about student progress.

The staff also took steps to ensure there would be clarity regarding what students are to learn. At the beginning of each unit, teachers who teach the same content identify the intended learning targets—the specific knowledge and skills students are to acquire as a result of that unit. The team of teachers advises students how they will be expected to demonstrate their mastery, creates a series of common formative assessments to monitor student learning, and stipulates the level of mastery a student must achieve on the assessment in order to be considered proficient.

Intervention and Enrichment at Prairie Star

The staff of Prairie Star has been particularly attentive to intervention and enrichment. During her first year at the school, Principal Rantz asked teachers to address the clear evidence that some students were not being successful and to devise strategies to support those students. The staff met that challenge, and the school has created a comprehensive process for monitoring student learning and providing intervention and enrichment for students who need those supports.

The Prairie Star process begins even before students arrive, when the school devotes some of its professional development days to giving teachers time to review vital information about the students they will serve in the coming year. Every teacher receives a notebook with data and information on the academic performance of his or her incoming students, both as individuals and as a class. The notebook includes analysis of longitudinal student performance on the state test, district benchmark assessments, and measures of academic progress (MAP) results by performance indicator. Results are color coded so that, at a glance, a teacher can identify students who are candidates for either intervention or enrichment. Students who score at the 95th percentile or above on MAP are highlighted in blue, while those scoring below the proficiency standard on the state assessment or who are one or more grade levels behind according to MAP are coded in red. Students deemed to be at risk are then cross-referenced with the school's intervention database to make certain they were identified as needing extra support.

The school also uses MAP to monitor each student's growth in reading and mathematics from the previous year. Teachers are able to determine if a student met, exceeded, or failed to reach the designated growth target during the previous year.

Teachers also receive the transition plan for each of their students, a plan created by the grade-level team that served that student in the previous year.

This review of the insights from former teachers, along with the careful analysis of past academic achievement, ensures each team has a plan in place for responding to students as soon as the school year begins. Counselors and administrators participate in each team's analysis of its students. Each team takes notes and documents intervention plans, which they will review periodically over the course of the year.

Each teacher also receives an analysis of the achievement of the students he or she taught in the previous year. Teachers are then able to assess the relative strengths and weaknesses of their instruction and work with content–area colleagues to build on strengths and address concerns. Finally, teachers receive an analysis of student achievement of the grade levels above and below theirs to come to a better understanding of where former and future students have found success and areas of challenge.

Building Relationships With a Caring Adult

Once the year begins, all students are assigned to a guided study period, which the teachers at Prairie Star have developed into one of the most potent weapons in their intervention arsenal. The goals of the program are 1) to ensure every student has a personal and supportive relationship with a caring adult in the building, and 2) to monitor and respond to the needs of each student. Teachers are assigned to guided study as a supervisory duty, and Principal Rantz makes those assignments very purposefully. She attempts to ensure that a math, reading, and special education teacher are available each period and creates a guided study for gifted students led by the school's gifted teacher.

The interdisciplinary PLC team reserves its team meeting each Monday for discussion with counselors, a school psychologist, and administrators about students experiencing academic difficulty. The guided study teacher, who monitors the academic performance of all the students assigned to his or her guided study, plays an important role in that conversation. The team can assign students to a particular guided study based on their findings. For example, one teacher may take the lead in supporting students who are having difficulty with organizational skills, while another works with students who are struggling with a particular math skill, and yet another works with students who need support in building the essential vocabulary for a unit. Teams create their guided study plan a month in advance and have the autonomy to adjust the activities as the situation dictates. For example, if the science teachers know they will be administering a comprehensive exam at the end of the third week of the month, they can prepare review materials and activities, and the interdisciplinary team will reserve that week to help students review for the exam during guided study.

Half of the students in each grade level attend guided study period every other day while their classmates are in physical education class. This rotation allows the school to limit the number of students in any guided study to fewer than fourteen so teachers can provide more personal attention. Students who are very deficient in a subject or who need help in more than one subject may be assigned to a second guided study period, that is, one each day. The school will adjust the student's schedule and even remove a student from an exploratory class, if necessary, to provide the additional time for intervention. The team works with the administration to determine who on the staff has the most positive relationship with the student—a teacher, counselor, or administrator. That person contacts the parents to recommend the schedule change and the reason for the recommendation. To date, every parent has agreed to support the recommended change.

As time has gone on, teams have tended to devote two days of guided study each week to supporting students with the "hard skills"—specific content from the core curriculum—using materials created by the subject area teachers. Two other days are reserved for "soft skills," such as building vocabulary and other skills that can be applied in multiple disciplines. Some of the soft-skill days are reserved for group guidance activities conducted by the school's counselors, school nurse, or school resource officer. Guided study also provides the gifted and special education teachers with access to their students as well.

Additional Layers of Support

If guided study does not resolve the problem, students can also be assigned to the Learning Lab located in the school's library. There they confront what Principal Rantz playfully refers to as a "designated nagger," an aide or specials teacher who monitors the students' work and insists that they complete their assignments each day. The one-on-one monitoring, mentoring, and support provided in the Learning Lab are particularly effective for students who are unable to stay organized, focused, or motivated to complete work after they leave school. Learning Lab teachers work in conjunction with the PLC teams to meet each student's needs, and content teachers provide the Learning Lab staff with essential learning targets and assignment details. Students are assigned to Learning Lab in place of an elective on a quarterly basis. As with other interventions, the teachers and counselors inform parents of this schedule change for intervention.

For students who continue to struggle, the school uses the Scholastic READ 180 program to provide more intensive support for students who are experiencing difficulty with reading. The program includes three components: using the computer to diagnose and remediate reading problems, participating in small-group reading activities led by the teacher, and reading highly engaging material at the appropriate reading level. Students in the program are guaranteed to receive two of the three components each day. READ 180 is scheduled in place of an elective course for students in sixth and seventh grades and replaces the standard reading class for eighth-grade students.

The staff has also made excellent use of Study Island, a web-based math and reading program designed to support the Kansas state standards. Students are taught how to use Study Island during their guided study period, and teachers can then assign students to complete work using that system. Students can access Study Island, which is designed to take advantage of student interest in video games, at home as well as at school. Some of the exercises build a video game activity into the work, while others reward students with access to a video game upon successful completion of an activity. Students are able to work at their own pace, and the program provides teachers with a thorough, real-time analysis of each student's progress in mastering state standards.

PACE (Providing Academic Challenges for Excellence) is the only part of the school's intervention plan that does not occur during the school day. It provides additional tutoring from certified teachers before and after school, Monday through Thursday. The school's parent-teacher organization (PTO) funds a late bus one day each week to provide transportation for students who attend PACE after school. On the other three days, students must arrange their own transportation.

The school monitors the effectiveness of each of its intervention strategies. Student participation and improvement in each of the various programs are documented and shared quarterly with the grade-level teams and parents.

The Need to Change Adult Practice

Principal Rantz asserts that creating a pyramid of interventions will have little impact on student achievement unless the adults in the building are also willing to make fundamental changes in their professional practice. To assist with those changes she created a leadership team consisting of two members from each of the three grade levels, two counselors, an exploratory teacher, the gifted teacher, and a special education teacher. The leadership team meets weekly, and any member of the team can request that a topic be placed on the agenda. Principal Rantz considers the team her eyes and ears to the needs of the staff and a sounding board for assessing ideas and proposals before they are presented to the staff. The agenda and notes from every leadership team meeting are emailed to the entire staff to ensure transparency. Some of the more profound changes in adult practice that the team helped to foster include the following.

Providing a Structure for Collaboration

Teachers at Prairie Star had always been provided time for collaboration, but they received little direction in terms of how they should use the time. The leadership team addressed that problem in several ways. First, every team was asked to create a foundation planning document that included a vision statement, SMART goal, norms, and a brief summary of the team's plan for addressing each of the four critical questions of a PLC. The foundation planning document for the seventh-grade team is presented in figure 6.1 (page 94).

The weekly wheel created by Principal Rantz and the leadership team was also used to help teams focus on the critical questions of a PLC. It designates certain topics for specific days of the week. For example, the seventh-grade team devotes Mondays to identifying the students who are experiencing difficulty and clarifying what steps they would take to intervene for those students. Other days of the week the focus is on clarifying intended outcomes for upcoming units, creating and analyzing the results of common assessments, and establishing plans for enriching and extending the learning of students who are already proficient. The grade-level special education teacher(s) join each grade-level team twice a week to participate in this dialogue and to assist with planning. This structure and the supporting documents the leadership team created to guide the collaborative process have helped eliminate the question that comes up all too often in schools when teachers are asked to collaborate: why are we here?

Using Assessment to Inform Students and Teachers, Not Merely to Assign Grades

One of the most significant changes that occurred in the school was in the use of assessments. Five members of the staff were given intensive training in the use of formative assessments, and they, in turn, became trainers for the rest of the faculty.

Seventh-Grade Vision Statement

We are a PLC committed to building a flexible, collaborative, student-focused culture empowering our students to be energetic learners, passionate leaders, and responsible citizens.

Seventh-Grade SMART Goal

By the end of the 2008–2009 school year, all seventh-grade students will be proficient (70 percent) on tested targets on one common assessment per quarter.

Our Plans to Address the Four Critical Questions of a PLC

1 **What do we want students to learn?**

- Study state curriculum, indicators, and learning targets.
- Plan units, lesson plans, and activities.
- Share research and best teaching strategies.
- Identify learning targets at instructional and assessment levels.

2 **How will we know if they have learned it?**

- Study the balanced assessment research (assessment *of* learning and assessment *for* learning).
- Develop common assessments.
- Perform an item analysis of those common assessments.

3 **What will we do if they don't learn it?**

- Use intervention pyramid for those not achieving success.
- Use student learning targets from beginning to end of unit.
- Share reteaching strategies.
- Study MAP data, grade distribution, and state assessment data to modify instruction.

4 **What do we do when they already know it?**

- Provide differentiated lessons and activities.
- Provide differentiated assessment modes.

Figure 6.1: A foundation planning document for seventh grade.

As teams became more specific and precise regarding the skills and knowledge students were to acquire as a result of each unit, they began to create a series of assessments *for* learning to monitor each student's acquisition of each specific skill. Teams also established the proficiency standards students were expected to achieve for each of those skills. Students unable to demonstrate proficiency were required to keep working on the skill and complete certain requirements in order to be reassessed, such as completing a reflection worksheet to analyze their performance on the skill, identifying the mistakes they made and the reasons for those mistakes, completing a study guide to provide practice on the designated skill, seeking support during guided study, and having parents sign a form.

Teachers were also asked to review the results of common assessments in their teams and to discuss such questions as the following: What learning targets are in need of improvement? What instructional strategies represent best practice for this skill? What strategies should be altered based upon poor results? Are there issues with the students' understanding of key vocabulary terms that may have impacted their achievement?

The clarity that each team established regarding specific learning targets students were to reach and the use of frequent team-developed formative assessments to monitor that learning began to change the way teachers, students, and parents looked at student achievement. Instead of merely receiving a grade on an assessment, students were able to determine their exact level of ability: "I can organize and interpret mathematical data, but I am not yet clear on how to calculate mean, median, and mode." With this clarity, and with additional opportunities to demonstrate their learning, students were able to take greater responsibility for their own academic success. Teachers began to change the way they reported student achievement. Instead of reporting a grade by the type of assignment ("Johnny earned a C on his last quiz"), they reported a student's proficiency level by skill learning target ("Johnny is not yet proficient in calculating mean, median, and mode"). Because teachers keep electronic gradebooks and make the information available to parents, parents can monitor the learning of their children, skill by skill, instead of merely receiving a generic grade.

This focus on mastery of skills rather than grading has also impacted traditional practices such as homework policies. Teachers no longer give students the option of taking a zero on assignments. Students who fail to complete an assignment on time are required to complete the assignment (usually during guided study) and are given 75 to 80 percent credit for the assignment. Furthermore, homework plays a much less significant role in determining a student's grade. Teachers assign grades at the end of each grading period primarily based upon the student's demonstration of proficiency on the team's common assessment *of* learning (summative assessments) after students have completed a series of formative assessments. Teachers focus on evidence of the students' ability to demonstrate proficiency on essential learning targets and view homework as a means to achieve that end rather than the end itself.

Results

Table 6.1 shows the percentage of Prairie Star students demonstrating proficiency on the state assessment compared to the percentage of students in the state who achieved proficiency. Note the steady improvement in student achievement that has occurred at Prairie Star since implementing the PLC process in the fall of 2004.

Table 6.1: Comparison of Prairie Star/State Proficiency on the State Assessment

	2003–2004	2004–2005	2005–2006	2006–2007	2007–2008	2008–2009
Math	82/65	82/65	93/75	95/79	97/82	99/tba
Reading	83/75	93/77	95/80	96/82	98/84	99/tba
Science	85/67		93/70		97/83	
Grade 6 Social Studies	81/65		86/74		99/83	
Grade 8 Social Studies	79/65		79/69		97/81	

The attention to ensuring each student's success on essential learning standards has not only moved previously failing students to proficiency, but has also moved formerly proficient students to higher levels of achievement. The Kansas state assessment identifies five different levels of performance: below standard, approaching standard, meets standard, exceeds standard, and exemplary. Figure 6.2 and table 6.2 illustrate that the percentage of Prairie Star students achieving the highest possible levels on the state assessment has skyrocketed in math. Figure 6.3 and table 6.3 (page 98) do the same for reading. In fact, *by far* the largest percentage of increase in both areas has occurred at the exemplary level.

As a result of its extraordinary success in helping *all* students learn at higher levels, Prairie Star Middle School has achieved Kansas Standard of Excellence recognition in every subject area at every grade level since implementing the PLC process. Furthermore, for each year from 2006 to 2009 it has been presented the Governor's Achievement Award honoring the top-performing schools in the state. Only five middle schools in the entire state of Kansas have been able to earn this distinction for three consecutive years.

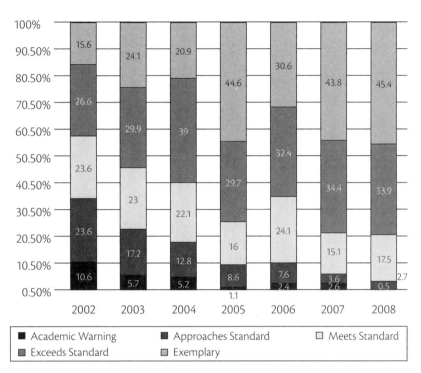

Figure 6.2: The performance of Prairie Star Middle School in math during the 2002 to 2008 school years.

Table 6.2: Comparison of Percentages of Students in Exceeds, Exemplary, and Below Standard in Mathematics, 2002 and 2008

Student Rating	2002	2008
Exceeds/Exemplary	40.2%	79.3%
Exemplary	15.6%	45.4%
Below Standard	34.2%	3.2%

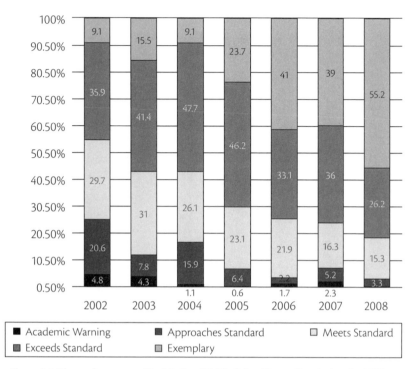

Figure 6.3: The performance of Prairie Star Middle School in reading during the 2002 to 2008 school years.

Table 6.3: Comparison of Percentages of Students in Exceeds, Exemplary, and Below Standard in Reading, 2002 and 2008

Student Rating	2002	2008
Exceeds/Exemplary	45%	81.4%
Exemplary	9.1%	55.2%
Below Standard	25.4%	3.3%

Concluding Thoughts

What sometimes gets lost in the presentation of achievement data is that those numbers represent real students with personal hopes and dreams. The staff at Prairie Star has made a tremendous difference in the lives of Prairie Star students, including students who would have been deemed failures only a few years ago. Prairie Star serves as a national model of effective implementation of the PLC process, providing valuable lessons for educators who hope to make a difference in the lives of their students.

Visit www.bluevalleyk12.org/education/school/school. php?sectionid=269 for more information on Prairie Star Middle School.

SUCCESS AND TRIUMPH IN A WORTHY ENDEAVOR: LAKERIDGE JUNIOR HIGH SCHOOL

Strong professional learning communities produce schools that are engines of hope and achievement for students.... There is nothing more important for education in the decades ahead than educating and supporting leaders in the commitments, understandings, and skills necessary to grow such schools where a focus on effort-based ability is the norm.

—JON SAPHIER, 2005

Lakeridge Junior High School in Orem, Utah, serves 1,200 students in grades 7 through 9. In 2002, it was the lowest-performing school in the Alpine School District, with only 55 percent of its students demonstrating proficiency in math and English on the state's end-of-level assessment. Staff tended to attribute the low performance to students. Thirty percent of the school's students came from low-income families, 15 percent had limited English proficiency, and many others lacked motivation.

The school's leaders recognized that structural changes would not help resolve the school's problems until staff members confronted some of their own assumptions impacting student achievement. Therefore, the leadership initiated a process to engage the faculty in the exploration of several questions:

- Do we believe all kids can learn?
- Do we believe that educators are key contributors to student learning?
- Do we believe education is critical to the future of our students?
- Do we believe we can make a difference in the lives of our kids?

As a result of that dialogue the staff established three shared beliefs with corresponding collective commitments:

1. We believe all students can learn. We will do all things in our power to help students learn.

2. We believe the answers to our issues are found within the collective knowledge of our staff. We commit to collaborate with each other to find those answers.

3 We believe teachers make the greatest difference in helping students learn. We commit to do things that are best for our students even if they might not be the most comfortable things for adults.

With those commitments in place, the school created a leadership team of eight teachers to help engage the staff in the consideration of the first three critical questions of a PLC: what is it we want students to learn, how will we know if they have learned it, and what will we do if they do not learn it?

In order to address the first question—what is it we want students to learn?—teachers in every course were asked to create a list of "I Cans"—agreed-upon standards for the course that students could use to monitor their own learning. For example, the algebra team list included the following:

I can . . .

- Find the missing side of a right triangle using the Pythagorean Theorem
- Simplify square roots
- Solve equations with square roots
- Solve proportion equations
- Graph linear equations using a table of values

Once collaborative teams of teachers had agreed on what students were expected to learn, they developed a series of common formative assessments that were intended to do the following:

- Ensure all students had access to a guaranteed curriculum regardless of the teacher to whom they were assigned. The premise guiding the staff was that teachers were more likely to teach a common curriculum if they had agreed on the knowledge and skills students should acquire and had created common assessments specifically designed to determine if each student could demonstrate proficiency.
- Inform students of their learning so students themselves could address problem areas in their learning.
- Inform teachers of their effectiveness in helping all students learn so they could improve their instruction.

Intervention at Lakeridge

Once the staff at Lakeridge had clarified what students were to learn and how teachers would monitor that learning, the faculty turned its attention to the question of how the school would respond when students did not learn. Initial efforts proved ineffective. For example, when intervention was held before and after school, it drained the energy of teachers and failed to reach some of the most at-risk students, who simply refused to participate. The Leopard Academy was another intervention program that proved ineffective. In that program, students who had failed a math or English course at the end of a semester were required to attend a one-hour after-school program for sixteen days to address their deficiency. Parents, however, could sign a refusal of service that exempted students from the program, and many parents simply signed the form rather than fight the battle of having their unwilling students extend their school day.

According to Principal Garrick Peterson, the turning point in the Lakeridge intervention program came when the staff recognized they had the power to take control of time during the school day. Teachers acknowledged that students learned at different rates and needed different levels of support. The school's traditional schedule, however, gave all students the same level of support (an individual classroom teacher) and the same amount of time (the same minutes of instruction each day) to master each essential skill. To their credit, the staff of Lakeridge concluded they could not develop a system of time and support for students unless they could create greater flexibility in students' schedules *during* the school day.

Moving to a modified A/B block schedule was one step in creating that flexibility. The new schedule assigned students to eight classes, with students attending four classes on alternating days. This new schedule increased the number of courses students could take from seven to eight, and with that extra period, Lakeridge could offer both supplemental time and support courses for those students who needed additional help to be successful. For example, some students were assigned to math and literacy courses each day to give them twice as much time to master the content. A study-skills course was created for students who needed assistance with that area, and a sheltered course was created for English language learners.

The Lakeridge staff also created a flex schedule, which carves out thirty minutes for intervention and enrichment every Tuesday through Friday. Students failing a course are required to spend that thirty minutes working with their classroom teacher to complete assignments and to acquire the intended knowledge and skills.

Students who are being successful in all their courses are provided with over twenty enrichment opportunities during flextime. Some of those opportunities take the form of high-interest cocurricular activities such as Model United Nations, mock trial, and math team. Other options are more social, such as intramural sports, dance revolution, or extended lunch. Students are allowed to elect the activity of their choice, and, with the exception of a few of the cocurricular programs, they may elect different options each day. As Principal Peterson explains, "We consider enrichment time as the students' time. They have demonstrated responsibility in passing all of their courses, and so we trust them to act responsibly and choose wisely during the flex period."

An instructional aide acts as the coordinator of flextime. Each day she runs a computer report to identify students who are failing a course. Any student on that report receives a white piece of paper that day, which signals that the student must participate in intervention during flextime. Students who are failing more than one class can choose which intervention session to attend. Students passing all of their classes receive a colored piece of paper, which serves as their admission to an enrichment activity.

Principal Peterson believes the administration is responsible for creating systems to ensure students report to intervention during flextime. It is then the classroom teacher's responsibility to use that time to provide students with the individualized instruction and support to acquire the essential knowledge and skills of the course. Math, science, and English teachers provide intervention support during all flex days. All other teachers provide intervention every other day and enrichment activities on the opposite day.

Making Time for Intervention

The Lakeridge staff made two minor modifications to the school schedule to create flextime. First, they eliminated Channel 1, the commercially sponsored television news program, which had consumed sixteen minutes each day. Second, they trimmed a few minutes off of each period in the block schedule. Originally, two of the four periods had been eighty-five minutes and two had been eighty-two minutes. The new schedule provides for four eighty-minute periods. Students follow a schedule determined by their assignment to one of two lunch periods. The schedule for Lakeridge on Tuesdays through Fridays is presented in table 7.1.

Table 7.1: Schedule for First and Second Lunch Students

First Lunch Students		Second Lunch Students	
8:15–9:35	First period	8:15–9:35	First period
9:40–11:00	Second period	9:40–11:00	Second period
11:00–11:30	Flextime	11:05–12:25	Third period
11:30–11:55	Lunch	12:25–12:55	Flextime
12:00–1:20	Third period	12:55–1:20	Lunch
1:25–2:45	Fourth period	1:25–2:45	Fourth period

Creating the flextime schedule was a major step on Lakeridge's PLC journey. It sent the message to students that they were expected to learn and were being held accountable for their learning. It gave staff access to students who needed more time and support for learning. It provided short-term, positive incentives for students to be academically successful. It did not, however, resolve all problems.

Reaching the Intentional Nonlearner

Some of the students who were not being successful at Lakeridge were intentional nonlearners. They didn't require more support to clarify a concept: they simply had no interest in doing the work that was necessary for academic success. The privileges available during flextime helped to motivate some of those students to apply themselves, but others remained unwilling to work. Therefore, Lakeridge added another layer of intervention for the intentional nonlearners. Many of these interventions were similar to those created at Stevenson High School. Students were assigned to the Counselor Watch program and would check in with their counselor on a weekly basis to discuss their progress. A "good friend" teacher or secretary was designated to take an intense personal interest in the student. Guidance support groups were held in an effort to help students confront the reasons for their self-destructive choices. Students were assigned to a guided study hall at which aides would monitor the completion of their work. The math department also created special sections of guided math classes that included monitoring the completion of all work as part of the daily activity.

The Lakeridge staff also concluded that a student's opportunities to learn and responsibilities for learning should not end at the conclusion of a term. Students who have failed a grading period are assigned to a special flextime program for the first two weeks of the next term to meet with the teacher whose course they failed. Those who are still unable to meet the requirements for passing the course at the end of the special program are assigned to the Principal's Academy. The Academy pulls students out of the regular school setting for a day during which they work with the principal, counselors, and aides in an effort to ensure they complete their work and demonstrate proficiency to pass their course. At the end of all this effort, students who still are not passing are assigned first to an after-school program, and finally to a summer school program to continue working until they can earn their credits. As Principal Peterson puts it, "We tell our students: 'We will give you some choice about when you learn, but ultimately you must learn. Learning is required rather than optional.'"

Lakeridge continues to explore strategies to provide students with additional time and support for learning. It offers jump-start English and math courses in the summer for students who are entering the school. It provides after-school tutoring and a late bus four days each week to provide transportation for participating students. It assigns students struggling with reading to intensive reading classes in seventh grade and offers study-skills classes as well. The multilayered pyramid of interventions illustrated in figure 7.1 is the school's systematic attempt to meet the needs of every student.

Building Staff Capacity to Function as a PLC

The Lakeridge leadership team was also attentive to providing teachers with the time and support they needed to work effectively in a PLC. Since the 2004–2005 school year, each of the five professional development days allotted to the school has been devoted to providing teachers with skills to create high-performing collaborative teams—skills such as clarifying standards, developing high-quality assessments, and analyzing data.

With the support of the central office, the school was able to adjust its weekly schedule to allow for an early dismissal each week. Every Monday afternoon the school day ends at 1:45 p.m. rather than 2:45 p.m. so that teachers are ensured at least one hour per week to collaborate. The district has also supported summer curriculum projects to provide teams with still more time to clarify what students must learn and how they will be expected to demonstrate that learning. Principal Peterson has, on occasion, also provided departments with substitute teachers on days when students are taking tests to provide additional blocks of time for collaboration. As he says, "It is amazing what a group of professional teachers can accomplish if they are given the time."

Most importantly, building the capacity of the staff to function as a PLC has been *the* focus at Lakeridge rather than one task among many. The school's leadership team has done an excellent job of protecting the staff from competing initiatives, so the faculty has been able to sustain its collective focus on the same process for six years. As Principal Peterson explains, "We felt if we were going to be successful in a collaborative model, then we needed to focus on building our capacity to collaborate on the right work. When schools try to do PLCs as a side project to everything else they do, they inhibit the success of the concept."

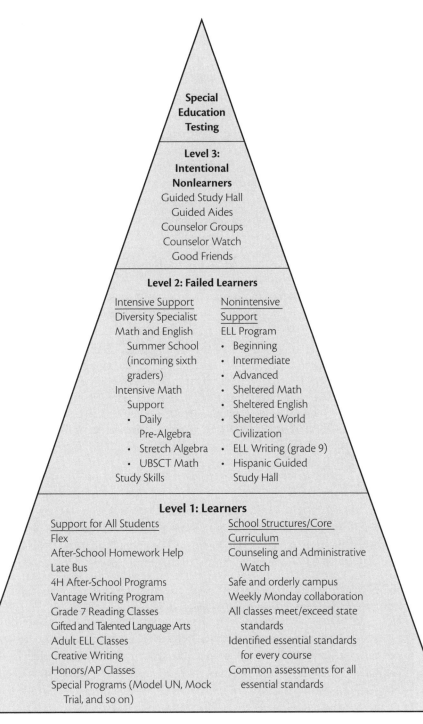

Special Education Testing

Level 3: Intentional Nonlearners
Guided Study Hall
Guided Aides
Counselor Groups
Counselor Watch
Good Friends

Level 2: Failed Learners

Intensive Support
Diversity Specialist
Math and English
 Summer School
 (incoming sixth
 graders)
Intensive Math
 Support
 • Daily
 Pre-Algebra
 • Stretch Algebra
 • UBSCT Math
Study Skills

Nonintensive Support
ELL Program
 • Beginning
 • Intermediate
 • Advanced
 • Sheltered Math
 • Sheltered English
 • Sheltered World
 Civilization
 • ELL Writing (grade 9)
 • Hispanic Guided
 Study Hall

Level 1: Learners

Support for All Students
Flex
After-School Homework Help
Late Bus
4H After-School Programs
Vantage Writing Program
Grade 7 Reading Classes
Gifted and Talented Language Arts
Adult ELL Classes
Creative Writing
Honors/AP Classes
Special Programs (Model UN, Mock
 Trial, and so on)

School Structures/Core Curriculum
Counseling and Administrative
 Watch
Safe and orderly campus
Weekly Monday collaboration
All classes meet/exceed state
 standards
Identified essential standards
 for every course
Common assessments for all
 essential standards

Figure 7.1: The Lakeridge Junior High pyramid of interventions.

Principal Peterson offers the following advice to those considering creating a process to provide students with additional time and support for learning according to a schoolwide plan:

- The process should ensure students receive the intervention in a timely fashion—at the first indication they are experiencing difficulty.

- The process should direct rather than invite students to devote the extra time and take advantage of the additional support until they are experiencing success. Additional time and support should not be optional for a student who is not being successful.

- Students should be guaranteed that they will receive this time and support regardless of who their teacher is. It must be a schoolwide plan rather than a teacher-dependent program.

- Intervention must occur within the school day. Schedules may need to be adjusted to allow for time and support *during* the school day.

- Qualified teachers should take the lead in intervention. Using instructional aides to intervene rather than the classroom instructor is not as effective.

- It must be a fluid model. Students failing a course should not be assigned to intervention for a designated period (for example, two weeks), but should instead know that as soon as they are passing the course, they will have immediate access to enrichment activities. Students should recognize the correlation between meeting their responsibilities as students and receiving the privileges the school is willing to offer.

Results

Tables 7.2 and 7.3 present the percentages of students demonstrating proficiency on the Utah state assessment in math. Table 7.4 presents results for English. Note that academic achievement has risen steadily at Lakeridge Junior High School—for all students, in all subgroups, and in all tested areas.

The 29 percent increase in student proficiency in math and 33 percent increase in English certainly speak to the effectiveness of the Lakeridge initiative. Note that the percentage of both Hispanic students and ELL students achieving proficiency has more than doubled in both math and English, and the percentage increases of low-income students achieving proficiency virtually mirror the school's overall increase. This staff's attention to the learning of each student has certainly benefited students in every group.

Table 7.2: Student Achievement Summary Data for Math: Percentages of Students Demonstrating Proficiency

	2002	2004	2007	2008
Overall Student Population	55%	71%	82%	84%
Caucasian Students	59%	79%	85%	87%
Hispanic Students	31%	50%	58%	68%
English Language Learners	31%	51%	61%	65%
Low-Income Students	49%	56%	68%	75%
Students With Special Needs	26%	33%	45%	45%

Table 7.3: Percentages of All Students Demonstrating Proficiency in Math by Course

	2002	2004	2007	2008
Geometry	55%	69%	95%	94%
Algebra	51%	77%	76%	80%
Pre-Algebra	58%	69%	75%	78%

Table 7.4: Student Achievement Summary Data for English: Percentages of Students Demonstrating Proficiency

	2002	2004	2007	2008
Overall Student Population	55%	81%	87%	88%
Caucasian Students	59%	82%	92%	92%
Hispanic Students	31%	49%	65%	72%
English Language Learners	34%	46%	68%	N/A
Low-Income Students	46%	65%	73%	78%
Students With Special Needs	37%	29%	49%	N/A

The school has also established a more challenging curriculum for students who are being successful. An advanced placement human geography course is a popular option for ninth graders, and the school offers an honors option in English and biology. Furthermore, like all of the schools featured in this book, the focus on the learning of all students has increased the percentage of students who are scoring at the highest levels on the state achievement test. From 2004 to 2009, the percentage of Lakeridge students achieving that distinction increased significantly in both English and mathematics. This increase occurred not only for the overall student population but also for *every* subgroup in the school. Seven of the eight subgroup categories have demonstrated double-digit percentage increases in scoring at the highest levels on state assessments.

Students and parents have recognized the improvement. Ninety-seven percent of students report that flextime has benefited them academically, and 93 percent of the school's parents believe the school's flex plan has benefited their children.

Finally, the state of Utah presents an annual Best of State award "to recognize outstanding individuals, organizations, and businesses" and to "share examples of success and triumph in worthy endeavors . . . so that others might be inspired to reach a little higher, to try a little harder, and to work a little longer for our dreams and goals" (Best of State, 2008). Lakeridge Junior High School was selected as the best K–12 school in the state in both 2008 and 2009. We hope that by sharing the Lakeridge story, we will inspire educators throughout the world to reach higher, try harder, and work longer as they pursue the worthy endeavor of helping all students learn.

Concluding Thoughts

It is not uncommon for educators to cite factors outside of their control as the cause of student failure. One of their most common laments is the lack of available resources. We understand their concern. There is no question that schools could benefit from additional financial support as educators struggle to meet the ever-increasing demands placed upon them. The staff at Lakeridge, however, elected to focus on what was within their sphere of influence rather than the factors they could not control. Despite the fact that Utah ranks last among the fifty states in per-pupil expenditures, this staff continues to bring a higher and higher percentage of students in all subgroups to proficiency. Educators at Lakeridge, like educators in all professional learning communities, do not look out the window for someone else to solve their problems—they look in the mirror.

Visit http://lakeridge.alpinedistrict.org/ for more information on Lakeridge Junior High School.

8

FROM STATE SANCTIONS TO NATIONAL RECOGNITION: HIGHLAND ELEMENTARY SCHOOL

Isolation is the enemy of learning. Principals who support the learning of adults in their school organize teachers' schedules to provide opportunities for teachers to work, plan, and think together. For instance, teams of teachers who share responsibility for the learning of all students meet regularly to plan lessons, critique student work and the assignments that led to it, and solve common instructional or classroom management problems.

—National Association of Elementary School Principals, 2002

Highland Elementary School . . . stands out among public schools in the Maryland suburbs for two reasons. It ranks first among those schools in the number of economically disadvantaged students who perform at advanced levels on statewide tests, a measure of its accomplishments. And it ranks second in percentage of students who have limited English proficiency, a measure of its challenges.

—Daniel de Vise, 2008

The Montgomery County School District in Maryland is one of the highest-performing large school districts in the United States. Covering almost 500 square miles, it serves approximately 139,000 students in 200 schools. Among the five strategic goals of the district are 1) ensuring success for every student, 2) providing an effective instructional program, and 3) creating a positive work environment in a self-renewing organization.

Unfortunately, in 2005 Highland Elementary School was one of the schools in the district falling well short of these ambitious goals. The school had failed to demonstrate adequate yearly progress on the Maryland State Assessment for four consecutive years and had been placed in corrective action by the state Department of Education.

The standard response in this situation is for districts to become highly prescriptive, demanding that teachers implement the decisions of others with fidelity and do what they are told. As Michael Fullan (2006) found, however, school improvement strategies based on sanctions, external pressure, and control may succeed in moving a school from "awful to adequate," but they will not build the capacity of a staff for continuous improvement. As he wrote, the punitive strategies "work on only a small part of the problem, violate everything known about change processes that lead to sustainable reform, cause the best teachers to abandon a 'failing' school, and actually create conditions that guarantee the improvements will not be sustained. There is, in other words, virtually no chance the approach will result in good, let alone great, schools" (p. 29).

Jerry Weast, the Montgomery County superintendent of schools, resisted the temptation to seek the quick fix of prescriptions and control. Instead, he recognized the need to provide struggling schools with the support, resources, and training to build the capacity of their staffs to engage in continuous improvement processes. In April of 2005, the district created the Professional Learning Community Project to help achieve its goals by building the capacity of the district's professionals. More specifically, the project was designed to do the following:

- Provide training on building high-performing teams with regard to focused school improvement.

- Provide professional development support to school staff in the development and/or refinement of strategic plans.

- Provide support to enable school teams to implement collaborative processes for data analysis and continuous improvement.

- Provide focused coaching to schools in order to attain critical student achievement, including achieving adequate yearly progress on state assessments and closing the achievement gap.

- Train principals and school staff on data collection and analysis, interpretation, and strategies for continuous improvement.

- Coach schools to initiate and implement focused improvement models and tools.

- Provide support to schools on meeting their performance measures based on identified goals.

- Develop measures and evaluate professional development opportunities related to school improvement support.

- Support the implementation of the Administrative and Supervisory Professional Growth System.

Highland Elementary was among the first schools in the county to participate in the Professional Learning Community Project. When Ray Myrtle was persuaded to come out of retirement to become principal of Highland in 2005, he found an alarming absence of the systems, coordination, collaboration, and collective effort that characterize professional learning communities. Myrtle recalls, "There were no standard procedures for anything; no vertical articulation, and no collaboration among teachers of the same grade level. Each teacher was free to do his or her own thing, and as a result, there was no consistency or continuity for students. For kids, every year was brand new because their experience of the previous year was irrelevant."

The other issue that was immediately apparent to Principal Myrtle was the low expectations of many staff members. Many teachers took little responsibility for the failure of their students, assigning the blame to conditions and characteristics of the students themselves. Seventy-five percent of the school's 700 students were Hispanic, 15 percent were African American, 5 percent were Asian, and 5 percent were white. They came from one of the poorest parts of the county, and 73 percent of the students lived in poverty. The student population was highly transient, and 60 percent of the students did not use English as their primary language. For some teachers, these conditions meant it was unrealistic for their students to achieve at high levels.

Principal Myrtle attacked the problem with an exemplary display of loose-tight leadership. He readily acknowledges he was "tight" in stipulating clearly that profound changes were needed in the structure and culture of the school, that the changes would impact everyone in the school, that teachers would work together collaboratively rather than in isolation, that procedures would be put in place to monitor student learning, and that the school would intervene in a systematic and timely way when students experienced difficulty. He also demonstrated that he was perfectly willing to confront any staff member who was not contributing to this new direction, and several opted to leave the school. At the same time, however, Principal Myrtle also committed to 1) engaging staff in the decisions regarding the implementation of the school's new direction and 2) providing staff with the training, resources, and support to help them succeed at what they were being asked to do.

The school created several different structures to ensure teachers played an active role in guiding the improvement initiative. Myrtle met with team leaders and the two school-level union representatives twice each month to monitor any issues arising from the staff. These same leaders were joined by reading and mathematics coaches, counselors, paraprofessionals, and parents every six weeks to review trends in school achievement and discipline data and to identify and address any concerns. Reading and math coaches helped grade-level teams become skillful in clarifying outcomes, gathering evidence of student learning, and addressing concerns. This widely dispersed leadership helped create a greater sense of ownership among staff regarding the direction of their school.

Creating the Schedule to Support Intervention

The staff began the school's transformation by adopting a common parallel schedule as the school's new master schedule (see figure 8.1). The school established large blocks of uninterrupted time for math and language arts instruction at every grade level each day. The new schedule also assigned all the students of a particular grade level to art, music, physical education, library, and writing classes at the same time so that the grade-level team could have common planning time for fifty minutes, four days each week. Principal Myrtle stipulated that the teams were to reserve one of those days to focus their collaborative work on reading and another to focus on mathematics. English language learner (ELL) and special education teachers were also assigned to particular teams and helped coteach in many of the classrooms.

Teams were not merely encouraged to "go collaborate," but were provided with a weekly template to guide their work. The template helped the teams establish the intended essential learnings for that week in reading, writing, phonics, fluency, vocabulary, and math, and to translate the learnings into specific statements regarding what students would know and be able to do as a result of the unit. Each team would also discuss whole group and small group instructional strategies and establish recommended topics and activities for each day of the week. Finally, the template asked teams to clarify action steps that they needed to take in order to implement their plan and assigned responsibility for each step to members of the team in order to divide the work and avoid duplicated effort. For example, at the conclusion of a meeting, one teacher agreed to develop writing prompts, another to create independent work that would allow students to demonstrate their ability to determine cause and effect, and a third to develop the parent conference materials that would be sent home to parents.

Principal Myrtle also supported the work of the teams by providing time for them to collaborate beyond their common planning period each week. Once each quarter he hired substitute teachers to give an entire grade-level team a full day of uninterrupted collaborative time to plan their work for the coming quarter.

Kindergarten	Grade 1	Grade 2	Grade 3	Grade 4	Grade 5
Reading/ Writing 8:50–9:50	Reading/ Writing 8:50–11:25	Math 8:50–10:15	Specials 8:55–9:40 Music, Art, PE, Library, Writing	Reading/ Writing 8:50–11:15	Math 8:50–10:30
Specials 9:55–10:40 Music, Art, PE, Library, Writing			Reading/ Writing 9:40–12:00		Intervention Team 9:00–9:30
Reading/ Writing 10:40–12:25	Intervention Team 10:20–11:00	Writing 10:15–11:00		Intervention Team 9:40–10:20	Science/ Social Studies 10:30–11:00
		Specials 11:00–11:45 Music, Art, PE, Library, Writing	Intervention Team 11:15–12:00	Lunch/Recess 11:15–12:05	Lunch/Recess 11:00–11:50
Intervention Team 11:25–12:25	Lunch/Recess 11:25–12:15	Lunch/Recess 11:50–12:40			Specials 11:50–12:45 Music, Art, PE, Library, Writing
Lunch/Recess 12:15–1:15	Math 12:15–1:25	Reading 12:40–2:30	Lunch/Recess 12:00–12:50	Math 12:05–1:45	
Math 1:15–2:30	Specials 1:25–2:10 Music, Art, PE, Library, Writing	Intervention Team 1:00–1:40	Math 12:50–2:30	Intervention Team 12:45–1:45	Reading/ Writing 12:45–3:00
Science/Social Studies 2:30–3:00	Science/ Social Studies 2:10–3:00	Science/ Social Studies 2:30–3:00	Science/ Social Studies 2:30–3:00	Science/ Social Studies 1:45–2:15	Intervention Team 1:40–2:20

Figure 8.1: Highland Elementary's master schedule.

Focused and job-embedded professional development was a major aspect of the improvement initiative at Highland Elementary. Staff members had access to both material and human resources to assist them in building shared knowledge about district and state learning standards, developing effective assessment practices, working collaboratively, and using curricular programs that were available to assist them. Grade-level teachers learned how to coteach more effectively with special education teachers, ELL teachers, reading specialists, math specialists, and intervention teachers.

With the benefit of this time and support, grade-level teams were able to clarify essential learning standards in reading, writing, and mathematics for each unit of instruction. They were also able to create common formative assessments to monitor student learning. Most teams used a quick math assessment virtually every day and a more comprehensive assessment every few weeks. The teams typically administered reading and writing assessments every week or two.

Initially, teams would analyze the results of the assessments and divide the students among the members of that team on the basis of student proficiency during the intervention period provided in the schedule each day. Teachers discovered that this strategy of short-term, focused intervention was effective in helping students acquire math skills, but it was not as effective in helping many of their students who were struggling to read. At that point, the teams recognized they needed to have more sustained and focused intervention for reading, and they created the structures to support that kind of intervention.

Reading Intervention at Highland Elementary School

Highland depicts its systems of interventions for reading in the form of a decision-making tree, as shown in figure 8.2.

For example, if a fourth-grade student is having difficulty, the grade-level team reviews the data from running records and common assessments to determine if the student is reading at or above the K/L level on the district's text gradient system (that is, approximately midyear of second grade). If the student is not proficient at that level, the team attempts to determine if the primary problem is decoding or comprehension. Students struggling with decoding are assigned to one of three options. The first is to provide the student with a double dose of guided reading instruction each day. The second option is to utilize the Wilson Reading System, a twelve-step system that provides direct, multisensory, structured reading instruction aimed at providing students with skills in phonological coding. The third option, the Lindamood Phoneme Sequencing Program, is another program aimed at developing phonemic awareness and phonics.

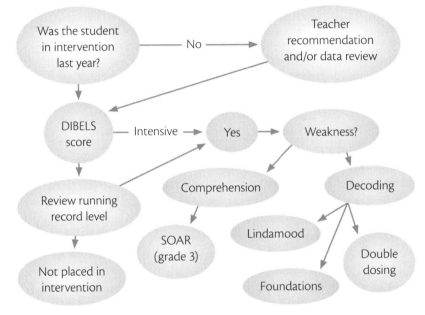

Figure 8.2: Highland Elementary School's K–3 reading intervention decision-making tree. Created by Melissa Wilkins, Meghane Murphy, and Danielle Bellizzi.

Students who have difficulty with comprehension rather than decoding are assigned to the SOAR to Success program, which provides additional small-group guided instruction in reading comprehension using level-appropriate trade books. This program is designed to increase students' understanding of what they read by engaging them in dialogue with the teacher to help them acquire the skills of summarizing, clarifying, questioning, and predicting.

In order to provide this additional time for reading instruction, each grade-level team carves out thirty to forty-five minutes in its daily schedule for intervention. The schedule for the 2008–2009 school year is shown in table 8.1 (page 116).

Table 8.1: Intervention Team Daily Schedule

	Papallo/ Casey	Whitthaus	Healy/Key	Chapman/ Lee
9:00–9:30 a.m.	Grade 5 Math	Planning	Grade 5 Math	
9:40–10:20 a.m.	Grade 4	Grade 4	Grade 4	
10:20–11:00 a.m.	Grade 1	Grade 1	Grade 1	
11:15–12:00 p.m.	Grade 3	Grade 3	Grade 3	Kindergarten 11:25–12:25
12:00–12:30 p.m.	Lunch	Lunch	Lunch	
12:30–1:00 p.m.	Planning	Grade 1 Math	Planning	Grade 4 Math 12:45–1:45
1:00–1:40 p.m.	Grade 2	Grade 2	Grade 2	
1:40–2:20 p.m.	Grade 5	Grade 5	Grade 5	
2:25–3:00 p.m.	Planning	Planning	Planning	

During intervention time, additional personnel descend on the grade level to provide students with intensive small-group and individual support. Principal Myrtle uses funding from Reading First, Title I, and discretionary district funds to hire part-time intervention teachers. Most of the intervention staff members are certified teachers whose family situation or lifestyle make part-time tutoring a particularly attractive option for them. The school's reading coach, reading specialist, special education teachers, and ELL teachers also participate in this effort to provide students with additional focused support.

During intervention, students from all of the classrooms in a grade level are regrouped, and the staff provides specific, differentiated instruction based on the needs of students. While some staff members focus on enrichment, others are implementing the intervention plan for a small group. The intervention teachers are assigned specific students, by name, and they know exactly which skills they need to address with those students. Because assessment is ongoing, student placement in groups is very fluid, and children are able to move into and out of groups as their proficiency dictates.

To ensure the communication essential to a coordinated effort, intervention teachers provide grade-level teams with scores from each embedded assessment as well as brief anecdotal feedback on the progress of each of the students they are serving. For example, one intervention teacher reported: "Lisa has shown *much* growth this marking period; now uses all strategies; participates often; high level of effort continues; uses text support in written responses; still hesitates to use her own words in retelling, but if encouraged will try; if she does not know the answer will search the text; oral reading is strong."

This coordinated effort to clarify the specific knowledge and skills students are to acquire, to monitor each student's proficiency, to respond to students in a systematic way, and to communicate results among all stakeholders has enabled teams to become what Principal Myrtle describes as "well-oiled machines." Students have clearly benefited.

Results

The improvement in the performance of Highland's students on the Maryland State Assessment has been amazing, as demonstrated in tables 8.2 through 8.4 (page 118).

Table 8.2: Percentages of Highland Students Meeting or Exceeding Maryland Proficiency Standards for Grade 3 Reading and Math

	Reading		Math	
	Highland Elementary	Maryland	Highland Elementary	Maryland
2004	55%	63%	65%	72%
2005	47%	76%	69%	77%
2006	78%	78%	79%	79%
2007	80%	80%	78%	79%
2008	95%	83%	92%	83%
Source: Maryland State Department of Education, 2008				

Table 8.3: Percentages of Highland Students Meeting or Exceeding Maryland Proficiency Standards for Grade 4 Reading and Math

	Reading		Math	
	Highland Elementary	Maryland	Highland Elementary	Maryland
2004	56%	75%	51%	70%
2005	76%	81%	74%	77%
2006	78%	82%	81%	82%
2007	90%	86%	85%	86%
2008	95%	88%	95%	89%
Source: Maryland State Department of Education, 2008				

Table 8.4: Percentages of Highland Students Meeting or Exceeding Maryland Proficiency Standards for Grade 5 Reading and Math

	Reading		Math	
	Highland Elementary	Maryland	Highland Elementary	Maryland
2004	56%	68%	45%	63%
2005	56%	74%	57%	69%
2006	76%	77%	80%	73%
2007	73%	77%	85%	78%
2008	93%	87%	92%	80%

Source: Maryland State Department of Education, 2008

As the tables demonstrate, in 2004 Highland Elementary students were performing well below the Maryland state average in reading and mathematics at every grade level tested; however, by 2008, the school's students outperformed students throughout the state in both subject areas in all grade levels. When compared to schools serving similar populations of ELL and high-poverty students, Highland ranked first in the state in both reading and mathematics. Furthermore, a higher percentage of Highland students achieved advanced proficiency in reading and math than the state as a whole. The difference in reading was particularly striking, with 55 percent of Highland students qualifying for advanced proficiency versus 36 percent of Maryland elementary students.

Within two years of beginning its school improvement process, Highland Elementary had been removed from the state's program improvement list. After its third year, the school was one of six in Maryland to be nominated for the United States Department of Education's Blue Ribbon Award. It received the award in 2009. In March of 2009, the National Center for Urban School Transformation named Highland Elementary as one of twelve schools in the nation to receive its Excellence in Urban Education Award. This school serves as a model of what schools can accomplish when clarity about purpose, priorities, and processes replaces ambiguity; when interdependence replaces isolation; and when systematic and collective efforts replace rampant individual autonomy.

Concluding Thoughts

Principal Myrtle reports that staff members are "cautiously elated" about the results the school is achieving and the recognition it has received. The caution comes from the fact that the staff recognizes the school cannot coast—every year new students will come to them with new needs and present new challenges. If, however, this staff continues to work collaboratively to clarify what students must learn, to monitor that learning on a timely basis, and to respond in a timely, directive, and systematic way to provide additional time and support for any student who struggles, we are confident Highland Elementary School will continue to serve as a model of what educators can accomplish.

We can only echo the tribute paid to the school by the district's superintendent, Jerry Weast (2008), who said, "Highland Elementary's overall success is helping to shatter the stereotype that students in poverty and those who are learning English cannot achieve at the highest levels. The academic performance of the school and its students are proof that race, ethnicity, and poverty need not and should not be predictors of academic success."

Visit www.montgomeryschoolsmd.org/schools/highlandes for more information on Highland Elementary School.

9
BUILDING TOWARD THE F.U.T.U.R.E.: CINCO RANCH HIGH SCHOOL

> Shared vision, collaboration, and learning together provide the foundation for teachers to take collective responsibility for students' success; the community's interdependent work structure allows teachers to act on this vision. . . . The learning of all students becomes the responsibility of all faculty, rather than individual teachers only . . . collective responsibility promotes collective growth.
>
> —MILBREY MCLAUGHLIN & JOAN TALBERT, 2006

Katy Independent School District, encompassing 181 square miles in suburban Houston, serves 55,000 students in its forty-six schools. The district has provided an overview of the professional learning community concept to all of its approximately 4,000 teachers and administrators, and many of the Katy schools have made excellent progress on their PLC journey. Cinco Ranch High School, serving over 3,000 students, is one of those schools.

A Focus on Freshmen

Principal Bonnie Brasic and the Cinco Ranch staff operate from the premise that freshman year is crucial to the ultimate success of students, and the school is committed to providing the support necessary to help each freshman have a successful year. Each spring the principals of the sending middle schools assist Cinco Ranch staff in identifying incoming students who will need additional time and support. Those students are recruited for a study skills course offered during the school year that is specifically designed to help them get off to a good start in high school. An extensive summer school program is also offered to all incoming freshmen, and scholarships are provided for students who cannot afford the cost.

The school year begins with Fish Camp—a freshman-only day of orientation to help incoming students become acquainted with the school. Upperclassmen assist freshmen as they follow their schedule, meet their teachers, move from class to class, find their lockers, and learn the layout of the building. Freshmen learn the day they enter high school that the four critical questions of a PLC are posted prominently in every classroom in their school.

A part of Fish Camp is reserved for persuading freshmen to join the cocurricular program of the school. The teachers at Cinco Ranch recognize that students who feel connected to an activity, club, or program are more likely to feel connected to their school and to be academically successful. Therefore they offer over sixty different clubs—from fencing, to ballroom dancing, to Guitar Heroes, to a variety of service organizations. The emphasis on participation has been successful. Over 85 percent of the school's 3,000 students participate in the school's cocurricular program.

In order to provide students with time during the school day for intervention and enrichment, all freshmen are required to reserve one of the seven periods of the day for study hall. A student may petition for permission to forgo study hall and enroll in a seventh course by presenting the principal with a letter, a four-year plan for graduation, a report card from eighth grade, and teacher recommendations. However, only a small percentage of students pursue that option.

Laying the Groundwork for Intervention

In order to provide teachers with time to collaborate, Principal Brasic and the leadership team created a schedule that gives every department common planning time every day. Wednesdays are considered sacred, the day that every course-specific team designates for collaboration on the critical questions of a PLC. Every teacher is expected to honor that commitment, and the administration protects teams from any intrusions on their Wednesday meeting time. Each administrator serves as a liaison to a particular department and supports the teams of that department.

Katy teachers have addressed the question, what do we want our students to learn, by becoming students of the Katy Management of Automated Curriculum—the district's online curriculum guide. This tool, created with the input of teachers throughout the district, suggests essential outcomes and recommended pacing for each course. It also includes lesson-planning tools and research-based strategies for differentiating instruction. The mathematics, English, and foreign language departments have also created vertical teams with the middle schools to ensure a strong scope and sequence in their curricula that avoid redundancy and address essential knowledge and skills.

Cinco Ranch uses a variety of tools to monitor student learning. Teachers are provided with a comprehensive overview of the assessment results for each of their students at the start of each school year. The district's science and mathematics teachers have created common core objectives tests and administer common district assessments in mathematics every nine weeks and in science every six weeks. The school also administers released sets of the state examination once each year to monitor the potential success of each student on this high-stakes test. Although the state sets the proficiency score at 2100, any Cinco Ranch student who scores below 2300 on the practice test is identified for intervention. Finally, each course-specific team at the school has developed a series of common formative assessments that it uses throughout the year to monitor each student's learning on an ongoing basis.

Intervention at Cinco Ranch High School

Students who are not being successful are provided additional time and support for learning in a variety of ways. The mathematics department offers a targeted study hall for students experiencing difficulty in mathematics one period each day, and students may have their schedules revised to participate in that study hall. Students may get a pass out of study hall to seek help from a teacher if that teacher is available or may attend a class to have a second opportunity to learn a concept. They may also receive tutoring from members of the National Honor Society and Mu Alpha Theta during their study hall or lunch period.

The school also assigns students to mandatory tutorial sessions that are held before and after school. Each teacher tutors twice each week as part of his or her weekly duties. The schedule for tutoring is posted in classrooms and on the school's website. Students can attend a tutorial session offered by any member of the course-specific team, but they are required to attend sessions until they are no longer failing. Parents are notified when a student is assigned to tutorials, and the school has found parents to be supportive of the additional help the school is providing their children. If a student does not report to the tutorial, the teacher writes a referral, and the administration assigns detentions after school. That student is advised, however, that the detentions will be waived if he or she attends tutorials. Given a choice between detention and receiving help with learning key concepts and completing their work, most students choose the tutorial session.

English language learners are also offered an extended-day program that targets their language development. Participating students meet with instructors after school four days each week during the spring semester. The school provides snacks and transportation.

If students continue to struggle or refuse to do their work, the school takes steps to determine the nature of their problems. For example, each year the administration and counselors identify thirty freshmen who continue to experience difficulty and invite them to a pizza party during the students' lunch hour. Once there, students complete a survey about their likes and dislikes regarding the school and offer their perspectives on why they are experiencing difficulty. The administration shares the results with department chairs and uses the findings to develop strategies for meeting the needs of individual students and assess the possibility of revising or adding programs to better serve students.

Each of the thirty students who attends the pizza party is assigned a mentor from a group of staff volunteers that includes assistant principals, teachers, counselors, security guards, custodians, and the campus police officer. The mentors visit with students twice each six weeks to discuss social and academic topics, monitor grades, and encourage students to take full advantage of the tutorials.

The school also creates student support groups that meet weekly to help students resolve the problems that are causing them to fail. For example, groups have been created for students recovering from an addiction, coping with grief, learning how to manage anger, needing academic support, and dealing with the challenges of transferring to a new school.

The Katy Online Learning Academy (KOLA) is designed to support students who must recover credits due to failing one or more courses. Students who fail a traditional course complete that course through an online computerized program that allows them to work independently at their own pace. Instructors facilitate the program, provide support to students, and monitor student progress. Students who complete all required online and offline assignments with a grade of 70 percent or better in a specified timeframe earn a credit and have the previous failing grade removed from their transcript. The program is offered during the instructional day in lieu of a class and is also available after school and during summer school. Ninety-seven percent of the Cinco Ranch students who participated in the program in 2008 earned their academic credit.

Technology as an Accelerator of the PLC Journey

In his examination of the practices of organizations that make the leap from "good to great," Jim Collins (2001) found that those who made the leap were very focused in their use of technology. They were not interested in having the latest technology for technology's sake, nor did they believe that technology alone could improve their organization. They were, however, keenly interested in finding technology that "fit with their core purpose," and then using it to advance their purpose. As Collins states, "Technology can *accelerate* a transformation, but technology can not *cause* a transformation" (p. 11).

Cinco Ranch High School has recognized that technology must always be a means to an end rather than the end itself. The staff there has done an exemplary job of using technology to accelerate momentum toward achieving the school's purpose of high levels of learning for all students. The district provides a data collection system, and teachers have been trained to access student scores by objective. Furthermore, some teachers have been released from a duty period to serve as data coaches for their department. They ensure that their colleagues receive the results of assessments on a timely basis and in a user-friendly format.

The district's science teachers have used video conferencing to create an electronic team that links them with all the other teachers of their course in the district. They have worked together to establish essential outcomes, create common assessments, and develop one common integrated lesson for each course. They then use video conferencing to review the results of their common assessments, reflect on the integrated lesson, and discuss best practices based on the results.

The school has also used both district funds and donations from its parent association to purchase Smart Boards™ that allow teachers to upload their lesson plans to their individual websites to help students review. Students also have access to an online discussion forum where they can post questions and seek assistance. As mentioned previously, technology is also used to provide students with the individualized instruction that allows them to recover their credits in the KOLA program.

A few of the school's teachers began to send a weekly email to the parents of their students advising them of upcoming topics and assignments. The parental response was so positive that all teachers have been trained to create email distribution lists to maintain steady communication with the homes of their students. Parents also receive either a progress report or a report card every three weeks from all of their children's teachers. Those who seek even more timely information can access teachers' gradebooks on the web to review their child's grades and completion of assignments. It is evident that parents sincerely appreciate the school's effort to make them partners in the education of their children, and parents devote over 10,000 hours of volunteer service to the school each year.

We have seen schools approach technology as if the primary goal was to collect the latest gizmos without consideration as to how the technology would align with the priorities of the school. The clarity of purpose that characterizes Cinco Ranch, and the constant focus on that purpose, has resulted in technology being used in a powerful way. This award-winning high school has demonstrated that technology can accelerate a school's progress on the PLC journey when it is used to provide teachers with the timely, specific, and user-friendly feedback that is essential to good instruction, foster greater collaboration with colleagues, create stronger links with parents by providing the information they need to be effective partners in the education of their children, and provide students with additional support and more opportunities to learn.

Results

Cinco Ranch has consistently scored among the top high schools in the state on the Texas Assessment of Knowledge and Skills (TAKS) tests, yet the percentage of its students meeting standards on all tests has increased each year between 2004 and 2009. Table 9.1 illustrates Cinco Ranch's scores are well above the state's overall performance on that assessment in every subject and every grade level.

Table 9.1: Cinco Ranch Texas Assessment of Knowledge and Skills (TAKS) Scores Compared to State Overall Performance

	Cinco Ranch 2008 TAKS scores	Texas 2008 TAKS scores
Grade 9 Reading	98%	84%
Grade 9 Math	91%	60%
Grade 10 English	98%	86%
Grade 10 Math	91%	63%
Grade 10 Social Studies	98%	88%
Grade 10 Science	98%	86%
Grade 11 English	98%	90%
Grade 11 Math	97%	79%
Grade 11 Social Studies	99%	95%
Grade 11 Science	97%	80%

High achievement characterizes every subgroup of the school's population. Minority students, economically disadvantaged students, and students with limited English proficiency at Cinco Ranch outperformed the state on every test except tenth-grade science, and their achievement is typically comparable to the overall school performance.

The school's attention to intervention when students experience difficulty has not come at the expense of its high-performing students. In fact, the greatest gains in the achievement scores of Cinco Ranch students on the state test have come at the commended level, which recognizes students who exceed the state standards. The growth in that category since 2004 is presented in table 9.2.

Table 9.2: Cinco Ranch Students Reaching the Commended Level on the Texas Assessment of Knowledge and Skills (TAKS)

	English Language Arts	Math	Science	Social Studies
2004	18%	40%	16%	46%
2005	29%	41%	23%	55%
2006	38%	43%	31%	63%
2007	40%	42%	32%	67%
2008	43%	49%	36%	66%

Cinco Ranch has also been successful in encouraging more students to pursue its most challenging curriculum. It begins making students and parents aware of the availability and benefits of advanced placement courses and dual enrollment college courses in the freshman year. Nonsequential AP courses are open to all interested students, and the number of AP exams written by Cinco Ranch students increased 25 percent from 2004 to 2008. The percentage of those exams earning the highest score (five on a five-point scale) has increased over 10 percent during that period and, in 2008, became the mode score for the first time in the history of the school.

The state of Texas recognizes schools for outstanding achievement, using a variety of indicators to monitor student learning. In 2008, Cinco Ranch received state recognition in English, mathematics, social studies, and advanced placement results. It was one of only four public high schools in Texas to receive the United States Department of Education's No Child Left Behind Blue Ribbon Award that year. Finally, in 2009 Cinco Ranch became one of the first high schools in the Houston area to receive Exemplary status from the Texas Department of Education. Despite the success of the school and the recognition it has received, the teachers of Cinco Ranch continue to look for new ways to ensure all students will learn at high levels. In the fall of 2008, a PLC 3 Committee made up of representatives from each department was created for the specific purpose of examining the third question of a PLC: what will we do when our students do not learn? The committee has been charged to review the school's current intervention practices and develop recommendations to improve them. One of the issues the committee members are grappling with is establishing greater consistency across the school in both retesting of students who have completed tutorials and acceptance of late work. The willingness of this staff to examine all of their practices to ensure those practices align with the purpose of learning for all students illustrates the commitment to continuous improvement present in all high-performing PLCs.

Concluding Thoughts

The Cinco Ranch website proudly proclaims the school is helping to create a new F.U.T.U.R.E. "by being Focused on academics, being User-friendly, engaging in Teamwork, being ever cognizant of individuals' Uniqueness, building Relationships, and fostering a safe and loving Environment." Educators who are looking for a model of a large high school that brings the PLC concept to life in an environment that is both caring and academically challenging can look to Cinco Ranch High School, a school that has rightfully been recognized as one of the best in the United States.

In the next three chapters we turn our attention to how district leaders are implementing systems of interventions in schools throughout their districts.

Visit http://kisdwebs.katyisd.org/campuses/crhs/Pages/Default.aspx for more information on Cinco Ranch High School.

For tools and templates from Cinco Ranch that you may find useful, visit go.solution-tree.com/PLCbooks.

10

FROM GOOD TO GREAT: IMPLEMENTATION OF PLC CONCEPTS IN KILDEER COUNTRYSIDE COMMUNITY CONSOLIDATED SCHOOL DISTRICT 96

At both school and district levels, administrative tasks essential to teachers' learning and learning communities include building a shared vision and common language about practice; convening and supporting reflective conversations, using evidence and data about student learning; and establishing norms and expectations about professional accountability and responsibility across the system for students' success.

—MILBREY MCLAUGHLIN & JOAN TALBERT, 2006

In the second half of the twentieth century, southern Lake County, Illinois, located about thirty miles northwest of Chicago, was transformed from a rural community with four one-room schoolhouses into suburbia. As a result of this metamorphosis, Kildeer Countryside Community Consolidated School District 96, which serves the area, has grown to seven schools with approximately 3,500 students in kindergarten through eighth grade. The district has historically served a predominantly (76 percent) white student population. Only 6 percent of its students are designated as limited English proficient, and only 4 percent qualify for free and reduced-cost lunch. Like many suburban Chicago districts that have very few students facing the issues of poverty or language, District 96 students have always done well on every measure of student achievement. When Illinois began testing its students with a state achievement test, District 96 students consistently scored well above the state average. Without question, it was a good district.

In the late 1990s, much of the district's attention was focused on construction of new schools and debates regarding boundary decisions that would determine which students would be assigned to which schools. Once those issues were finally resolved, Superintendent Tom Many led an initiative to switch the district's focus from *where* students would be educated to *how* they would be educated.

Superintendent Many organized a community search project to examine the district's practices and, more importantly, to clarify the future it was trying to create. Representatives of the board of education, administration, teachers, support staff, parents, and community leaders all participated in this intensive project. At its conclusion, they articulated their collective hopes for the district, which they summarized in the succinct statement of mission, vision, and values presented in the following feature box.

The Foundation of District 96

Our Mission

Ensure that every child achieve his or her maximum potential.

Our Vision

Become the premier elementary school district in the nation.

Our Values

Model *for* others what we expect *from* others.

Every child, every school, every day.

Best practice, not first practice.

Learning has no boundaries.

Celebrate success.

The board of education then established a stretch goal, setting a standard the district had never come close to achieving: "At least 90 percent of students will demonstrate proficiency on the state assessment." In short, a collective commitment was made to move the district from good to great.

Superintendent Many concluded there were three keys to realizing the ambitious aspirations that had been articulated. First, leaders throughout the district had to communicate—clearly, consistently, effectively, and unequivocally—a passionate commitment to the learning of *each* student. Every practice, policy, program, and department had to align with that purpose, and the staffs in each school needed to be protected from competing initiatives and mixed messages. Second, each school would need to be transformed into a professional learning community in order to fulfill the commitment to ensure the learning of all students. Third, principals would play the critical role in leading the implementation of the PLC process in each building. He was convinced that if the PLC concept were to come alive in the schools of District 96, principals would need a deep understanding of the concept. In his words, "every principal had to really *get* it."

Dr. Many realized that without a deep understanding, educators could regard the various elements of the PLC concept as a series of disparate and disconnected tasks to be completed at the behest of the central office rather than a comprehensive and coherent approach to changing school culture. Assigning people into teams, asking teams to write norms and SMART goals, developing common assessments, and creating systems of interventions could be regarded as projects to be accomplished as part of the never-ending to-do lists descending upon schools. He knew the cultural change that was necessary required school leaders who could bring coherence and connectedness to the process—principals who could consistently and persistently articulate, promote, and protect a common priority of learning for all and a clear, comprehensive process for addressing that priority.

To his credit, Superintendent Many acknowledged that if he intended to hold principals accountable for leading the PLC process in their schools, he had an obligation to provide them with the knowledge, tools, support, and resources essential to their success. One of his earliest steps toward that end was to make dramatic changes in the focus and format of the district's principals' meetings. No longer were these meetings to be one-directional presentations *to* principals about managerial issues. Now every meeting was designed to model the shared learning, collective inquiry, collaboration, teamwork, and intense focus on results that were expected in each of the schools. The entire administration engaged in book studies to explore professional learning community concepts, and each member took responsibility for leading the dialogue on different chapters. Rehearsal, role-playing, and hypothetical (but likely) scenarios became a regular part of the agenda. Administrators were challenged to articulate not only *how* they were implementing key PLC components in their buildings, but also *why* those components were vital.

As the district and building leaders engaged in this process of learning together, they discovered the need to become more and more precise with their professional language to ensure they were speaking with one voice and establishing a common vocabulary across the district. As Superintendent Many reflected, "We wanted absolute clarity of language. If principals were to make this happen in their buildings, they needed a deep rather than superficial understanding of key terms. Lots of educators throw around terms like *professional learning community, formative assessment, systems of interventions,* but those terms can mean very different things to different people. We wanted to ensure we were all certain not only of what the terms meant in our context, but exactly what it would look like for those terms to come to life in each school."

Systematic Intervention in District 96

The district's approach to creating systematic interventions in each school is illustrative of its attempt to place specific initiatives within a broader, coherent context and to provide the clarity and specificity to guide the work of educators in each building. As District 96 educators built shared knowledge about the PLC process, they recognized it would be a mistake to move forward with systematic interventions until they took these preliminary steps:

1   Build shared knowledge among teachers and staff regarding the elements of the PLC process and the rationale for implementing those elements.

2   Develop the leadership capacity of key teachers to ensure they play a significant role in the implementation of the PLC process. Teacher leaders were identified in every school to serve as the guiding coalition of the PLC process for their building. Training was provided to support those leaders. For example, an outside consultant offered training in facilitating the collaborative team process. Learning retreats were established to train the trainers and provide teachers with the skills to advance the PLC process in their buildings.

3   Assign teachers into meaningful teams whose members work interdependently to achieve common goals for which they accept mutual accountability. A system of interventions that supported six grade-level teams in an elementary school or a few interdisciplinary or content teams at the middle schools was viable. Responding to twenty-five to fifty individual autonomous classrooms was not.

4   Ensure the members of each team are clear on the knowledge, skills, and dispositions each student is to acquire as a result of their course or grade level. A system of interventions to support student learning could not be effective unless there was clarity regarding exactly what students were to learn.

5   Establish common pacing to monitor student proficiency of the same knowledge and skills. Common pacing made it possible for a system of interventions to identify students who needed support with the same skills at the same time.

6   Develop a series of district-level and building-level common as-
    sessments to monitor the learning of each student. A process for
    monitoring each student's learning of specific knowledge and skills
    on a frequent and timely basis was an absolute prerequisite for the
    success of any system of interventions. Therefore, the district co-
    ordinated a process for teachers to create four district benchmark
    assessments that were to be administered to students across the
    district. Furthermore, grade level and course specific teams in every
    building were asked to develop and administer short-cycle, interim,
    common formative assessments every two or three weeks.

Only after these processes were in place to ensure teachers were clear on
what students were expected to learn and each student's learning was being
closely monitored through a series of common assessments, were teachers
asked to address the next, logical question: how will we respond in our
school when students experience difficulty in their learning? Once again,
an effort was made to ensure clarity regarding the elements of effective
systems of interventions. Representatives from each school participated
in a process to establish criteria for intervention that would be evident in
every building, while leaving the particulars up to each faculty to resolve.
The result was the creation of the SPEED Intervention Criteria (page 134),
which called upon each school to create a process of intervention that had
common characteristics.

Schools were also asked to take a two-pronged approach to students who
experienced difficulty. First, results from the team-developed common formative assessments were to trigger short-term interventions that were highly
fluid. Students would receive additional time and support immediately, but
only until they demonstrated proficiency. Second, if a student's performance
on a district benchmark assessment lagged well below the proficiency standards, the school was to provide ongoing remediation with double doses of
instruction in the subject area over an extended period of time.

The district's two middle schools adjusted their schedules to build time
for intervention into the regular school day. On two days each week, they
adjusted the nine periods of their school day from forty-eight minutes to
forty-five minutes in order to create an academic enrichment period. During that period, students who are being successful in all of their classes are
given options such as additional time for band and orchestra sectionals,
computer lab, study halls, group projects, and student leadership seminars.
Students who are failing a class are assigned to intervention until they have
resolved the issue and are passing their classes.

SPEED Intervention Criteria

Systematic: The intervention plan must be schoolwide, independent of the individual teacher, and communicated in writing (who, why, how, where, and when) to everyone: staff, parents, and students.

Practical: The intervention plan must be affordable within the school's available resources (time, space, staff, and materials). The plan must be sustainable and replicable so that its programs and strategies can be used in other schools.

Effective: The intervention plan must be effective, available, and operational early enough in the school year to make a difference for students. It should have flexible entrance and exit criteria designed to respond to the ever-changing needs of students.

Essential: The intervention plan should focus on agreed-upon standards and the essential learning outcomes of the district's curriculum and be targeted to a student's specific learning needs as determined by formative and summative assessments.

Directive: The intervention plan should be directive. It should be mandatory—not by invitation—and a part of the students' regular school day. Students should not be able to opt out, and parents and teachers cannot waive the student's participation in the intervention program.

Source: DuFour, DuFour, Eaker, & Many, 2006, p. 84.

In addition, four days each week the middle schools offer a forty-five min-ute program called ASAP (After School Assistance Program) to provide ongoing support for students who need more intensive remediation. The district provides transportation for all students who attend this program, and principals stress its importance to parents. Although parents can elect to exempt their student from participation, most choose not to do so.

The elementary schools in the district have focused their intervention efforts on language arts and mathematics. Twice each week students who are experiencing difficulty work in either a literacy lab or a math lab for more intensive, small-group instruction, while their classmates report to the learning center. Some of the schools also use a 9-1 model of instruc-tion and intervention. The teams create a pacing guide designed to provide eight days of instruction on a key skill or concept. On the ninth day they administer a common formative assessment, and on the tenth day they regroup students for intensive intervention or enrichment. Some of the schools assign students who have not completed their work to "Ketchup

Cafes" during lunch, at which students receive assistance in catching up (as the name implies). One of the elementary schools has created a partnership with the local high school that brings high school students to its campus for after-school tutoring for students who need one-on-one support. Once again, the district provides late buses for students who take advantage of this opportunity for tutoring.

District 96 educates all of its 300 kindergarten students in one center, and that school, too, is attentive to systematic interventions. Most students attend kindergarten either in the morning or the afternoon. The moment they arrive on campus an adult greets them, escorts them to a room, and assists them with their "welcome work," to monitor the students' learning before classroom instruction begins. Every adult in the building, with the exception of one secretary and one custodian, assists in this process. Students who persist in having difficulty are assigned to "Double Dose"—that is, morning students stay an hour later, and afternoon students arrive an hour earlier to receive an additional five hours of instructional support each week. If students in the Double Dose program continue to struggle, they are assigned to Kindergarten Plus, which means they attend both the morning and afternoon sessions, as well as Double Dose. If this step does not resolve the difficulties the students experience, they are assigned to integrated kindergarten, a mainstream class taught by a special education teacher. This intense focus on the proficiency and success of students entering the school system has paid enormous dividends for schools throughout the district.

PACE

A districtwide PACE Program (Providing Academic Challenge for Excellence) has been created in District 96 to provide all students with a challenging curriculum. The PACE team—composed of an extended learning specialist, a technology integration specialist, a learning center specialist, and classroom teachers—meets once a trimester with grade levels to help design lessons, extend the learning of teachers, lead small-group instruction, coteach, research ideas, and gather resources. The PACE team has been instrumental in helping teachers develop assessments at the start of a unit and then utilize differentiated instructional strategies and appropriate adjustments in content to challenge individual students based on their readiness, interest, and learning style.

Attention Is All There Is

Leaders do not communicate their priorities through pronouncements, no matter how eloquently those pronouncements are expressed. The *only* way leaders reveal their priorities is by what they pay attention to; or put another way, "Attention is all there is" (Peters & Austin, 1985, p. 266). Principals who did not respond to the district's PLC process were confronted by Superintendent Many, who made it clear that failure to establish a systematic plan for intervention would be cited as a major concern in their evaluations, a concern that would have implications for both their compensation and their continued assignment as principals. Building-level administrators were expected to shift the focus of their annual goals for their schools from completion of projects to evidence of improved student learning. Annual day-long retreats were established to bring teacher leaders, principals, and district leaders together to assess the implementation of the PLC process in each building and to establish specific plans for moving each school forward.

The most powerful expression of the new priority of the district was the establishment of a quarterly meeting between each principal and the central office cabinet to review the evidence of student learning in that school and the specific plan for supporting students who were experiencing difficulty. Initially, principals tended to focus on achievement data—reporting, for example, that 84 percent of the students in a grade level were proficient in math according to the benchmark assessments. The questions posed by the cabinet helped principals learn that they needed to dig deeper into the data. The cabinet was not satisfied with a general number and a general statement of proficiency. Members asked, "Who are the students that are not proficient?" Principals learned to prepare a review of each student who was experiencing difficulty. When the cabinet probed, "Which skills are causing problems for this student?" principals understood that neither *math* nor even *integers* would suffice as a response. They needed to know that this individual student was unable to demonstrate proficiency in the subtraction of two-digit integers.

This digging deeper with principals led them, in turn, to probe more closely with their teacher teams in preparation for the quarterly cabinet meeting. Principals began to use the same questions in regular meetings with their teams, and personnel throughout the district began to monitor each student's learning, skill by skill.

Results

This intensive and coordinated effort to move a district from good to great has had a tremendous impact on student achievement in District 96, as illustrated in figure 10.1.

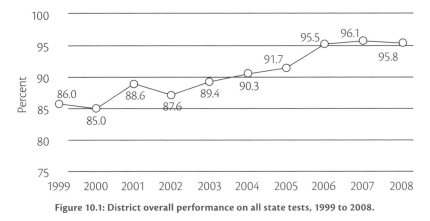

Figure 10.1: District overall performance on all state tests, 1999 to 2008.

Helping All Students Learn at Higher Levels

The improved achievement has benefited all groups of students in District 96. For example, 59 percent of the students in the district exceeded the state standard in mathematics and 49 percent exceeded the standard in language arts. The percentage of the district's special education students meeting the state standard has increased from 64 percent to 80 percent in reading and from 81 percent to 88 percent in mathematics. As a result, in 2008, students with disabilities in District 96 not only scored significantly higher on the state assessment than other students in the state with disabilities, but they also performed comparable to or better than all students in Illinois in both areas in every grade level. Table 10.1 (page 138) indicates the percentage of the district's special education students who are meeting or exceeding the state standards in reading and mathematics.

Whereas fewer than one in ten of the special education students in Illinois in grades 3 through 8 achieve at the exceeds standards level on the state assessment in reading, almost one in three of District 96 special education students meet that standard. In math, approximately 17 percent of the state's special education students earn the "exceeds expectations" distinction, while 40 percent of District 96's students achieve at that level.

Table 10.1: Percentages of Students Meeting the Illinois State Proficiency Standard

	Illinois Students With Individualized Education Plans		All Illinois Students		District 96 Students With Individualized Education Plans	
	Reading	Math	Reading	Math	Reading	Math
Grade 3	42.8%	67.8%	71.7%	85.1%	70.5%	95.1%
Grade 4	41.5%	71.6%	73.2%	84.6%	78.0%	96.7%
Grade 5	38.5%	54.5%	73.5%	81.4%	84.8%	85.3%
Grade 6	42.9%	52.1%	79.0%	82.6%	84.7%	86.4%
Grade 7	34.9%	45.2%	77.7%	80.4%	85.3%	80.3%
Grade 8	42.3%	43.2%	81.4%	80.4%	78.0%	84.0%

As a result of this steady improvement, District 96 has reaped the following benefits:

- Moved from fifty-seventh to ninth place among elementary school districts in the state in student achievement on the state test

- Had three of its four elementary schools listed among the top elementary schools in the Chicago area, with a special citation for having the lowest per-pupil expenditure of any qualifying schools

- Had four schools listed among the top fifty schools in the state in 2008

- Was featured by the United States Department of Education on the *Doing What Works* website for its exemplary middle school math program (see http://dww.ed.gov/)

- Became one of the few public school programs in the state to have its preschool and kindergarten center accredited by the National Association for the Education of Young Children

Finally, District 96's success in moving from good to great has brought it national attention. No school in the district had ever received the U.S. Department of Education's Blue Ribbon Award during the first twenty-four years the award was offered (1982–2005). Three of its schools won the award between 2005 and 2009. Furthermore, educators from around the country visit District 96 every month to learn more about its transformation.

It is important to note that this steady improvement occurred despite a state-initiated early retirement incentive that has created massive personnel changes in District 96. Fourteen of the nineteen building and central office administrators who helped launch the good-to-great effort are no longer with the district, and 43 percent of its teachers have been in the district less than four years. Nevertheless, student achievement continues to improve. As Superintendent Many says, "It is not a few charismatic individuals who are responsible for our transformation. It's the fact that we put systems in place to focus the attention and efforts of everyone in the organization on the right work."

Concluding Thoughts

We have worked with educators throughout North America who argue that they cannot generate interest in improving student learning because they work in "good" schools. Student achievement is high enough to avoid sanctions and compares favorably to other schools in the area. Parents seem satisfied. "How," they ask, "can you convince colleagues to invest the effort and energy to help more students learn when there is no sense of urgency because the school is good enough?" We offer District 96 as an example of what people can accomplish when they decide "good enough" isn't good enough.

Visit www.district96.k12.il.us for more information on District 96.

11
WHATEVER IT TAKES—STAYING THE COURSE: WHITTIER UNION HIGH SCHOOL DISTRICT

> Leaders should stand for a high purpose with quality, hire talented individuals along those lines, create mechanisms for purposeful peer interaction with a focus on results, stay involved but avoid micromanaging. Put differently, once you establish the right conditions and set the process in motion, trust the process and the people in it.
>
> —MICHAEL FULLAN, 2008

Whittier Union High School District, located in Los Angeles County, is comprised of five comprehensive high schools, a continuation school, an alternative studies program, and an adult high school. Whittier is 2,000 miles from Kildeer Countryside Community Consolidated School District 96 geographically, but even further removed from the suburban Chicago district in virtually every characteristic. It is four times larger, serving 14,000 students. It is a high school district rather than an elementary district. Whereas 76 percent of Kildeer's students are white, over 80 percent of Whittier's students are Hispanic. Whereas only 4 percent of Kildeer's students are eligible for free and reduced-cost lunch, the percentage of economically disadvantaged Whittier students increased from 31 percent to 72 percent from 2004 to 2009. In most regards, these two districts could not be more different, yet they share a commitment to helping all students achieve at high levels, a determination to provide students who experience difficulty with additional time and support for learning in a systematic way, and steadily increasing student achievement. In fact, despite the tremendous increase in the number of its students living in poverty from 2004 to 2009 and the huge fiscal challenges California districts have confronted during that time, Whittier Union schools have demonstrated significant gains in every indicator of student achievement.

The Whittier Union Journey

Sandy Thorstenson, the superintendent of Whittier Union, has been connected to the district and its schools for most of her life. She attended the district's oldest high school, Whittier High, worked in a variety of roles in three of the other schools, and sent her daughter to another. She had worked in the district for over a quarter of a century when, as superintendent, she launched its professional learning community journey by accompanying an administrative team to a conference on the Professional Learning Communities at Work concept. They became convinced that the best hope for sustained and substantive improvement in their schools was to build the capacity of staff to operate as PLCs, but they faced the challenge of how best to initiate the dialogue. Superintendent Thorstenson began building shared knowledge among administrators and teacher leaders by asking them to read and discuss one of our favorite books, *Whatever It Takes* (DuFour, DuFour, Eaker, & Karhanek, 2004).

Superintendent Thorstenson then arranged multiple fieldtrips to Adlai Stevenson High School in suburban Chicago so dozens of the district's teachers and administrators could see the PLC concept in action at a high school that was even larger than any of Whittier's schools. She specifically chose the most respected and influential teacher leaders to visit Stevenson, and has since concluded that those visits were the turning point in the district's journey because of the enthusiasm they generated among key educators in every school. In their study of how leaders are able to influence the beliefs, expectations, and ultimately the behavior of others, Patterson, Grenny, Maxfield, McMillan, and Switzler (2008) suggested taking skeptics "on a field trip—or several of them" because "personal experience is the mother of all cognitive map changes" (p. 51). Superintendent Thorstenson used that strategy to full advantage.

After making school-based leaders at each of the five comprehensive high schools aware of the PLC concept, Superintendent Thorstenson urged them to begin closing the gap between *knowing* about the PLC process and actually *doing* what PLCs do. She supported their efforts on the opening day of school for all staff in 2005 by explicitly stipulating three expectations for all Whittier Schools (Cox, 2008):

1   Every school would implement common assessments created at both the district and site levels.

2   Every school would provide and protect time for teacher collaboration.

3   Every school would implement academic interventions within the daily schedule.

Superintendent Thorstenson stressed that while the details of implementation could vary from school to school, the intended outcomes could not—and three measurable indicators were established to monitor each school's success in helping more students achieve at higher levels. She pledged to provide additional training and support to schools as they identified their needs. She also committed to stay the course, promising the district would not deviate from its commitment to the PLC concept.

Leadership pronouncements will only go so far in terms of changing the practices of an organization. Administrative and teacher leaders throughout the district also engaged in ongoing dialogue with staff to address concerns, answer their questions, and, very importantly, reinforce both *why* the PLC initiative was being undertaken and *how* people throughout the district would be asked to contribute. The honest assessment of the current reality of student achievement in the district, the clearly articulated vision of what the schools were expected to become, the sharing of the research and rationale in support of PLC practices, the creation of a core group of teacher and administrator advocates, and the continuing effort to bring concerns to the surface and work collaboratively to address them gradually built support for the PLC process among staff throughout the district.

Dispersing Leadership

The central office staff and the district's six principals became their own learning community as they moved forward with the PLC process. Every principal attended institutes on the PLC concept and made the pilgrimage to Stevenson. The job description and evaluation process for Whittier principals were changed to emphasize that the primary responsibility of each principal was to address the three district initiatives—teachers working collaboratively, common assessments, and systematic intervention—and to demonstrate progress on the indicators of effectiveness that the district was tracking. As Loring Davies, the district's assistant superintendent and former principal of Whittier High School explains, "Sandy left no doubt in any principal's mind what the priorities were in the district and that our effectiveness as principals would be evaluated on the basis of tangible evidence of improved student learning."

Superintendent Thorstenson and the district's three assistant superintendents met, and continue to meet, with all the principals as a team once a week to monitor what Thorstenson refers to as "mission critical" work and share ideas for addressing problems they encounter. The central office administrators and principals also participate in an annual retreat to assess progress and plan the next steps in moving forward on the PLC journey. The clarity of purpose, priorities, and the indicators to monitor progress have helped create a wonderfully cohesive administrative team in which principals work as partners to ensure all schools are effective rather than competing with one another. As Superintendent Thorstenson says, "If we are going to ask teachers to work collaboratively, share best practices, and demonstrate a willingness to learn from one another, we need to model those behaviors as administrators."

The central office also coordinated a collaborative effort among science, mathematics, English, and social studies teachers from each school to create four district common assessments to be administered to all students annually. Schools were also asked to create at least four of their own interim common assessments in the core courses of those subject areas. Initially, department chairs took the lead in coordinating the development, implementation, and analysis of these site-based common assessments for their departments. Soon, however, schools recognized that the task required more time than a single person with a full teaching load could devote to it. So the district created the position of lead teacher for each course and asked that teacher to assume the responsibility for leading both the implementation of common assessments and the team analysis and dialogue after they were administered. This strategy significantly increased the number of people in each building who accepted responsibility for leading the PLC process. In 2009, 123 teachers in the district held the position of lead teacher.

When the district discovered that it lacked the capacity to provide teachers with timely and user-friendly analysis of the results from common assessments, it purchased new software to accomplish that goal. It also assigned one person in each school to assist teachers in learning how to use that software to organize and retrieve the data they needed to identify strengths and weaknesses in student learning.

As each school's system of interventions became more sophisticated, the district created the position of intervention specialist to coordinate the response to students who were experiencing difficulty. Specialists were available for one period each day during the 2006–2007 school year. In 2007–2008 specialists were available for a second period and were provided a clerk to assist in monitoring interventions.

The role of guidance counselor was significantly altered to give counselors key leadership responsibilities in the system of interventions in each school. Counselors from each building were asked to work together to identify three key indicators all schools would track to monitor the effectiveness of the system of interventions. The three they chose—the percentage of students eligible to enter the University of California or California State University systems upon graduation, the percentage of underclassmen on target for graduation, and the actual graduation rate—became the benchmarks each school used to monitor its improvement. Counselors took the lead in establishing greater coordination with the sender schools so that the high schools could be more proactive in meeting the needs of incoming students rather than waiting for them to establish a cycle of failure in their new school. Most importantly, counselors played a critical role in creating the specific steps and strategies that constituted the system of interventions in their schools. The district provided counselors with ongoing staff development from Gayle Karhanek (one of the authors of this book) over a four-year period to ensure each had a deep understanding of the PLC process and how systematic intervention contributed to that process. Gayle tailored that training to the specific needs of each school site, and the training was later expanded to include the leadership team at each high school.

The Whittier teachers union has also played an important leadership role in supporting the PLC journey. Union leaders were part of the leadership coalition that built shared knowledge by reading the same books and articles, analyzing the same data, participating in focus group dialogues, and taking the field trips to Stevenson. They also took on key roles as lead teachers and intervention specialists. As Superintendent Thorstenson acknowledges, "We would not have been successful in our efforts to create PLCs without the support and leadership of our union."

Finally, the transparency of results and open dialogue that characterized the work in Whittier allowed different schools in the district to assume a leadership role in different areas. A practice that proved effective or a new schedule piloted successfully in one school soon spread to other schools. Competition among the schools diminished. Educators demonstrated a willingness to learn from one another and became interested in the success not only of their own school, but also of all the schools in the district.

This same openness and focus on results also made it possible for individual leaders to emerge from within the ranks and have a profound impact on practice throughout the district. For example, Dan Esquerra, a mathematics department chairman at Whittier High School, was one of the first in the district to embrace the idea of common assessments, advocating that strategy even before the district launched its PLC process. In the fall of 2003, he began to lead his colleagues in identifying skills and concepts that were proving problematic for students by engaging teachers in the analysis of the results from common assessments. The department created a three-part protocol for that collective analysis, including reviewing the content and standard that had been assessed, analyzing the results, and discussing implications for effective teaching and intervention.

The school's dramatic gains in student achievement in mathematics on the state test after only one year of this process sparked great interest in other departments. Esquerra was asked to make presentations at schoolwide faculty meetings to explain the department's use of common assessments and its protocols for effective analysis of results by teams of teachers.

Esquerra and the math department also pioneered the practice of allowing students to retest if they had failed an assessment, a practice that led to a lower failure rate and improved student achievement on high-stakes testing. These assessment and grading practices soon spread—first throughout the school, and then throughout the district. By 2009 Esquerra became a districtwide trainer in the use of common assessments and effective grading practices.

Promoting Prevention

The Whittier district operates from the premises that the initial focus of a school must be on prevention rather than intervention and that the best way to limit the need for intervention is to ensure students receive effective, high-quality instruction in their classrooms each day. The emphases on using common assessments, so that each teacher can identify strengths and weaknesses in his or her instruction, and providing teachers time to collaborate to learn from each other were both specifically intended to promote best instructional practice.

Each campus was given considerable latitude regarding the structures they would establish to support collaboration and a focus on results. All schools had to create time for teachers to collaborate, but schools had great autonomy regarding the schedules they would develop to provide that time. Whittier High School created an early dismissal on Friday afternoons that provided teachers with time to collaborate, while La Serna High School arranged for a late start to its school day once each week. All schools became adept at finding creative ways for making time for collaboration. For example, several times each year counselors at Whittier High School conduct group guidance sessions by class. Freshmen, for example, report to the auditorium for a guidance activity rather than report to their English class. Because the school follows a modified A/B block schedule, this provides the freshman English teachers with two full days for working in their collaborative teams.

Systematic Intervention at Whittier

Initially, many of the interventions put into place at Whittier were very similar to those their staff had observed during their visits to Stevenson High School. Whittier schools created their own versions of Freshman First Day to give incoming students a day to become familiar with the campus before other students arrive, Campus Watch to identify students who will need additional support in making the transition from eighth grade to high school, and Link Crew to provide each freshman with an upperclassman mentor.

Whittier has also developed its own unique programs to provide an intensive focus on and support for ninth-grade students. The Summer Bridge Program was created to support students who had struggled in eighth grade by providing them with the academic and social skills to succeed in high school. The program has been extended into the school year and is offered as an elective class for students to ensure they have additional support throughout their freshman year.

Whittier schools increased the reporting of student achievement from once every nine weeks to once every four-and-a-half weeks. This more frequent reporting not only provides students and parents with more timely information, but, very importantly, it also enables the school to respond more quickly to students who are struggling.

One of the most unique aspects of Whittier's approach to systematic interventions is the way schools have adjusted their schedules to provide time for intervention. For example, the faculty at Whittier High School voted to move to a modified block schedule proposed by some of their colleagues. On the first day of the week, all six periods meet for forty-eight minutes. One Monday each month, classes meet for only thirty-five minutes, and students are dismissed at 12:15 to give teachers a large block of time for collaboration. Tuesdays through Thursdays, three classes meet in 100-minute blocks. For the first five weeks of the school year, all students remain in class for the entire 100 minutes; however, from that point on, students who are passing the class and have completed all their work are released from each period twenty minutes early to enjoy free time, a longer lunch period, or the privilege of leaving school early. Students who are not passing or have not completed their work remain in the class for intensive small-group work with their teachers. On the initial vote to move to this schedule, two-thirds of the faculty supported the move. After one year of experience with the schedule, over 90 percent of the faculty voted to support it.

At La Serna High School, on the other hand, the tutorial system is incorporated into a fifty-eight-minute lunch period. Students who meet the prerequisite requirements enjoy an extended lunch, whereas those who are not passing their classes or completing their work spend a portion of the lunch period in a study hall or in a subject-specific tutorial. Again, the specifics of intervention are left to each school, but every plan must be particularly attentive to incoming freshmen and provide all students with intervention that is timely, directive (rather than invitational), and systematic.

Whittier has also designed specific classes to provide students who are struggling with the support they need in order to be successful. Incoming students whose reading scores fall below established standards are automatically placed in a reading enrichment course. A guided study course is the Whittier program for entering students who failed to graduate from eighth grade. Students in this program are taught study skills and have their work monitored on a daily basis. Students who fail to pass, or are in danger of failing to pass, the California High School Exit Examination (CAHSEE) are placed into a support class specifically designed to help them succeed on that high-stakes assessment.

Whittier schools continue to tweak their programs and procedures in a constant effort to improve student achievement. Staff members have been asked to embrace the ongoing cycle of success which calls upon them to A-I-M. They gather information and evidence to *assess* the effectiveness of their efforts to help all students learn; *intervene* when students experience difficulty; and *monitor* the effectiveness of each strategy, program, and process in resolving those difficulties and helping students be successful learners.

The constant search for better ways to meet the needs of students is also exemplified in the district's best-practices dinners held each quarter. At these events, teachers from each school share the best practices they have developed to improve student achievement. Once again, data on student achievement and the practices that lead to those results are openly shared among educators from all of the schools. This lateral capacity building is yet one more tool used to convey the message that helping all students learn is a collective responsibility that cuts across not only classrooms, but also schools.

Results

The leaders of the Whittier Union PLC process have never lost sight of the fact that their purpose is to help more students learn at higher levels. Today they can celebrate the progress they have made thus far.

Academic Performance Index Scores

California establishes the Academic Performance Index (API) as a measure of student achievement for each school and district in the state. For high schools the score, which ranges from 200 to 1000, is based on a formula that includes student results on California Standards Tests in English-language arts, mathematics, science, and social studies, as well as the California High School Exit Examination.

Since 2004, Whittier Union's API score has risen from 635 to 728, and all five of the district's comprehensive high schools have experienced significant gains that range from 71 to 104 points. California also ranks schools in deciles to establish how a school performs compared to other schools with similar student populations. All of the district's schools rank in the top half of the state, and three of the five rank in the ninth decile.

Closing the Achievement Gap

Whittier Union is one of the most effective districts in California in terms of closing the achievement gap. The largest gains in student achievement have been for ethnic minorities and economically disadvantaged students, and the difference in achievement between the highest and lowest groups has been reduced to 10 percent.

High School Completion Rates

Whittier has reduced its dropout rate to 9 percent, compared to a county average of 28 percent and a state rate of 24 percent. The percentage of freshmen who are on track for graduation at the completion of ninth grade has increased from 76 percent to 83 percent since the end of the 2005 school year. From 2005 to 2008, over 99 percent of Whittier's students passed the California High School Exit Examination required for graduation.

Pursuit of More Rigorous Curriculum

The attention to the success of all students has increased the number of Whittier Union students willing to pursue a more challenging curriculum. The percentage of students completing all requirements for admission to the University of California and California State University system has risen from 27 percent to 40 percent from 2006 to 2008. The number of advanced placement examinations written by Whittier Union students jumped more than 30 percent from 2004 to 2009. The district has doubled the number of students qualifying for its honors program in ninth grade and expects to have steadily higher percentages of its students pursuing the school's most rigorous curriculum.

A study of the district conducted by researchers from the University of Southern California lauded Whittier for being one of the few districts in the state where *every* school was outperforming similar schools. The researchers attributed Whittier's success to "the District's unwavering 'laser-like' focus on implementing its 'Whatever It Takes' initiative and its tremendous leadership at all levels—from the Board and Superintendent to teachers"—and for creating "a culture of success" that demonstrated "demographics do not determine destiny" (Whittier Union High School District, 2008, p. 1).

Concluding Thoughts

What is particularly striking about the steadily improving student achievement in Whittier is the context in which it is occurring. The percentage of economically disadvantaged students has skyrocketed, and the instability of the California state budget presents districts with fiscal challenges that are as severe as anywhere in the United States. Yet despite all the obstacles, student achievement continues to climb—and not in an isolated school, but in every school in the district. In its continuing focus on reshaping high schools, *Educational Leadership* featured Whittier Union High School District in an online article (Cox, 2008). The title of the article was "What's Working in Whittier." The answer to that question is, "Quite a lot!" We encourage other districts to take a close look at Whittier and, more importantly, to embrace the district's publicly stated philosophy: "Whatever It Takes—Staying the Course."

Visit www.wuhsd.k12.ca.us/whittieruhsd/site/default.asp for more information on Whittier Union High School District.

12

UNDER NO CIRCUMSTANCES BLAME THE KIDS: SANGER UNIFIED SCHOOL DISTRICT

Effective superintendents created a normative climate in which teachers and principals were collectively responsible for student learning and in which the improvement of instruction and performance was the central task and other distractions were reduced.

—RICHARD ELMORE, 2006

Teaching without learning isn't teaching at all. It is just presenting.

—MARK JOHNSON, SUPERINTENDENT OF SANGER UNIFIED SCHOOL DISTRICT

Sanger Unified School District is a sprawling, diverse district covering approximately 180 square miles in Fresno County, California. Some areas of the district are classified as "urban fringe," while others are distinctly rural, reflecting the county's status as one of the leading agricultural areas of the United States. Sanger is comprised of nineteen schools—three charter schools, eleven elementary schools, one middle school, one high school, an alternative education school, a community day school, and an adult school. Seventy percent of its approximately 10,000 students are Hispanic, 18 percent are white, and 10 percent are Asian. More than 75 percent of students qualify for free and reduced-cost lunch.

At the end of the 2003–2004 school year, Sanger became one of the first districts in California designated for Program Improvement by the state. Five of its elementary schools and the middle school had also been placed in Program Improvement. Superintendent Mark Johnson admits that Sanger Unified was "in dire straits" as the 2004–2005 school year began.

Superintendent Johnson recognized that educators at all levels of the district had good intentions and were working hard. He believed that the district had made progress in ensuring that every student in every classroom was under the tutelage of a caring teacher every day. He also recognized, however, that the district's efforts to help all students learn were uncoordinated. Good things happening in some parts of the district had not been enough to prevent it from being designated for Program Improvement, and random acts of innovation would not be sufficient to overcome what he regarded as systemic obstacles to raising student achievement. He looked upon the potential sanctions facing the district as a moral imperative to address those obstacles in a very direct way. He began to communicate a consistent message, as steady as a drumbeat: 1) the job of every person in this district is to ensure student learning, 2) hoping things will get better is not a strategy, 3) don't blame the kids, and 4) the best strategy for sustained, substantive improvement is developing our capacity to work as members of a professional learning community.

Johnson immediately set out to reinforce that message by building shared knowledge among principals and teacher leaders about the elements of a professional learning community. He personally accompanied each group of educators that he sent to intensive two-day training sessions on the Professional Learning Communities at Work process sponsored by the Riverside County Office of Education. Not only did he recognize his presence signaled his own commitment to the process, but he found the five-hour drive each way to be an invaluable experience for reflecting, sharing, debriefing, and planning with principals and key teacher leaders. By 2009, he had sent over 300 of the district's educators to the training. Furthermore, the district had brought additional trainers into Sanger to work with schools on particular elements of the PLC process. In short, there was a very purposeful decision to build shared knowledge among Sanger educators as a prerequisite for improvement.

As Sanger educators became more familiar with the PLC process and began to assess their own district's practices in light of that process, they confronted a series of brutal facts:

- Teachers were not clear on what students were to learn. Not enough attention had been paid to ensuring teachers had studied and clarified essential state standards for their course or grade level.

- The district had no process for monitoring student learning on a timely basis. Hoping for good results at the end of the year on state assessments had not proven to be an effective strategy for helping all students develop proficiency.

- Schools lacked any coherent sense as to how they should respond when students did not learn.

Superintendent Johnson coordinated a districtwide effort to engage teachers in addressing each of these issues, and he stipulated that certain things were to occur in every school. For example, teachers were to work in collaborative teams that took mutual responsibility for the success of their students. Teams were not only to administer the new assessments created at the district level three times each year, but they were also to create their own common formative assessments to monitor the learning of each student. Finally, each school was to create a systematic plan to assist students who experienced difficulty in their learning. As he put it, "The questions that drive a learning community—what is it we want kids to learn, how do we know if they have learned it, what will we do when they don't learn it, and what will we do to deepen and extend the learning for those who are proficient—are what drove our entire improvement effort."

Systems of Interventions in Sanger

Superintendent Johnson insisted that each school create a plan for providing additional time and support for students who experienced difficulty. He also stipulated that the time for intervention had to occur during the school day and that students were to be required rather than invited to use this additional support for learning. He stopped short, however, of specifying a particular plan that every school was required to adopt. The staff at each school was free to develop their own coordinated process to assist students.

Elementary schools focused on training staff in explicit direct instruction and differentiated instruction to ensure all students had access to a foundational level of effective teaching in every classroom, every day. Grade-level teams monitored each student's learning through a wide variety of assessments including team-developed common assessments, district assessments, and commercially developed assessments that support particular programs. When students began to experience difficulty, the teams attempted to identify the specific nature of the problem and assigned students to interventions specifically designed to address that problem.

Intervention in elementary schools takes an "all hands on deck" approach. Schools devised ways to bring a team of supportive adults to each grade level during a period of the day when students of that grade level could be assigned to different stations. Student teachers, college students, adult volunteers, school psychologists, speech therapists, and teacher aides worked with proficient students to enrich their learning or to "front load" them for the next unit. Meanwhile, classroom teachers and special education teachers for that grade level created fluid groups to ensure a student who was experiencing difficulty works with the teacher on the team whose students achieved the best results based on the common assessments. As a result, the team began to think of students as "our kids" rather than thinking "these are my kids and those are your kids."

The staff at Washington Academic Middle School found their plan of intervention had to address not only students who experienced difficulty in learning despite their best efforts, but also behavior and work ethic issues that contributed to the failure of some students. These "intentional nonlearners" (Buffum, Mattos, & Weber, 2009, p. 98) had made the choice to opt out of learning and were perfectly willing to fail. Therefore, the staff recognized their plan had to address the needs of both groups of students.

One of the strategies the middle school adopted was referred to as *rectification*. In brief, all students missing work or in danger of a failing grade were required to "rectify" the situation by completing all of their work during a mandatory homework lab during their lunch period. The week the policy was initiated, almost 300 students were assigned to the lab. By the third week, the number had been reduced to forty students, and by the end of the month it was down to twenty-five students. By then, students who were passing their courses were accompanying their friends to the lab to help them complete their work and earn back the privilege of extended lunch. The school also created academic seminars during the school day to assist chronic procrastinators with getting organized, managing their time, and completing their work. The staff at Washington created the expectation that students must do their work and that opting out of learning is no longer an option.

The staff at Sanger High School recognized the first step in a system of interventions was to promote effective instruction in each classroom every day. Toward that end, the faculty adopted three instructional norms that were to characterize their teaching each day: 1) teachers will utilize learning objectives derived from content standards, 2) they will employ checking for understanding to ascertain whether or not the student has learned the material, and 3) they will use effective strategies that ensure student engagement in the curriculum.

The school also became more proactive in its approach to intervention. The district assesses the learning level of every incoming ninth-grade student and transfer student. Those who are not proficient readers are assigned to a corrective reading course until they can pass the California Standards Test. The number of students needing this support has declined each year, despite the fact that the district has raised the standard students must achieve to opt out of the course.

As part of the second level of the pyramid of interventions, the high school offers both semester-long intervention courses and three-week intensive courses to support eleventh- and twelfth-grade students who have not passed the English and/or math portions of the state test required for graduation, the California High School Exit Examination. The school also assigns low-performing tenth-grade students to CAHSEE intensive courses and has established a CAHSEE intensive course specifically designed for the school's English language learners.

Sixty-five members of the certified staff also volunteer to serve as mentors to at-risk students. Each of those staff members takes responsibility for up to five students. Mentors make regular contact with their students, monitor homework completion, and keep parents informed.

Departments have also created their own systems of response for students who are not being successful or not completing their work. For example, the science department has created "purgatory," the stipulation that students who fail a test must report to a tutoring session at lunch until they learn the material and retake a test. The English department also uses lunch sessions for students who have not completed their homework.

Developing Principals as Leaders

One of Sanger's core strategies for improving student achievement was developing the leadership skills of the district's principals. Johnson was convinced that the competency of the principal was the primary vehicle for moving a school forward, and he accepted responsibility for building the capacity of principals to lead PLCs.

All of the district's principals have received intensive training in leading the PLC process and additional training in data analysis and intervention approaches. Some of the greatest learning for principals, however, has occurred from ongoing processes initiated in the district rather than through formal training.

Each fall, the Sanger Summit brings building principals and central office staff together for a structured review of student achievement. Principals from three schools at a time (grouped by similar school characteristics) meet for a dialogue with Superintendent Johnson, the associate superintendent for human resources, and Rich Smith, the deputy superintendent for curriculum and instruction (whom Johnson cites as a key leader of the PLC process in Sanger). The conversation takes place in full view of curriculum coordinators, program directors, guests from other districts, county office representatives, and staff and students of local universities who come to observe the process. Other principals from the district are also invited to attend to observe their colleagues.

Each principal provides a forty-five minute overview of trends in student achievement in his or her school and the progress the school is making in implementing PLC concepts. The three central office staff members at the table and, eventually, the other participants observing the process pose questions. Johnson contends the constant transparency of results and the collective approach to problem solving have caused the depth of knowledge of the district's principals to grow exponentially. Furthermore, principals have been able to transfer the skills they have learned through their participation in the process back to the teams in their schools.

To provide clear expectations and parameters regarding the summits, Superintendent Johnson provides each principal with written guidelines regarding how the program will operate (fig. 12.1).

Sanger Summits 2008–2009

What Is a Sanger Summit?

Sanger Summits are an opportunity for principals to present their school's past and current levels of student achievement, review their plans for improving achievement, and receive feedback and suggestions from their peers. The Summits also allow the district office and district support providers to better understand the distinct needs, goals, programs, and direction of all schools. Summits are a dialogue from which all participants grow and improve for the benefit of the children of Sanger Unified.

Items to Bring to the Summit for Discussion

Participants are to create their presentations in PowerPoint. Please make graphs clear and concise. Each graph should be on a single page/frame. The total presentation is to be contained in a handout of fifteen or more pages. Participants are to bring no fewer than fifteen photocopied sets of their presentation. Items to be included in your presentation are as follows:

A graph or diagram showing—

1   Your school's overall API for the past seven years.

2   AYP levels for all significant subgroups over the past six years using *percentage and number* of students who are proficient/advanced in language arts. Point out any achievement gaps and discuss your plans to address these achievement gaps. *Secondary schools should use their 2007–2008 sophomores' CAHSEE data.*

3   AYP levels for all significant subgroups over the past six years using *percentage and number* of students who are proficient/advanced in mathematics. Point out any achievement gaps and discuss your plans to address these achievement gaps. *Secondary schools should use their 2007–2008 sophomores' CAHSEE data.*

Figure 12.1: Participation guidelines for a Sanger Summit.

4   Show the percentage of English language learners (ELLs) who are proficient/advanced in the areas of language arts and mathematics for the past four years. *Secondary schools should use their 2007–2008 sophomores' CAHSEE data.*

5   The number of students in each ELL classification as compared to the prior year (A, B, EO, and so on). Clearly show the number of students who advanced levels, stayed the same, or regressed from each classification using your 2006–2007 and 2007–2008 CELDT data.

6   The percent and number of students moved from performance band to performance band for language arts (plus or minus) from 2004–2005, 2005–2006, 2006–2007, and 2007–2008.

7   The percent and number of students moved from performance band to performance band (plus or minus) for mathematics from 2004–2005, 2005–2006, 2006–2007, and 2007–2008.

Synopsis

Your synopsis should include no more than one page per item. Please make your synopsis reader-friendly using diagrams, tables, and bullets with clear, thoughtful statements.

1   Provide a brief synopsis of *why* your school made improvements in academic achievement last year. Include key areas of focus to continue to improve student achievement this year on this same sheet.

2   Clearly state the status of implementation of professional learning communities at your school site. Include how you monitor the creation and assessment of SMART goals. Explain how your grade levels/departments respond when students do not meet a SMART goal. Describe your efforts to embed PLCs into the culture of your school.

3   Describe your plan to ensure effective ELL instruction is taking place in all classrooms and how you plan to frequently and effectively monitor ELL student achievement throughout the year.

4   Present your pyramid of interventions. Clearly state what steps you have taken to ensure that classroom teachers provide the first level of interventions. Also give entry and exit criteria for each level of the pyramid.

5   Present the steps you have taken to ensure that the elements of effective direct instruction are used in the instruction of your students.

Participants will be given *forty-five minutes* to present their graphs and talk about their plans. A discussion period will take place immediately following each presentation.

Principals also meet with the deputy superintendent on a monthly basis. An ongoing topic of conversation is student achievement on the district-administered assessments. Every other month the principals and the PLC leadership teams from each school are brought together for ongoing training on the PLC concept.

At approximately the midpoint of each school year, principals are called upon to make predictions regarding how their students will perform on the state assessments. The message is unmistakable: principals are expected to monitor the learning of each student very closely and to make adjustments to the student's schedule and the school's curriculum based on that ongoing monitoring. There are to be no unpleasant surprises on the state assessment for Sanger students.

Administrative Retreats

Sanger also brings all of its administrators together every August for an annual retreat. Principals, vice principals, program coordinators, directors, and top-level managers of classified staff all attend the two-day event that is intended to clarify expectations and goals for the year and build a sense of team among leaders at all levels. At one retreat, for example, the entire group was divided into teams that were charged with developing an opening day presentation to staff that would establish a positive tone and clarify the sustained commitment to the direction the district had taken. The event was just one more attempt on the part of the district to ensure administrators at every level were speaking with one voice and communicating a consistent vision.

Superintendent Johnson has made his expectations of principals very, very explicit. Each receives a written statement establishing academic goals and stipulating principals must provide evidence that they have established certain structures in their schools. For example, the Statement of Administrative Expectations directs all principals to:

- Ensure the PLC implementation is deepening at your site, at all grade levels, in all departments, and that all staff are involved.

- Ensure that collaborative teams review achievement data, there is collaborative planning, common assessments, and that SMART goals are developed and utilized.

- Develop and implement a pyramid of interventions designed to ensure the instructional needs of all students are met.

- Monitor student progress through assessment data designed to inform instruction and target effective interventions.

Principals understand that their evaluations each year will be based on their attentiveness to these expectations. There is no ambiguity regarding priorities among Sanger administrators.

Ongoing Support and Focus

The Sanger school board and administration have demonstrated a willingness to support schools as they attempt to address and overcome obstacles. The board has been very explicit in establishing its commitment to the PLC process. One of its goals calls upon every school to "strengthen the culture of collaboration." Every year the board supports providing intensive training in the PLC concept to a new group of the district's educators. Those educators inevitably feel validated by the training because it reinforces the steps they have been taking to improve their schools. Furthermore, Johnson believes that each group that returns from the training "reignites the spark and energizes the process all over again." When some of the more rural schools faced the obstacle of difficulty in teaming because their small size often resulted in a single instructor teaching a course or grade level, the district implemented the First Class Communication Suite to allow collaboration across the district in virtual teams. When schools pushed for more collaborative time, the board supported early dismissal one day every other week to provide the time.

Another important factor in Sanger's steady improvement has been the ongoing focus on and support of the improvement process. From 2004 to 2009, the district has sustained a fixation on the critical questions of a PLC, making it more and more difficult for cynics to contend, "This, too, shall pass." Resistance to the initiative has diminished in the face of concrete evidence of steadily improving results.

Superintendent Johnson is a gifted storyteller, and he describes the cultural shift that has occurred in the district with a story of a sixth-grade team of language arts teachers who presented to the principals and leadership teams at one of the district's ongoing PLC training sessions. At the end of their presentation the team was asked, "If given the option, would you ever return to your former practice and give up collaboration?" The response was enthusiastic and unanimous: "Never!"

Johnson describes how Reggie Wagner, a veteran member of that sixth-grade team, offered his personal reflection on the PLC process. He reminded the group that the sequoias, the largest living things on the planet, were located less than fifty miles from the district. He pointed out that these massive trees live for thousands of years and seem to stand in isolated splendor. What the casual observer does not realize, Wagner pointed out, is that the root structure of the giant sequoias is very shallow, making them susceptible to falling in strong winds. The trees only flourish in groves where they can intermingle their roots and rely on the strength of neighboring trees. It is their combined strength that enables them to withstand the ravages of nature. He concluded by saying, "I used to be like that sequoia standing alone, strong and confident in appearance. Now, because of our professional learning community, I am like the sequoias standing in a grove, stronger because of those around me and the support we provide each other."

Results

The sustained focus on building the capacity of staff throughout the district to transform schools into PLCs has had a tremendous impact on student achievement in Sanger. Sanger's API score as a district has risen from 599 to 778 since 2002, and the percentage of students scoring at or above proficiency has risen 40 percent in math and 30 percent in language arts (see fig. 12.2).

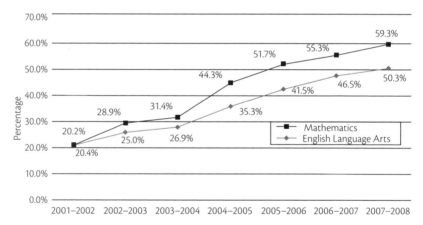

Figure 12.2: Percentages of students at or above proficiency on state assessment.

Every population has reflected these gains. The percentage of English language learners, special education students, and children of poverty demonstrating proficiency has increased in language arts by 28 percent, 26 percent, and 32 percent, respectively, and in mathematics by 40 percent, 33 percent, and 40 percent, respectively. Furthermore, the district's emphasis on focused instruction, frequent monitoring of student learning, and effective systems of interventions has reduced the number of students assigned to special education by 50 percent because students are finding success in the general education program.

Table 12.1: Sanger Unified School Performance Information

School Name	Academic Performance Index			State and Similar School Rankings			
	2002 API	2008 API	Improvement	State 2002	State 2007	Similar Schools 2002	Similar Schools 2007
Centerville	675	839	164	5	7	3	10
Del Rey	532	753	221	1	6	2	10
Fairmont	677	810	133	5	7	4	8
Jackson	624	845	221	3	8	2	10
Jefferson	531	815	284	1	6	2	10
John Wash	744	862	118	7	9	5	9
Lincoln	536	766	230	1	4	2	10
Lone Star	643	817	174	4	6	3	6
Madison	644	808	164	4	6	3	7
Quail Lake	756	925	169	7	10	1	10
Sanger Academy	721	865	144	6	9	4	10
Wilson	533	763	230	1	5	2	10
WAMS	549	740	191	2	6	2	10
Sanger High	592	750	158	4	6	6	8
Hallmark*	486	732	246				
Community Day*	363	546	183				
Kings River*	414	683	269				

*Hallmark, Community Day, and Kings River are alternative schools and therefore not included in the similar schools ranking of the state.

The tremendous improvement in student achievement has not been limited to a few schools. Table 12.1 illustrates *every* school in the district has increased its API score by at least 118 points, with an average increase of 194 points. What is even more striking is each school's decile ranking with schools of similar student populations. In 2002, thirteen of Sanger's fourteen schools ranked in the bottom half of the state when compared to similar schools. In 2007, all fourteen ranked in the top half of the state, and ten schools placed in the highest decile or among the top 10 percent of similar schools in California.

Six of the district's schools have been recognized as Title I Academic Achieving Schools. Sanger High School was named a Bronze Medal Award winner as one of America's best high schools by *US News & World Report* and was designated a California Distinguished School in 2009. A project by the American Productivity and Quality Center and the GE Foundation to establish benchmark districts for best practices in implementation of the PLC concept recognized Sanger as a model district.

Clearly, the Sanger mantra—1) the job of every person in this district is to ensure student learning, 2) hoping things will get better is not a strategy, 3) don't blame the kids, and 4) the best strategy for sustained, substantive improvement is developing our capacity to work as members of a professional learning community—has benefited the students served by this district. May that mantra become the norm in districts across North America.

Concluding Thoughts

The preceding chapters have described wonderful success stories at both the district and school levels. We have shared the steps these educators have taken and the wonderful results they are achieving in very different schools. What we have not examined adequately are the pragmatic and philosophical challenges they confronted when they proposed that schools should operate as PLCs and that students who were not being successful should receive additional time and support in a systematic process. In the next chapter we examine the concerns that are almost certain to be expressed in any school or district that considers implementing the process of systematic intervention that is so vital to the PLC concept. We then offer explanations regarding how we would respond to those concerns.

Visit www.sanger.k12.ca.us/education/district/district. php?sectionid=1 for more information on Sanger Unified School District.

13
"YAH, BUT . . . ": CONSIDERING CHALLENGES TO SYSTEMATIC INTERVENTION

> What people resist is being controlled, being told what to do without being told why, and not being able to affect the change process. An organization that is inclusive, open with information, clear about expectations, and forthcoming with support provides the framework for leaders and team members to commit to change together.
>
> —ROSABETH MOSS KANTER (KANTER, IBM, COUNCIL OF CHIEF STATE SCHOOL OFFICERS, & NATIONAL ASSOCIATION OF ELEMENTARY SCHOOL PRINCIPALS, 2002)

In this book, we have argued that if schools are to fulfill their mission of helping all students learn at high levels, they must monitor each student's learning on a timely basis and create procedures to ensure that students receive additional time and support when they experience difficulty in learning. We also contend that this time and support should be provided in a systematic way rather than left to the discretion of individual teachers, that the system should include a number of interventions based on increasing levels of support, and that students should be directed rather than invited to avail themselves of the support system. We recognize that this proposal will generate significant reservation on the part of some educators. Some of those reservations will be pragmatic and typically begin with a "Yah, but"— "*Yah*, this sounds good, *but* we can't do it because . . ." Other reservations are based on philosophical concerns about what is best for all students. Therefore, this chapter examines and responds to questions that are likely to emerge as a staff considers the implications of creating their version of a system of interventions for students.

Pragmatic Concerns

Question 1: Yah, but we have neither sufficient staff to create a system of interventions nor resources to hire new staff.

As we wrote in the introduction, creating a system of interventions relies more on determination and a willingness to accept new roles and responsibilities than it does on resources. Utah ranks last among the fifty states in per-pupil expenditures, spending less than 60 percent of the national average (United States Census Bureau, 2008b), yet Lakeridge has built a powerful system of interventions. California has been ravaged by budget cuts, and both Whittier Union and Sanger Unified spend 25 percent less in per-pupil expenditures than the state average. Nevertheless, these two districts have created effective systems of interventions. Boones Mill is located in a county with one of the lowest per-pupil expenditures in Virginia, yet the staff was able to shift dollars that had been spent on ineffective after-school programs and summer remediation to fund its floating tutors. The Blue Valley School District in which Prairie Star Middle School is located spends 15 percent less than the state average in per-pupil expenditures. Stevenson ranked last among the surrounding high school districts in per-pupil expenditures when it began to develop its pyramid of interventions and continued to rank last after its pyramid was developed. Additional resources are wonderful, and we hope that schools will receive additional financial support in the future. In the meantime, however, they can take steps to create effective systems of interventions within their current resources.

Question 2: Yah, but the schedule won't let us devote time to intervention.

The pronouncement, "The schedule won't allow it," is the single most proffered explanation as to why a school has not created a systematic plan of intervention when students do not learn. It has the benefit of demonstrating our good intentions—"We would love to intervene when kids do not learn"—while at the same time absolving us of responsibility—"Alas, it is simply impossible given our schedule." Blame is assigned to an inanimate, abstract concept (the schedule), while people are exonerated for failure to act.

We find this argument puzzling, and we offer these questions to educators across North America:

● Did you mean it when you said the purpose of your school or district is to help *all* students learn? Was that a sincere declaration of intent and priority or politically correct hyperbole?

● Do you recognize that some students will require more time and support for their learning than others? We are unaware of any researcher who has concluded that *all* students can learn if time and support are constants rather than variables in the learning process.

● Do you agree a school's schedule should reflect its purpose and priorities?

- Have you created a schedule that ensures you have access to all students who experience difficulty in order to provide them with additional time and support for learning?

When we pose these questions, one at a time, to educators, it is disheartening to hear them say, "Yes, we are committed to helping all students learn; yes, we recognize some will need more time and support if they are to learn; yes, a school's schedule should reflect its purpose and priorities; but, no, we do not have a system of interventions in place because the schedule won't let us." A school's schedule should be regarded as a tool to further priorities rather than an impediment to change. Our advice to educators is simple: your schedule is not a sacred document. If your current schedule does not allow you to provide students with something as essential to their academic success as extra time and support for learning, you should change it!

The schools we have examined in this book rely on different schedules. Stevenson has eight fifty-minute periods in its school day, with one of the periods reserved for lunch. Cinco Ranch offers a seven-period day with thirty minutes for lunch. Three Whittier Union high schools have six periods that meet on Mondays, then alternate periods on a block schedule Tuesday through Friday. Two of the other Whittier schools use different schedules. Both Lakeridge and Prairie Star operate a modified A/B block schedule, but their schedules are unique. Boones Mill and Highland Elementary schedules have some similarities, but they are not identical. Schedules can differ. However, schedules should 1) give school personnel access to students who are experiencing difficulty in their learning during the school day, and 2) ensure students receive additional time and support for learning in ways that do not require them to miss new direct instruction.

Philosophical Concerns

Question 1: Doesn't this system of interventions simply enable students to act irresponsibly?

Those who voice this legitimate concern often put it in the following terms:

"We want our students to learn more than content. One of our most important goals is that students learn responsibility, and this system is at cross-purposes with that goal. It calls upon us to take on more responsibility for student learning rather than placing the burden where it belongs—with the student. If we come swooping in to solve their problems by offering increasing levels of time and support when they have not done what is necessary to be successful, we are simply enabling and reinforcing irresponsible behavior.

Students must learn there are consequences for failing to act responsibly. We deprive them of the opportunity to learn if we shield them from those consequences."

Educators can readily agree that it would indeed be preferable if every student who entered a school had the prerequisite knowledge, skills, and dispositions to be successful. They can also agree that among those skills and dispositions students should demonstrate are self-discipline, a strong work ethic, the ability to manage their time in order to meet deadlines, diligence, and a host of other qualities that might come under the general heading of personal responsibility. Finally, there is virtual unanimity among educators that, unfortunately, many students lack one or more of those prerequisites. The disagreement comes from their views on the best strategy for responding to these students.

The traditional strategy is to apply the consequence of failure for those who do not demonstrate responsibility. This strategy is based on the premise that if students fail to study, fail to complete their work, or fail to meet deadlines they should suffer the logical consequence of their actions—failure. This consequence, the argument goes, will, in turn, teach the student to become more responsible in the future.

We suggest that this strategy is not only illogical, but has been demonstrated over time as completely ineffective. We argue that it is time for a new strategy based on a new story.

Anyone who has ever taught will acknowledge that if students are told, "You must do this work and turn it in on time, or you will fail," some students will be perfectly content to fail. Allowing them the option of not doing the work merely reinforces their irresponsibility. A school that was committed to helping all students learn—helping all students acquire the knowledge, skills, and dispositions essential to their success—would teach students to demonstrate responsibility by insisting students do what responsible people do.

In some of our workshops we ask educators to consider this analogy: assume you are the parent of a fourteen-year-old child. You issue the following directive to your child: "I want you to mow the lawn by noon on Saturday, and if you don't have it mowed by noon on Saturday, you will never have to mow at all!" The statement typically brings howls of laughter. No effective parent would consider presenting his or her child with such an option. We then remind participants that, as educators, their legal status with students is in loco parentis—they stand in the place of the parent while the student is in school. We ask, "Why is it laughable to take this approach with your own child but justifiable to take the approach with the children of other people when they are in your school?"

Occasionally, a participant will point out a flaw in this analogy. In the school setting we are applying a consequence—failure—whereas in the lawn-mowing analogy there is no consequence. The point is valid, so we extend the analogy. As a parent, you tell your child that if the lawn is not mowed by Saturday at noon, he won't be allowed to take the three-hour drive with the family to Grandma's house for the weekend. He will instead be grounded and left alone at home for the weekend, unsupervised.

Most fourteen-year-olds would prefer the consequence of being left at home alone to either doing the work or going to Grandma's. In fact, the parent is likely to return home to find their child has not spent his time in his room vowing to be more responsible in the future, but has instead engaged in inappropriate behavior that is not in his best long-term interest. We contend that there is a long history that many students *prefer* the consequence of failure if it means they will not have to do the work. Thus, it is not an effective consequence. Once again, allowing the student the option of acting irresponsibly does not teach responsibility.

Consider two very different schools. The staff of the first school exhorts students to study for tests, complete their homework on time, and persevere if they experience initial difficulty. Alas, some of their students elect to ignore these admonitions. Teachers then impose a penalty—a failing grade or zeros on missed assignments. In effect, students are free to opt for the penalty rather than do the work. The second school offers no such option. If students do not put sufficient time into their studies, the staff requires them to spend time in a tutorial situation. If students do not complete their homework, they are placed in an environment where completion of homework is carefully monitored. This school strives to teach students responsibility by insisting students act responsibly—even if under duress—in the hope that students will ultimately internalize the lesson. Which of these schools is holding students accountable? Which has "enabled" irresponsible behavior?

A pyramid of interventions is not the same as saying that students should not experience consequences for lack of effort or irresponsible behavior. It is reasonable to provide students with incentives for completing their work on time and consequences for failing to meet deadlines or achieve the acceptable standard of work. A school that made learning its primary focus, however, would never consider absolving the student of the responsibility for completing an assignment as an appropriate consequence—particularly if the assignment was given with the assumption that it would promote student learning.

When schools make working and learning optional, both students and teachers can take the easy way out. Conversely, when schools create a system of interventions similar to what has been described in this book, students are held accountable. Their schools bombard them with the message, "We will not let you off the hook. We will see to it that you do what is necessary to be successful. We won't place you in a less rigorous curriculum, nor will we lower our standards for this course or grade level. We will give you the support, time, and structure to help you be successful, but we will not lower the bar." This approach is the antithesis of *enabling*. For example, one study of Stevenson High School lauded its pyramid of interventions as an effective model for teaching "diligence, a strong work ethic, a positive attitude, and perseverance" (Lickona & Davidson, 2005, p. xv). In another, Tom Sergiovanni (2005) found the school has created "covenants of obligations" among faculty and students that resulted in a "community of responsibility" (p. 60), and he called for other schools to do the same.

In *Influencer: The Power to Change Anything* (Patterson, Grenny, Maxfield, McMillan, & Switzler, 2008), the authors make a compelling case that there is one powerful strategy for shaping the thinking, dispositions, and actions of others. Those who are masterful in the art of influencing others always identify a few *vital behaviors,* asking, "What must people actually *do* to improve this situation?" They then coach the specifics of each behavior through *deliberate practice*; align systems, processes, and structures to support the behaviors; and create appropriate reward structures to reinforce the behavior until it becomes internalized.

We contend that there is widespread agreement among educators that "completing the work" is a critical element in the ultimate success of their students. It is indeed a *vital behavior*. Furthermore, virtually all school and district mission statements express a commitment to helping all students become "responsible citizens." Responsible people can be counted on to do their work. If demonstrating responsibility is a vital behavior in the current and future success of students, schools cannot continue with the laissez-faire tradition of allowing students to opt out of this vital behavior.

The hard fact is, left to their own devices, students will often make bad choices. As economist Richard Thaler and legal scholar Cass Sunstein (2008) note, "Individuals make pretty bad decisions—decisions they would not have made if they had paid full attention and possessed complete information, unlimited cognitive abilities, and complete self-control" (p. 5). Certainly this observation applies to students in the K–12 setting, where students routinely make bad decisions. Thaler and Sunstein contend, however, that effective leaders can influence people's behavior and increase the likelihood that they will act in ways that improve their lives.

One of the most powerful strategies Thaler and Sunstein (2008) identify for nudging people in the right direction is what they refer to as the *default option*. Simply put, the default option is how the organization responds when a person does not, for whatever reason, make a good decision.

For example, imagine that a school district provides its employees with options regarding health insurance. Does the employee prefer the Preferred Provider Organization (PPO) option or the Health Maintenance Organization (HMO) option, family coverage or individual coverage, inclusion or exclusion of dental insurance, and so on. Each year the district sends forms to every employee allowing him or her to select the options he or she prefers for the coming year. They even remind employees several times of the pending deadline for submitting their option forms. Unfortunately, some employees fail to meet the deadline. If the district default option was, "Those who fail to meet the deadline will receive no insurance this year," there certainly would be an outcry. The consequence of that default position puts people at risk and could be damaging to their overall well-being. A better default option would be to advise those employees, "We will provide you with the same options that you requested last year" because that option is less harmful to people.

The lifetime earnings of a student who drops out of high school today will equate to thirty-two cents for every dollar a college graduate will earn and sixty-six cents for every dollar a high school graduate will earn based on mean household incomes. When the calculation is based on median household incomes, the disparity is even worse, with the dropout earning sixty-one cents for each dollar the high school graduate will earn and twenty-nine cents compared to college graduates (United States Census Bureau, 2008a). The dropout will be less able to provide for his or her family and will be less employable in a volatile job market. He or she will live a shorter life and will be more prone to ill health than those who continue their education (Kolta, 2007). The dropout's children will have only a one-in-seventeen chance of ever graduating from college (Brooks, 2006). If a school's default position when students do not engage in the behavior vital to their success is to give students license to continue to make bad decisions, the school has chosen an option that is clearly harmful to the students it serves.

Here is a question we urge every reader to consider: what is the default op-tion in your school when a student fails to make good decisions regarding applying himself, completing his work, giving his best effort, and in general, doing what responsible people do? If it is merely to allow the student to go on making bad decisions and applying a consequence that has no relevance to the student, we contend it is a bad option. If the default option is harmful to the best interests of the student's long-term well-being, we contend it is a bad option. The schools that we have featured in this book applied a very different default option. Their position was, "As a result of your series of bad decisions, we will now intervene and insist that you act more responsibly." They did not merely bemoan a lack of responsibility on the part of their students, they taught their students to do what responsible people do.

Finally, we must reiterate that the power of the default option requires a coordinated and systematic response rather than an individualized response. There are limits to what the best-intentioned classroom teacher can do in terms of *requiring* students to demonstrate the vital behaviors essential to their success. When intervention reaches a point that it becomes *directive*, advising students that they *must* complete their work and report to a place or program that monitors that completion, it must be the entire school and not merely an individual teacher that is doing the nudging.

Question 2: How does all of this support prepare our students for the next level of schooling they will encounter? No one will hold their hands there! They need to learn to be responsible for their own learning.

It is incredible to us how pervasive this sentiment is at every level of school-ing. High school teachers justify leaving students to fend for themselves because that is what students will face if they enroll in college. Middle school teachers warn students they must be accountable for themselves because that is what is expected of them in high school. Elementary teachers advise students they are expected to be responsible for their learning because they will not be babied when they arrive in middle school. We have no doubt some prenatal physician somewhere is warning an unborn child that it is a tough world out here.

There is widespread agreement among organizational theorists that the most effective organizations base their decisions upon the best evidence that is available. These organizations "face the hard facts" (Pfeffer & Sutton, 2006, p. 13), "confront the brutal facts" (Collins, 2001, p. 70), refuse to "duck the facts" (Kanter, 2004, pp. 208–209), and "subject all decisions to a ruthless and continuous *judgment by results*" (Champy, 1995, p. 120). Consider some hard, brutal, ruthless facts about the effectiveness of the premise that each level of schooling must prepare students for the indifference of the level above it:

- In 2008, 1.23 million students dropped out of high school in the United States—the equivalent of one student every twenty-six seconds. Although the calculation of the dropout rate is subject to manipulation and debate, about 70 percent of students who enter high school in the United States graduate on time with a regular diploma. The percentage in urban areas drops to about 50 percent (Swanson, 2008).

- Sixty-eight percent of the 70 percent who graduate from high school will pursue college education. Sixty percent of those students will enroll in a four-year institution, and the remainder will enroll in a two-year community college (Bureau of Labor Statistics, 2008).

- One-third of the students who do enter college are required to take remedial courses to acquire the knowledge and skills they should have learned in high school (Alliance for Excellent Education, 2006). More than 75 percent of four-year public institutions and virtually all two-year public colleges offer remedial courses to address this need (National Center for Education Statistics, 2007).

- Thirty-four percent of the students who enroll in college do not return to that school for their second year. The percentage is increasing (ACT, 2009).

- Only 29 percent of those who enter a two-year community college in the United States will earn an associate degree within three years (ACT, 2008).

- Only 40 percent of those who enter a four-year public university will earn a bachelor's degree within five years (ACT, 2008).

Now apply these facts to a hypothetical kindergarten class of 100 students. If their experience reflects the national statistics:

- Seventy of the 100 will complete the process the K–12 system was designed to accomplish and will earn a high school diploma with their class.

- Forty-eight of the seventy will pursue higher education. Twenty-nine will enroll in a four-year college, and nineteen will enroll in a two-year community college.

- Sixteen of the forty-eight will require remedial courses in college because they did not acquire the skills the K–12 system was designed to give them.

- Six of the seventeen students who enrolled in the community college will earn an associate degree within three years of entering the college.

- Twelve of the twenty-nine students who enrolled in a four-year college will earn a bachelor's degree within five years of entering the college.

We suggest that the facts should speak for themselves. If three of every ten students who enter the K–12 system do not graduate when expected, if one-third of those who do graduate and enter college are required to enroll in remedial courses, if more than one-third of college freshmen do not return to their college for a second year, and if there is only an 18 percent chance that students entering kindergarten will earn either an associate or bachelor's degree, then *the traditional way in which that system is preparing students for success in higher education is not working.*

There will be those who argue it is a dangerous overgeneralization to cite the experience and results of a few schools and districts to argue educators are more effective in teaching students to be responsible and to learn at higher levels when they create systems of interventions and enrichment. Perhaps that point is valid. We suggest, however, the experience of thousands of schools over more than a century has demonstrated beyond any question that the absence of a systematic response to support and challenge students and allowing them, instead, to choose to fail, neither teaches students responsibility nor prepares them for future success. *It is time to confront the brutal facts. It is time to embrace a different strategy. It is time for a new story.* If educators continue to assert they are committed to high levels of learning for all students and acknowledge there are certain steps students must take in order to learn, they will create systems to ensure those steps are taken.

Question 3: Are we forgetting the whole child?

Another objection to creating a system of interventions to assist students who experience academic difficulty argues the emphasis on academic success is misplaced. "All of this attention to academic achievement is a case of misplaced priorities. We need to address the needs of the whole child. What about the emotional needs of our children? What about their artistic side? What about developing their character? This focus on academic achievement is just another example of the fixation with test scores and trying to reduce a child to a statistic."

In *Built to Last: Successful Habits of Visionary Companies,* Jim Collins and Jerry Porras (1997) identify the characteristics and qualities that differentiate organizations that were able to sustain high performance from their less-successful counterparts. They discovered that ineffective organizations succumbed to the "Tyranny of Or," while their extraordinary counterparts embraced the "Genius of And." Low-performing companies created false dichotomies: "We must be either this or that, but we cannot be both." High performers recognized that such perceptions were needlessly limiting and, instead of choosing between A *or* B, figured out ways to have both A *and* B. They note:

> We're not talking about mere balance here. Balance implies going to the midpoint, fifty-fifty, half and half. . . . A highly visionary company does not want to blend yin and yang into a gray, indistinguishable circle that is neither highly yin nor highly yang; it aims to be distinctly yin *and* yang—*both* at the same time, all the time. (pp. 44–45)

Schools are particularly prone to the Tyranny of Or. Educators often assume they must choose between strong administrators *or* autonomous teachers, phonics *or* whole language, emphasis on core curriculum *or* commitment to the arts, leadership anchored in the central office *or* site-based management, and so on. One of the most damaging examples of the Tyranny of Or is the belief that a focus on academics leads to indifference to all of the other factors that constitute the well-being of a student.

Thomas Lickona (2004), director of the Center for Respect and Responsibility and noted author on character education, calls for educators to create a "school of character," which he describes as:

> A community of virtue, a place where moral and intellectual qualities such as good judgment, best effort, respect, kindness, honesty, service, and citizenship are modeled, upheld, celebrated, and practiced in every part of the school's life—from the examples of the adults to the relationship among peers, the handling of discipline, the content of the curriculum, the rigor of academic standards, the ethos of the environment, the conduct of extracurricular activities, and the involvement of parents. (p. 219)

Lickona recommends three resources to help educators create such schools, and *Professional Learning Communities at Work: Best Practices for Enhancing Student Achievement* (DuFour & Eaker, 1998) is one of those resources. Clearly he does not believe that a PLC's commitment to the academic achievement of students interferes with the development of the whole child. In fact, when he and Matthew Davidson (2005) identified twenty-four diverse high schools in the United States that demonstrated a commitment to promote character, they included Stevenson as one of those schools that fosters both "excellence and ethics" (p. xv).

The culture of excellence created in the schools and districts we have featured is not limited to a few students or to the core curriculum. Among those schools are recipients of state and national recognition for the arts, athletics, and community service. We contend the students in these schools have a more positive attitude about school than most of their peers around the country because they are being successful and because they are surrounded by people who demonstrate they care about them through their collective efforts to support every student. We concur with Lickona and Davidson that those who contend schools must focus on either academic achievement or the well-being of students are presenting a false dichotomy.

Question 4: But aren't we neglecting the gifted and high-achieving children?

Educators who ask this question believe that focusing all this attention on needy, lazy, or low-performing kids deprives our more gifted students of the resources and time essential to their development. The assumption behind this thinking is that education is a zero-sum game. Schools have finite resources and energy, and therefore addressing the needs of a particular group of students means the school is not addressing the needs of others. For some students to win, others must lose.

We reject that assumption. The PLC model is based on the premise that *all* students benefit when placed in a challenging and supportive environment. The staff of a PLC attempts to create a culture that stretches all students beyond their comfort zone and then provides the support to help them be successful in meeting the challenge. Students who have become comfortable in self-contained special education classes or remedial classes are called upon to meet the challenge of the standard curriculum. Students comfortable in the standard curriculum are called upon to stretch to meet the challenges of an accelerated curriculum. Students in the most rigorous curriculum are challenged to see how far they can go in extending their learning. In a PLC *every* student is urged to pursue more challenging levels of learning, but at the same time, the school assures those students that they will receive the additional time and support they need to be successful to meet that challenge.

One of the most consistent themes that emerged from our investigation of the schools and districts in this book is that their attention to ensuring every student becomes proficient *dramatically increased the percentage of students able to achieve at advanced levels*. We have referenced this phenomenon in each of the chapters that explore the various schools and districts, and we will return to the topic again in the next chapter on the stretch culture of PLCs. In brief, we found absolutely no evidence that being attentive to students who experienced difficulty diminished the achievement of traditionally high-performing students and abundant evidence in every case to refute that theory.

Question 5: Isn't this what special education is designed to do?

Some people think the PLC concept is just another version of special education. They suggest, "If the kids can't cut it, why not just put them in special education? That's why we have it."

Veteran educators will quickly acknowledge that student failure is often not a result of a disabling condition, but rather a function of student indifference to school, unwillingness to do the work, or a host of personal problems that interfere with a student's ability to do what is necessary to be successful in school. If a school was able to identify every student who truly required special education services and did a wonderful job of providing those services, it would continue to face the harsh, cold reality that a number of its students were still not being successful.

Furthermore, as the President's Commission on Excellence in Special Education (2002) concludes, in many schools special education has become a "first response" rather than a "last resort." Psychologist Abraham Maslow (1966) observed, "If the only tool you have is a hammer, it is tempting to treat everything as if it were a nail" (p. 15). If special education is the only significant intervention tool available in a school, it is inevitable that the school will come to rely upon that tool too frequently. A school with a multistep system of interventions arms itself with a variety of tools for meeting the needs of its students and, thus, is more likely to find the appropriate strategy.

Boones Mill is an excellent example of this principle at work. Prior to building its system of interventions for students, individual classroom teachers worked diligently to help students meet the standards of their grade levels, but when students continued to lag far behind despite the best efforts of their teachers, the students were recommended for special education. In 2000, Boones Mill ranked first among the eleven elementary schools in Franklin County in the number of students referred for special education testing. Within one year of building its system of interventions to provide students with additional time and support for learning through a number of different strategies, Boones Mill ranked last in the county in terms of new referrals for special education.

Sanger Unified District provides another excellent example of meeting the needs of students through intervention rather than special education. It has been able to cut its referrals for special education by 50 percent.

There are some very pragmatic reasons for looking for alternatives to special education. Systems of interventions and enrichment are more cost effective and far more fluid than traditional special education programs. Most importantly, the President's Commission on Excellence in Special Education (2002) reports that too often schools have been forced to focus on compliance with regulations rather than the effectiveness and agility of the response when students struggle. But if timely, directive, and systematic interventions are in place in a school, a student can be shifted from one level of support to another within minutes.

This flexibility also extends to the duration of services. It is not unusual for a student identified with a disabling condition in third grade to still be receiving special education services as a senior in high school. When a school develops a system of interventions, the goal is to provide the services only until students demonstrate they are ready to assume greater responsibility for their learning. The focus is on gradually weaning the student from the extra time and support as the student becomes successful in classes. The interventions, then, serve as a safety net if the student should falter, but they are not intended to be a permanent crutch.

Finally, the response to intervention initiative outlined in the latest version of the Individuals with Disabilities Education Improvement Act was specifically intended to reject the premise that a student's academic difficulties represent a "special education problem." RTI, like the pyramid of interventions we have advocated for years, operates under the assumption that whenever any student is having difficulty, it is a "school" problem, that students are not to be divided into general education versus special education or "my kids" versus "your kids." Every student should be considered "our student," and all of the resources of the school should be available to resolve the problem. Thus, those who would hope to deflect this problem to special education must recognize that the provisions of RTI now call for schools to have a coordinated, multilayered, systematic plan of intervention for *all* students.

Special education serves a tremendously important role in a school committed to success for all students, but special education staff, alone and in isolation, cannot ensure all students will learn. When schools create a systematic process to provide additional time and support for students who experience initial difficulty in learning, all students can learn in "the least-restrictive environment" within a cost-effective and flexible framework.

Concluding Thoughts

Those who begin the PLC journey and the cultural shifts it requires should not only anticipate challenges, but also welcome the challenges to PLC concepts. As Michael Fullan (1997) states:

> Learning organizations will legitimize dissent. . . . The value of resisters has been missed. Trying to manipulate the change process to eliminate resistance is futile. A more successful process is listening to those who are resisting and seeking to understand what lies behind their resistance. (p. 223)

Challenges to PLC concepts provide leaders of the initiative with the opportunity to model the collective inquiry that characterizes a learning organization. Effective leaders will initiate dialogue, a process whereby participants seek to understand each other's perspectives, assumptions, and thought processes. They will advocate for their position, explain why they came to their conclusions, and present evidence to support them. They will also, however, encourage others to question their conclusions and invite them to share the reasoning and assumptions behind their reservations. They will build shared knowledge with those who oppose systems of interventions by examining all evidence in the belief that if people have access to the same pool of knowledge, they are more likely to arrive at the same conclusions.

Honoring the challenges of a resister and engaging in collective inquiry is not just a strategy for reaching consensus; it is a powerful tool for deepening one's own understanding of an issue. The benefits of the PLC concept will speak for themselves if educators demonstrate good faith toward one another as they honestly assess both best practices for helping all students achieve at high levels and the current reality of their own schools.

14

FINDING COMMON GROUND: THE SHARED PRACTICES OF HIGHLY EFFECTIVE SCHOOLS AND DISTRICTS

"Academic Press" means that the faculty and staff press the students to do well, and they do so in multiple ways. Students are consistently sent messages that they are able and that academic achievement is important for them now and in the future. Persistence and pursuit, support and push show up in the students' experience in equal measure.

—JONATHON SAPHIER, 2005

The key to achieving a simultaneous tight-loose organization lies more in purposeful peer interaction than in top-down direction from the hierarchy. This does not require less leadership at the top, but rather more—more of a different kind.

—MICHAEL FULLAN, 2008

The preceding chapters tell the stories of six very distinct schools and three very different districts. In fact, we chose the districts because they were so different from one another. One is structured K–8, another 9–12, and the third K–12. Some of the students served by these districts come from suburban settings, others live in urban areas, and still others reside in rural communities. One has low rates of poverty, another has the majority of its students living in poverty, and the third has three of every four students living in poverty. One serves a predominantly white student population, whereas the other two serve a student population that is predominantly Hispanic. The Sanger district covers three times the area of the Whittier and Kildeer districts combined. Two of the districts are led by men, and one is led by a woman.

The six schools we feature also represent different grade levels, different sizes, different geographical areas, different communities, and students from very different backgrounds. At first glance, these schools and districts seem to have far more differences than commonalities; however, closer examination reveals that they are similar in many important ways. They share:

- Clarity of purpose and a clear sense of how to achieve that purpose more effectively

- Collaborative culture
- Collective inquiry into best practice and current reality
- Action orientation
- Commitment to continuous improvement
- Focus on results
- Strong leaders who empower others
- Willingness to face adversity, conflict, and anxiety
- Perseverance in the face of obstacles

The first seven characteristics are addressed in the following sections; the final two characteristics will be addressed in chapter 15.

Clarity of Purpose

Staff members in each of the schools and districts are clear about and focused on the fundamental purpose of their organizations: high levels of learning for all students. There is no ambiguity and no hedging. There is no suggestion that all kids will learn *if* they are conscientious, responsible, attentive, developmentally ready, fluent in English, and come from homes with concerned parents who take an interest in their education. There is no hint that staff members believe they can help all kids learn *if* class sizes are reduced, more resources are made available, new textbooks are purchased, or more support staff are hired. In these schools and districts, staff members embrace the premise that the very reason the school exists is to help *all* of their students—all the boys and girls who come to them each day—acquire essential knowledge and skills given the current resources available to the school. . . period. People throughout the organizations understand that not only their programs and procedures, but also their personal actions each day, must align with and advance this commitment to the success of each student.

Because the educators in these organizations held that fundamental conviction in common, they developed a shared vision of the schools they needed to create to help all kids learn, made collective commitments regarding what they were prepared to do to help all kids learn, and set goals and monitored data to assess their progress in helping all kids learn. The point to understand, however, is that the journey to becoming a professional learning community begins with an honest assessment of our assumptions regarding the ability of students to learn and our responsibility to see to it that they do.

Collaborative Culture

Each of the schools was designed to promote a collaborative culture by organizing teachers into teams and building time for them to meet in the routine schedule of the school. Members of these teams were asked to be more than congenial. They were expected to work *interdependently* to achieve *common goals* for which members were held *mutually accountable.*

When Mike Schmoker (2001) interviewed Stevenson High School teachers to find the secret of the school's sustained success, he heard a consistent response: "our collaborative teams." Boones Mill teachers cited the creation of a schedule that gave teachers time to collaborate with their teammates for seventy minutes each week as the catalyst that launched them on the road to becoming a PLC.

The importance of providing the structures to support meaningful collaboration among teachers is difficult to overstate. As McLaughlin and Talbert (2001) conclude:

> Chorus and refrain in our study of teaching and our understanding of the conditions that support teachers' learning and change is the critical importance of professional discourse and inquiry. Opportunities for teachers to talk with colleagues about teaching, consider new ways of doing things, and hammer out shared understandings about goals were common across diverse environments where practices were rethought in ways that benefited both teachers and students. (pp. 131–132)

In every instance, however, collaboration was viewed as a means to an end—higher levels of learning for students—rather than the end itself. As Fullan (2001) observes, "Collaborative cultures . . . are indeed powerful, but unless they are focusing on the right things they may end up being powerfully wrong" (p. 67). The schools and districts we have featured created a systematic process to ensure educators focused on the right work—work specifically designed to analyze and impact their practice in order to improve results.

Collective Inquiry Into Best Practice and Current Reality

In each of the schools and districts, building shared knowledge was a critical step in finding common ground. Teachers were more likely to acknowledge the need for improvement when they jointly studied evidence of the strengths and weaknesses of their school. They were more likely to arrive at consensus on the most essential knowledge and skills students should acquire when, together, they analyzed and discussed state and national standards, district curriculum guides, and student achievement data. They were more likely to agree on the most effective instructional strategies when they worked together in examining results from their common assessments. Teachers in these schools certainly had disagreements and differences of opinion, but they were able to find common ground on critical questions because they engaged in collective study of best practice and concrete evidence of results rather than simply sharing their opinions.

Action Orientation

Teachers and principals in most schools can reflect upon the school year each June and conclude that, once again, their school has been characterized by an action orientation. They can point to the launching of new initiatives, the diverse professional training they have received, and their response to the myriad directives that descended upon them from the central office as evidence of their often frenetic activity. As the Consortium on Productivity in the Schools (1995) concludes:

> The issue is not that individual teachers and schools do not innovate and change all the time. They do. The problem is with the kinds of change that occur in the education system, their fragile quality, and their random and idiosyncratic nature. (p. 23)

What distinguishes the schools and districts in this book is not their "busyness," but the fact that their efforts were guided by what Fred Newmann, BetsAnn Smith, Elaine Allensworth, and Anthony Bryk (2001) describe as *coherence*—"the extent to which the school's programs for students and staff are coordinated, focused on learning goals, and sustained over a period of time" (p. 5). The unrelenting focus on the four critical questions helped these schools bring coherence to their efforts. Assessments became linked to common essential outcomes. Staff development became linked to specific skills teachers needed to help students achieve those outcomes. Team goals became linked to the school's purpose and priorities. These schools illustrate that the shift from a focus on teaching to a focus on learning is a "powerful coherence-maker" (Fullan, 2001, p. 117).

It is important to recognize the focus and coordination that guided the work of these schools and districts, but it is equally important to understand that, ultimately, the teachers and principals were required to *act*. The process of changing the culture of any organization begins by changing the way in which the people of that organization behave (Bossidy & Charan, 2002;

Kotter & Cohen, 2002). None of the schools experienced gains in student achievement merely by writing a new vision statement or developing a strategic plan. These schools did not see improvement until staff members began to *act* differently. They worked collaboratively rather than working in isolation. They developed common assessments and applied consistent standards rather than acting autonomously. They changed instructional pacing and strategies based on new insights into pedagogical effectiveness. They recognized that, until they began to *act* differently, to *do* differently, there was little reason to expect different results. These schools were not characterized by studied, deliberate musings. They were places of action, experimentation, and a willingness to test ideas that seemed to hold potential for improving student achievement.

Commitment to Continuous Improvement

Each of the organizations we have featured has been recognized as exemplary by external sources, yet there is no evidence that any of them have elected to rest on their laurels. The perpetual disquiet and constant search for a better way that characterizes these schools results from the continuous improvement processes that are embedded in the routine practices of the school. Although each is attentive to celebrating the success of individuals, teams, and the school at large, the systems that are in place call upon every team and every teacher to identify and attack areas for improvement.

If a team analyzes student achievement data and discovers that a particular math concept is the most problematic for its students, the team discusses the issue, develops strategies for addressing the problem, implements the strategies in members' classrooms, and gathers new information to assess the impact of the strategies on student achievement. If the team's efforts have been successful, members can (and should) celebrate the improvement, but they also shift their efforts to identifying and addressing the next, most problematic concept. There will always be an area where students do "least well"—an area that can be targeted for improvement.

Embedding continuous improvement processes into the routine practices of the collaborative teams is also critical to the sustainability of the PLC process. As we mentioned in the introduction, each of the four schools that were featured in *Whatever It Takes* has had at least one change in the principalship since 2004. Yet each of the four has built upon and exceeded the exceptionally high standards the school exemplified when we told its story in *Whatever It Takes*. The widespread leadership, shared responsibility, and improvement processes that characterized those schools drove PLC concepts so deep into their cultures, that the PLC journeys have continued despite the departure of the principals who helped to begin them. The transformation in the schools was the result of the altered assumptions, beliefs, expectations, and practices of an entire staff rather than the result of a single charismatic champion. A study of Stevenson High School illustrates the point. The author of that study concludes that the school has "built a culture of learning that is far more enduring than a shrine to a single man and his ideas. The vision and beliefs that make Stevenson High School what it is today are deeply embedded in the daily practices of its teachers, counselors, and administrators" (Richardson, 2004, p. 115).

It is important that those who seek to emulate the success of these schools and districts understand that their challenge goes far beyond the implementation of a series of tasks. They must instead recognize that they are working to create a process of perpetual learning, ongoing renewal, and continuous improvement for the entire organization and all of its members. It is a constant challenge that is never quite completely solved. Yet talk to the educators in these schools and they will tell you the PLC process is energizing rather than frustrating because month by month and year by year, they see new evidence that their collective efforts do indeed have a positive impact on student learning. These educators have a clear purpose and a powerful sense of self-efficacy. They will attest to the fact that becoming a PLC is a wonderful journey, even if the journey has no final destination.

Focus on Results

Each of the schools and districts assesses the impact of its efforts and decisions on the basis of tangible results. When educators in a school are truly focused on student learning as their primary mission, they inevitably seek valid methods to assess the extent and depth of that learning. In John Hattie's (2009) extensive analysis of factors that impact student learning, he discovered that the teachers and principals in excellent schools constantly gather evidence of student learning and work together to ask, "'What is working best?', 'Why is it working best?', and 'Who is it not working for?'" (p. 240). The educators in the schools and districts we studied all found that frequent, locally developed common assessments were a vital resource in their efforts to answer those questions. Doug Reeves (2004) found that "schools with the greatest gains in student achievement consistently used common assessments" (p. 70). He contends that common assessments, collaboratively developed and scored by every teacher at a grade level, represent "the gold standard in educational accountability" because these assessments are used to "improve teaching and learning, not merely to evaluate students and schools" (pp. 114–115).

Another study found that schools most successful in closing the achievement gap structure teacher conversations around evidence of student learning gathered within the school rather than relying solely on external tests. The use of common formative assessments helps educators build their collective capacity to meet the needs of all students (Little, 2006). Our own work with schools has led us to conclude that teacher-developed common formative assessments are one of the most powerful vehicles a school can use to advance on the PLC journey.

The educators in the schools and districts featured in this book embraced data and information from their common assessments because the assessments provided timely and powerful insight into the learning of their students and the effectiveness of their professional practice. They can attest to the fact that these assessments *for* learning give them greater power, individually and collectively, to meet the needs of their students. They do not denigrate data that suggest all is not well, nor do they blindly worship means, medians, and modes. They have a healthy respect for information that can help them understand areas of strengths and weaknesses in the learning of each student, skill by skill, because they are keenly interested in results.

A fixation on results will ultimately, inevitably, lead educators to immerse themselves in the question, how will we respond when, despite our best efforts, our students experience difficulty in learning key concepts? What is so striking about these schools and districts is that each has addressed this question so directly. Each has created plans to monitor students on a *timely* basis; but more importantly, each has developed a *systematic* process of intervention that provides students with additional time and support for learning. Furthermore, because they are committed to the success of each student, these schools do not simply offer time and support; they *direct* students to devote the time and avail themselves of the support that will lead to success.

Strong Leaders Who Empower Others (Simultaneous Loose and Tight Leadership)

As Michael Fullan (2007) has observed, the primary challenge facing those who hope to bring about substantive change in an organization is the "too loose/too tight problem" (p. 11). Do change initiatives work best when they are "top down" or "bottom up?"

The schools and districts we feature resolved this dilemma in a very consistent way as we illustrate in the following sections.

Positive Assumptions About Others

In his study of effective organizations, Fullan (2008) discovered leaders of those organizations "love" their employees. We concur. One of the most striking trends that emerged from our examination of these schools and districts was the enthusiasm, admiration, and genuine affection the superintendents and principals expressed for their staffs. They consistently described the people with whom they worked as "amazing," "incredible," "tremendously dedicated," and "awesome." They did not believe that teachers were incompetent, uncaring about their students, or unconcerned about their own effectiveness. They did not approach their job as supervising subordinates into better performance. They believed their colleagues were well-intentioned, cared about students, and were willing to work very hard to help students learn. As a result, these leaders were committed to giving teachers and principals the knowledge, skills, support, and systems to help them be more effective.

One of the ways leaders demonstrate love for employees is to "create conditions for them to succeed" (Fullan, 2008, p. 25). The term *capacity building* is being used loosely these days, but that term accurately depicts how these principals and superintendents met the challenge of improving their organizations. They purposefully set out to create the conditions that would enable teachers and principals to build their capacity to succeed.

Widely Dispersed Leadership

A comprehensive study of the restructuring movement in education found that "leaders in schools with strong professional communities . . . delegated authority, developed collaborative decision-making processes, and stepped back from being the central problem solver. Instead they turned to the professional communities for critical decisions" (Louis, Kruse, & Marks, 1996, p. 193). Leadership was indeed widely distributed in each of the schools we feature. Each had the benefit of a guiding coalition for its change process, and all of the schools made a conscious effort to give teams and individuals the authority and autonomy that is often reserved for the highest levels of leadership.

The guiding coalition for both Stevenson and Cinco Ranch is made up of the principal, assistant principals, and the chairperson of each department. Cinco Ranch also utilizes a Campus Advisory Team composed of the principal, four to six teachers, two or three nonteaching professional staff, five to seven parents, two community members, and a representative of the business community. People volunteer to serve on the team for a two-year term, and members are chosen through a random drawing. Both schools also create periodic task forces of parents, community members, staff, and students to focus on a particular school improvement issue. Those task forces are charged to help build shared knowledge regarding alternatives, to build consensus for the preferred option, and to present recommendations to the administration and/or board of education for action.

At Boones Mill, the PLC process is led by a comprehensive school improvement committee made up of the principal, a teacher from each grade level, and representatives of the support staff and parent community. Highland Elementary's guiding coalition includes the principal, a member of each grade-level team, and two representatives of the teacher union.

The Prairie Star leadership team includes the principal, two members from each of the three grade levels, two counselors, an exploratory teacher, the gifted teacher, and a special education teacher. The leadership team meets weekly, and any member of the team can request that a topic be placed on the agenda. The leadership team of Lakeridge Junior High includes a representative of each of the eight departments. Members oversee and support the work of teams in their department, develop the plan for the five school days devoted to staff development, and meet regularly to assess the progress the school is making on its PLC journey. A community council made up of teachers and parents also plays a key role in monitoring the progress of the school.

There are many schools across North America that could point to similar structures, and we recognize that merely creating the structure does not ensure truly dispersed leadership. Several other factors contributed to the shared leadership evident in the schools we have featured.

1 **The collaborative team process created a format for both formal and informal leadership.**

    Most of the schools assigned a specific leader for each team to help guide the PLC process at the team level. This assignment significantly expanded the number of people in the school with formal responsibility for leading. Furthermore, the collaborative team process in place in each of the schools was designed to encourage very fluid *situational* leadership. If the team discovered that one of its members had special expertise in a particular content area, in teaching a concept, in developing effective assessments, or in meeting the needs of a particular kind of learner, that member would naturally assume temporary leadership based upon expertise, rather than on position, when the team focused on that topic. As a result, every teacher in the building had the potential to assume a leadership role.

2   **The schools developed leaders by providing staff members with the opportunity to lead and the support to be effective.**

The best strategy for developing the leadership potential of others is to assign them significant responsibilities and then provide them with ongoing support (Hernez-Broome, Hughes, & Center for Creative Leadership, 2004; Pfeffer & Sutton, 2006). All of the schools utilized this strategy. The collaborative team process in each school was specifically designed to empower teachers to make important decisions regarding curriculum, pacing, instruction, and assessment. Teachers were called upon to analyze student achievement data, share their insights, and develop strategies for improving their individual and collective effectiveness. Throughout the process they were given ongoing training, feedback, and support. In short, they were given both authority and assistance, and in return, they were asked to accept greater responsibility for student learning. And as John Gardner (1990) observes, "The taking of responsibility is at the very heart of leadership. To the extent that leadership tasks are shared, responsibility is shared" (p. 152).

Launching the PLC journey will almost inevitably require tremendous personal energy and courageous patience on the part of school or district leaders. Ironically, however, the ultimate success of the initiative will depend to a larger extent on the ability of administrators to delegate authority and develop widespread, shared leadership throughout the district or school. If the PLC concept is fueled solely by the energy and effort of a superintendent or principal, it will last only as long as that person remains in the position. When the concept is owned by the entire staff and led by people throughout the staff, the district or school can endure changes in key leadership positions without missing a beat. In the final analysis, the real effectiveness of school leaders in building a sustainable PLC culture will not be determined until after they are no longer there to support it.

Autonomy Within Clearly Defined, Nondiscretionary Parameters

The principals and superintendents we have featured in this book were highly adept at "simultaneous loose and tight leadership." Creating a PLC presents an interesting paradox for those who hope to lead the process. On one hand, they must disperse rather than hoard power because "shared or 'distributive leadership' brings the learning community together in a common commitment and shared responsibility for sustaining improvement" (National Commission on Teaching and America's Future, 2003, p. 17). Unless educators feel that they have a voice in the improvement process, they will view change as something that is done *to* them rather than *by* them. Most educators will be unwilling to accept responsibility for the success or failure of an initiative unless they have had some authority in making key decisions and some discretion in implementing those decisions.

On the other hand, at the same time that they are encouraging autonomy and discretion, leaders must insist on adherence to certain tenets that are essential to the PLC concept and make it clear that individual autonomy does not extend to disregarding those tenets. Throughout our writings we have referred to this paradox of strong and forceful leaders empowering others while demanding adherence to certain core principles as "simultaneous loose and tight leadership." The superintendents and principals we have featured were masters of this leadership style. They clarified the core concepts of the organization for its members, concepts that were sacred and not to be violated. At the same time, however, they gave those within the organization tremendous autonomy in applying those concepts on a day-to-day basis. These leaders encouraged freedom within parameters—"an ethic of entrepreneurship within a culture of discipline" (Collins, 2001, p. 124).

The superintendents in each of the three districts were not reluctant to stipulate the conditions they expected to see in all of their schools. Recall how Whittier's Sandy Thorstenson established three expectations for all of the district's schools: "(1) every school will implement common assessments created at both the district and school site levels, (2) every school will provide and protect time for teacher collaboration, and (3) every school will implement academic interventions within the daily schedule" (Cox, 2008). Consider Mark Johnson's insistence that in every Sanger school 1) teachers would work in collaborative teams that took mutual responsibility for student learning, 2) teachers would administer both district and team-level common assessments to monitor each student's learning throughout the year, and 3) the school would develop a systematic plan to respond immediately to any student who experienced difficulty. Remember Tom Many's steps to ensure that teachers in every school in District 96 were assigned into meaningful teams; that each team clarified essential outcomes, established common pacing, and developed common formative assessments; and that every school had a system of interventions that reflected the criteria spelled out in the district's SPEED model. In every instance, these leaders provided a detailed rationale for their directives. They used a variety of strategies—providing written materials, sending staff to workshops, accompanying teachers and principals on fieldtrips to successful PLCs, devoting time to answering questions—to help build shared knowledge of the research and reasoning that supported the initiative. But in the final analysis, they were emphatic about how schools in their districts must operate.

These three superintendents were also very purposeful in the way they monitored and supported the work of the principals in their districts. They were committed to providing principals with the training and tools to lead the PLC process, but the attention they paid to the ongoing monitoring of the progress in every school communicated to principals, clearly and effectively, that developing the capacity of staff to function as a PLC was a priority.

The principals of the schools in this book were also adept at loose-tight leadership. They were not laissez-faire leaders who allowed individuals to establish personal kingdoms; but rather, they articulated clear parameters and priorities that allowed individuals to work within established boundaries in creative and autonomous ways.

Marcus Buckingham (2005) argues that the "one thing" every leader must know to be effective is the importance of clarity—communicating clearly and consistently the purpose of the organization, the primary clients it serves, the future it is creating, the indicators of progress it will track, and the specific actions members can take immediately to achieve its long-term purpose and goals. The success of the superintendents and principals we have highlighted flows from such clarity. Simultaneous loose and tight leadership is a powerful concept, but it requires leaders who are crystal clear regarding the fundamental purpose of their organizations and who can effectively communicate that purpose through their actions as well as their words.

Concluding Thoughts

Those who carefully read the stories of these very different schools and districts will note the strikingly common approaches they took to improving their effectiveness. In fact, in some ways their stories are redundant. Details may vary, but the driving force for change and the strategies they used to lead the change process were remarkably consistent. They each were committed to ensuring all students learn at high levels, and they had clear and specific strategies to support that learning. Staff members were expected to work collaboratively to clarify what students were to learn and to monitor that learning. Each organization was focused on results and used those results to improve professional practice and respond to students who needed intervention and enrichment. The response to students was to be timely, directive, and systematic. Unlike most schools and districts, they had a plan for responding to a student who experienced difficulty in mastering key concepts. Furthermore, their plan did not end with one or two steps. If Plan A did not work, there was a Plan B, and a Plan C, and so on. This series of steps was taken on behalf of any student, in any class, whenever that student struggled. And, while leaders in these organizations encouraged and supported a great deal of autonomy and empowerment in every school, they were also emphatic that some critical elements of schooling were nondiscretionary.

Finally, perhaps the most common theme among the schools and districts we have featured is the fact that in every setting there were significant barriers that needed to be confronted and overcome. The next chapter examines the obstacles that these educators faced and the strategies they used for moving forward.

15 WHATEVER IT TAKES: HOW EFFECTIVE SCHOOLS AND DISTRICTS OVERCOME BARRIERS TO SYSTEMATIC INTERVENTION AND ENRICHMENT

> Advice about implementation is consistent. It all amounts to focus, persistence, implementation, monitoring, corrective action, and humility in the face of change.
>
> —MICHAEL FULLAN, 2007

> I know that the urge to try something new is often born of a fear that we've chosen wrong and a frustration that we aren't getting quick results. . . . In hindsight, I see that moving forward and doing something innovative often won out over painstakingly measuring our progress and adjusting our strategies. My advice? Stay the course. Work the plan. Monitor progress and analyze results. It's not glamorous; it doesn't make headlines. But patience and persistence work when trying to achieve success at this most difficult of tasks.
>
> —HUGH BURKETT, 2006

In each of the schools and districts featured in this book, educators faced the challenge of formidable logistical barriers. In fact, any school or district that commits to creating a collaborative culture and a system of interventions and enrichment will certainly be confronted with similar issues. The question facing educators, then, is whether they will respond to these challenges with resignation or determination, with explanations as to why it can't be done or a collective resolve to make it happen.

Stevenson High School

As Stevenson teachers began the dialogue regarding steps the school might take to provide students with additional time and support for learning, they confronted the reality that there were no staff members available to take on the roles of advisors or tutors and no funding available for new staff to assume those roles. The contract called for each teacher to teach five periods and to supervise students for one period each day. The contract also stipulated that a teacher could be assigned to study hall, hall duty, or cafeteria duty as their supervision. Because almost all of the school's 1,600 students were assigned to a study hall, and because the study halls were in traditional classrooms with seating for approximately twenty-five students, sixty-four teachers were needed for study halls. The remainder of the staff was assigned to hall duty or cafeteria duty. There was simply no one available to assume responsibility for advising or tutoring no matter how beneficial those programs might be.

But instead of saying, "We can't," the Stevenson staff looked for creative solutions. If juniors and seniors who were passing all of their courses with grades of C or better and who had no disciplinary problems were exempt from study hall and provided with free time instead, the school not only could offer students an incentive for good grades and behavior, but also could cut the number of study halls in half. Furthermore, if freshmen and sophomores remained in study hall, but study halls were moved to the auditorium rather than individual classrooms, a single teacher could supervise 100 students rather than twenty-five. These two changes had the potential to reduce the number of staff needed to supervise study hall from sixty-four to eight and could thus free teachers to take on new assignments as advisors and tutors.

The teachers union raised some legitimate concerns. First, they questioned whether advising and tutoring would be considered teaching assignments. If so, the contract stipulated staff who taught an extra course would be paid an additional 10 percent of their base salary. The administration assured the union that no advisor or tutor would ever be required to prepare a lesson or grade a paper or perform the tasks associated with classroom teaching. Advisors were merely to monitor the academic progress of each of their twenty-five students, consult with and counsel each student on that progress every three weeks, and assist students in finding solutions to their problems. Tutors would simply work with students individually and in small groups to review key concepts and address any confusion the students were experiencing. The administration proposed the assignments were more analogous to supervising than they were to teaching and, therefore, should substitute for the study hall, cafeteria duty, or hall duty to which teachers had traditionally been assigned.

The union pointed out that the contract made no provision for assigning staff to advising or tutoring and argued that to assign teachers to those duties could be considered a violation of the contract. The administration proposed a written agreement with the union allowing interested teachers to *volunteer* for these duties and stipulating that only volunteers would be assigned.

Union leaders were also concerned regarding how advising and tutoring would be scheduled into the school day. Neither teachers nor administrators favored extending the school day, which ran from 8:05 to 3:25 for students. The union offered a solution. Stevenson students had traditionally received fifty minutes for lunch. Union leaders proposed that the advisory period for freshmen meet for twenty-five minutes four days each week during the lunch period, thereby reducing the time freshmen were allotted for lunch from fifty to twenty-five minutes. One day each week, however, freshmen would receive fifty minutes for lunch with the promise that if they passed all their courses with grades of C or better and avoided serious discipline problems, they would earn the privilege of extended lunch as sophomores. It was also decided that tutoring services for all students would be provided during their study hall or free period rather than at the end of the day.

Working together, the administration and union were able to create a win-win situation for students and teachers. Students received the additional support of advising and tutoring services. Teachers were presented with additional options for fulfilling their supervisory assignment, and most teachers preferred working with students as advisors and tutors to supervising them in hallways, study halls, and the cafeteria.

Several members of the staff were convinced the advisory program needed the support of upperclassman mentors if it was to be effective, but the school faced the challenge of how to persuade juniors and seniors to meet with freshmen during lunch periods. Two teachers came up with a solution. First, students would be invited to serve as mentors through a formal letter stipulating they had been identified as potential role models for younger students. Second, students who agreed to serve as role models would be granted one request regarding their schedule for the coming year, such as specifying a teacher for a particular course, designating when their free period would occur during the day, coordinating their lunch period with another student, and so on. By stressing the honor of selection and offering the "one wish" scheduling option, the school had no difficulty in recruiting enough upperclassmen to serve as mentors. After three years, when every student in the school had enjoyed the support of a mentor as freshmen, Stevenson dropped the one-wish incentive. Today, over 500 students volunteer for the position of mentor, about twice as many as the school requires.

The proposal to change the grading practices of the school from two nine-week grading periods with optional progress reports to three six-week grading periods with mandatory progress reports for *all* students at the midpoint of each six-week period met with initial opposition from teachers and students alike. Teachers were concerned that the new system would result in unreasonable demands on their already limited time. The teacher task force that proposed the change attempted to address this concern in several ways. First, they presented evidence that their proposal was more consistent with the frequent monitoring of student progress and strong parent partnerships that characterized high-performing schools. Second, they demonstrated that the use of appropriate technology made it possible for a teacher to send a computerized progress report to every student in a class in less time than it was taking to send written failure notices to the 10 percent of the students who were receiving notification under the current system.

The student council objected, saying that the change would mean teachers would assess students more frequently, which, from the student perspective, would mean more quizzes, more tests, more papers, and more projects than they were accustomed to. When the student council was unable to persuade the administration to abandon the new grading proposal, its leaders appealed directly to the board of education to reject the new grading proposal.

The reservations on the part of some teachers and many students led to a compromise of sorts. The board approved the new grading calendar, but only on a pilot basis for two years, until its impact could be determined. After two years the evidence of reduced failure and higher levels of achievement was so apparent that neither students nor teachers objected to the pilot becoming the standard practice of the school.

Boones Mill Elementary

The transformation of Boones Mill Elementary School did not occur without some pushback from staff. The most frequent concern expressed by some staff was the loss of individual autonomy. In the past, each teacher had been free to determine at what point in the day he or she would teach a particular subject area, and when students would take recess. Each classroom teacher had been able to negotiate with the teachers of specials classes regarding the day and time his or her students would take those classes. Assertive teachers were able to secure their preferred time for specials, while other teachers were left to take whatever was available. As a result, on some days of the week a teacher might have his or her students assigned to several specials classes while on other days the students had no access to specials. Despite the inconsistencies, many teachers had established a comfortable routine regarding their schedule, and they were reluctant to abandon the familiar.

The school's new schedule required coordination. Teams were called upon to make collective decisions regarding when particular subjects would be taught. All of the students of a grade level would have specials, eat lunch, and have recess at the same time. Common blocks of time for intervention and enrichment were to be established. Furthermore, the need for coordination of the schedule to support intervention and enrichment meant not every grade-level team could teach language arts and math in the morning, and some teachers were convinced students could not learn language arts in the afternoon.

When the staff raised these objections, the principal returned to the dialogue she had conducted with each team over the course of the summer. The primary concern that had emerged from the teachers during these conversations was the lack of time—to teach, to collaborate with colleagues, and to provide additional support to students who were struggling. A secondary concern was the constant interruptions to their teaching as students were pulled from classes for resource services. As one teacher observed, "You may as well put a revolving door on my classroom."

Based on the dialogue, the principal had developed a parallel schedule to address teacher concerns. The new schedule ensured large blocks of protected time for teaching and learning, daily specials for all students, collaboration time each week for teachers of the same grade level, and an intervention and enrichment block each day for every grade level. In effect she said, "I have listened to you and created the schedule that met all the criteria you articulated about your priorities. I am willing to consider an alternative schedule as long as you can demonstrate that it reflects those priorities." At that point, when the faculty was unable to present a workable alternative, the school went forward with the new schedule. This approach of engaging in dialogue, listening to concerns, establishing criteria for a better alternative, and insisting that solutions meet the criteria is a powerful strategy for addressing barriers.

Another issue that arose at Boones Mill was the shifting of funds designated for instructional materials to hire a part-time floating tutor to assist with intervention. While the staff recognized the benefits of the tutor, some were disappointed that they would not be able to purchase materials they felt would benefit their students. The principal addressed this concern by persuading the parent-teacher organization to break with its tradition of how it provided support for the school. In the past the PTO had raised funds for a large gift to benefit the entire student body, such as computers or playground equipment. At the urging of the principal, the PTO agreed to devote the funds it raised to support grade-level grants that allowed each collaborative team to purchase the supplementary instructional materials and resources it desired.

Prairie Star Middle School

Prairie Star faced the challenge of using staff members in new ways. If the Learning Lab and guided study programs were to be effective in supporting students, they needed the contribution and support of some of the teaching staff. When enrollment in some of the elective programs did not support a full-time teacher, the school had traditionally assigned those teachers an extra period of preparation. Principal Rantz now asked some of them to work in the Learning Lab to help students. She was also able to assign paraprofessionals from special education to the Learning Lab to assist with accommodations in testing for those students and to provide more adult supervision in the lab. Foreign language teachers whose enrollment did not require a full-time teacher were asked to assist with the guided study program to help students learn to become more organized and more responsible for their learning.

Special education teachers at Prairie Star had never been provided with collaborative time to work as members of a special education team. So Principal Rantz worked with counselors to create a new schedule that ensured those teachers received one hour each week during the school day to work in their own collaborative team to address how they could better support both special education students and their general education colleagues. Once again, changes in roles and responsibilities and changes to the schedule were vital to the success of the initiative.

Lakeridge Junior High

Lakeridge Junior High School had to address both contractual issues and parental concerns. When it was proposed that the school move to a modified block schedule in order to build time for intervention and enrichment into the school day, some teachers argued that the new schedule would violate the contractual provisions regarding teacher contract hours. The administration worked through the issue with the union representative, and when the faculty voted on the new schedule, the vote was an overwhelming forty-eight to one to support it.

A community council made up of parents and teachers has played an important role in transforming the Lakeridge school culture in a way that has moved the school from one of the lowest performing in the district to a school recognized as the best in Utah. Initially, however, the parent members on the council were skeptical of the idea of the flex period. They questioned the loss of instructional time, the number of students who would have very little direct supervision, and the need for intervention and enrichment. When they were presented with the data on student achievement and came to a better understanding of how the period would work for students depending on their needs, they became more receptive to the proposal. They were ultimately persuaded when they accompanied Lakeridge staff on a visit to a school that had a similar program in place to see how it operated. Principal Peterson believes today that not only are the parents on the community council among the biggest advocates for the school's system of interventions and enrichment, but they also are able to explain how it operates and the rationale behind it as well as any member of the staff.

Kildeer Countryside

In Kildeer Countryside Community Consolidated School District 96, both time and tradition became barriers to effective systems of interventions and enrichment. As district and building leaders built shared knowledge among staff about the benefits of systematic rather than random approaches to intervention and enrichment, the limits imposed by the contractual workday presented significant barriers to moving forward. The board of education and the teachers union resolved to work together to address the issue through the negotiating process. They were able to agree that an additional hour would be added to the teacher workday with the stipulation that the time would be used for teacher collaboration and student support. The details were left to each school to work out.

At that point, however, implementation of the intervention program stalled as principals struggled with finding ways to use the time creatively. It wasn't until the teachers themselves became involved in designing an effective system that schools began to experience breakthroughs. Superintendent Many considers the leadership of both the teacher union and teachers in each building as vital to the success that the district has experienced.

The other issue that challenged progress was less tangible, but potentially more problematic. In some of the elementary schools, veteran teachers had a difficult time letting go of the paradigm that each teacher is personally responsible for his or her own students. They struggled with the idea of a team of people working together to address the needs of students, and they were reluctant to release "their kids" to other teachers or staff. The schools pushed forward, despite the reservations of some teachers, and no teacher was permitted to opt out of participation in the program. As the results began to demonstrate the positive impact of systematic intervention and enrichment, reservations and opposition diminished.

Whittier Union

When Whittier Schools began to consider how they might create a new schedule to provide teachers with time to collaborate and students with time for additional support, they faced an immediate hurdle. The teacher contract stipulated that any proposed change to the schedule required the approval of the majority of the staff. The district met that challenge by providing a core group of teacher leaders and administrators with the opportunity to attend training on the professional learning community concept, to share readings on the concept, and to visit Adlai Stevenson High School to witness the concept at work. These leaders became the advocates for bringing PLCs to Whittier and played a key role as the district engaged in the training and dialogue to make all staff aware of the potential impact of PLCs. When the vote to change the schedule was taken at each school, over 70 percent of the staff approved the change in the first year. When a vote was taken in the second year, over 90 percent voted in favor of continuing with the new schedule.

A second obstacle at Whittier was the demands that the new systems were placing on already overburdened department chairmen and counselors. As we described in chapter 11, Whittier was able to resolve this issue and expand the leadership base by creating the positions of lead teacher and intervention specialist—a step that engaged more than 125 staff members to the collective effort to provide leadership to the improvement process.

Sanger Unified

At one point in the history of Sanger Unified School District, the teacher contract stipulated that administrators could only meet with teachers for a total of ten hours per year. If an administrator went beyond that threshold, teachers were entitled to additional compensation. To move from that mentality to one in which teachers were expected to meet regularly as part of their routine work practice required some major shifts in thinking. To facilitate that shift, the district leadership made certain the union leaders played a key role in the PLC process. Union leaders were included in the early training to introduce the concept, and they continue to participate in the annual administrative retreat to monitor the progress of the initiative and set goals for improvement.

The district was able to address the time issue by extending the school hours a few extra minutes each day in order to allow for a 12:30 student dismissal twice per month. On those days, teachers are provided with a four-hour block of time to work together collaboratively. The central office administration has committed to the teachers union leadership that this time will be spent in meaningful work rather than administrivia, has asked those leaders to alert them to any situations in which teachers feel this commitment is not being honored, and has pledged to address the situation to ensure that this precious time is being used for the right purpose.

Another challenge Sanger confronted was the disparate progress that different schools were making on the PLC journey. While some schools were moving forward, others seemed stuck. While some faculties seemed to embrace PLC practices, others seemed entrenched in traditional practice. District leaders at Sanger had to decide whether to limit the PLC process to the schools where staffs were inclined to embrace the concept or to insist that all schools were to reflect a focus on the learning of each student, a collaborative and collective effort to ensure each student was learning, and a commitment to providing a systematic response when any student struggled. When leaders opted to press on with a *districtwide process*, it meant they had to provide some principals with intensive support to build their capacity to lead the initiative.

Yet another obstacle confronting Sanger was the sprawling nature of the district and the small size of some schools, conditions that resulted in many teachers being the only ones in their school to teach a particular course or grade level. These teachers did not have the benefit of a collaborative team in the same building. Sanger addressed this challenge in two ways. First, the large blocks of time set aside for collaboration every two weeks allow teachers from different schools to gather together to work collaboratively. Second, the district has implemented the First Class Communication Suite to support electronic collaboration of teachers across the district.

A Universal Issue: Not Everyone Initially Embraces the PLC Process

The one common obstacle that *every* school and district confronted as they implemented the PLC concept was the unwillingness of some staff to support the implementation. The faculties cited in the preceding chapters ultimately became enthusiastic advocates for the collaborative culture and systematic interventions that are so critical to the PLC concept. In every case, however, the school and district leaders faced the challenge of one or more staff members who were either aggressively or passively resistant to the new direction of their organization. The points we wish to make here are 1) every school had to address this issue, 2) leaders anticipated the resistance and did not vilify those who offered objections, 3) leaders used similar strategies in how they dealt with the challenge, and 4) leaders were willing to confront behavior that was misaligned with the PLC process and to direct individuals to change that behavior.

As Principal Garrick Peterson of Lakeridge said, "I don't know how you could expect to implement PLCs and not deal with resistance. How can you think you will ask people to change and not expect them to resist? Resistance in most cases is just coming to grips with how you can be successful in this new thing. Just because someone questions the new thing does not mean they are resisting. It means they are trying to figure things out. The job of administration is to help them figure it out."

The initial response of leaders at both the school and district level to resistance was to attempt to build shared knowledge. Bonnie Brasic remembers that presenting staff with data on the rapidly shifting demographics of the student population at Cinco Ranch was a "real eye-opener that convinced most that business as usual would no longer suffice."

These leaders also built shared knowledge by engaging in dialogue and encouraging resisters to both articulate their assumptions and provide research and evidence to support those assumptions. This strategy of bringing assumptions to the surface for examination and dialogue has been described by organizational theorists Pfeffer and Sutton (2000) as "one of the most powerful interventions" to free people from the unconscious power of "mindless precedent" (pp. 91–92).

Leaders in these schools and districts not only called upon others to articulate their assumptions, but also recognized the importance of communicating their own assumptions and presenting their own evidence and research in support of their position. They presented staff with articles and books on PLCs. They sent staff to workshops on the concept. They offered testimonials from schools that had created systems of interventions and arranged for staff to visit those schools. They conducted pilot studies in their own schools to gather evidence. They were convinced that an honest examination of best practice would support their initiatives.

As one of the nation's leading researchers on the change process concluded, most leaders undercommunicate the need for and the specifics of the necessary change by a factor of ten (Kotter, 1996). The leaders of the organizations we featured avoided that mistake. Principal Rantz offered a common refrain when she recalled, "Every chance I got, I stressed that every student is deserving of our collective best, not just the best that each individual teacher has to offer. I wrote about it in my weekly newsletters and provided many articles and books for discussions and study. I stressed it at faculty meetings, leadership meetings, and chance encounters in the hallway."

In their work on how to influence the thinking and behavior of others, Kerry Patterson and his colleagues (Patterson, Grenny, Maxfield, McMillan, & Switzler, 2008) described personal experience as "the great persuader" (p. 51). In addition to ongoing dialogue, these leaders utilized the power of personal experience by moving forward even though some on the staff remained unconvinced the intervention process would be beneficial to the school. They did not wait for unanimity because they realized that "attitudes *follow* behavior. That means people accept new beliefs as a result of changing their behavior" (Pfeffer & Sutton, 2000, p. 65).

Principal Garrick Peterson described what happens when the strategy of personal experience is effective:

> Once you get them to experiment, they will have success. All of a sudden they will realize that low-income students can learn, minority students can learn, all students can learn. Most educators got into this business because they wanted to make a difference for their students. I think one reason educators become cynical is because they lose hope that they can make a difference. They would never say it, but they don't think they can make a difference with these kids. Once PLCs empower them and they recognize they are making a difference, teachers become the champions of PLCs. You celebrate, publicly acknowledge progress, and allow people and teams that have had success to share their practice. This sharing will cause others to want to experiment. Excitement will rise and a culture of change and continual improvement will be created. Teachers become leaders, and promote the process to other teachers in the school.

The goal, of course, is to create a critical mass, to reach a tipping point where momentum accelerates and people embrace the change out of commitment rather than compliance. As Principal Peterson puts it, "You can either let resisters put pressure on the organization, or you can put pressure on them. Eventually the pressure from the team, the school, the administration, and the parents will force big resisters to change or leave."

Alas, it is probable that not every person will be converted, regardless of how much evidence is presented or how many success stories are shared. At some point in the process it is likely that leaders will confront the reality that the behavior of some staff members is undermining the PLC process, and at that point those leaders must be willing to engage in a "crucial conversation."

The consistent way in which these school and district leaders addressed this challenge offers important insights into leading the PLC process. In every case, the leader met with the teacher or principal privately, stated concerns very directly, and identified the specific steps the teacher or principal must take to remedy the situation. Finally, the leader asked how he or she might help the person make the necessary changes. They did not equivocate. They made it clear that the current behavior was unacceptable and that the need for change was imperative. They did so without rancor, but they left no room for doubt regarding their expectations. The educators of these schools and districts came to understand that their organizations stood for certain principles that every staff member was expected to honor.

Perhaps there are schools that have made the transition to a PLC without conflict or anxiety, but we are unaware of any. Expect disagreements and tension. The question schools must face is not, how can we eliminate all potential for conflict as we go through this process; rather, the question is how will we react when we are immersed in the inevitable conflict that accompanies significant change? In *Crucial Conversations* (Patterson, Grenny, McMillan, & Switzler, 2002), the authors contrast how teams respond when faced with conflict. Ineffective teams will ignore the problem, letting it fester and build until resentment and frustration lead to an explosion of accusations and recrimination. Good teams will take the matter to the boss and ask that he or she deal with the problem and find a satisfactory solution. Great teams deal with the issue themselves, engaging in open dialogue and applying positive peer pressure to bring about the desired change.

Seldom, however, do all the teams in a school start out as great teams. Before they can get to the point where team members can work together to resolve the matter, it is likely that they will need the "boss" or principal to help remedy the situation. If, at that critical moment, the staff observes their principal is unwilling to confront obvious violations of PLC concepts, the initiative will soon begin to unravel. Principals must place a higher priority on promoting PLC concepts than on getting along with staff or avoiding conflict.

In some of the schools we have featured, a few staff members chose to leave rather than act in accordance with the new culture. Principal Myrtle found that some teachers at Highland Elementary were not acting according to any philosophical positions, but had merely sought out a low-performing school because it offered the comfort of low expectations and little parental involvement. They had no interest in staying in a school committed to a collective effort to ensure all students learn. Principal Rantz acknowledges that two teachers left Prairie Star at the end of the first year. Stevenson also had 2 of its 135 teachers opt to leave when it launched the PLC process. One teacher was counseled out of the profession at Boones Mill at the conclusion of the second year of their PLC journey. In almost every instance, not everyone was convinced of the need for change, and a very few chose to leave to seek out more comfortable environments where they would not be expected to embrace the premise that they had a responsibility to help all students learn, collaborate, or provide evidence of student learning.

So, while we can offer advice and strategies regarding how to persuade skeptics to embrace the assumptions of the PLC culture, we cannot offer a guaranteed method for ensuring success in that effort. We can, however, offer this observation to every leader: *the culture of your organization will be shaped, to a large extent, by the behavior you are willing to tolerate.* An unwillingness to confront inappropriate or incongruent behavior sends the message to everyone in the organization that the behavior is acceptable and actually reduces the levels of trust teachers express in their principals (Bryk & Schneider, 2004).

Confronting those whose actions violate what is held sacred in your organization may not always bring about the desired change in their behavior, but it does communicate to everyone in the organization what you stand for. As Principal Myrtle advises, "Any principal who doesn't get this will not accomplish anything. Your faculty makes the school what it is and makes you who you are."

In short, school and district leaders play a pivotal role in implementing the PLC concept, a role that includes carefully monitoring and celebrating progress and responding to those whose actions are incongruent with PLC principles. As Rick DuFour notes in an article for *The School Administrator*:

> Much is required of school leaders if they are to build the capacity of people throughout the organization to help more students learn at higher levels. They must encourage people throughout the organization to examine and articulate their assumptions. They must help build shared knowledge and encourage learning by doing. They must create new experiences for people that call upon them to act in new ways. They must build continuous improvement processes into the routine practices of each school. They must demonstrate fierce resolve and consistent commitment to a sustained direction over an

extended period of time. And, very significantly, *they must be emphatically assertive when necessary and use the power of their position to get people to act in ways that are aligned with the mission of higher levels of learning for all.* (DuFour, 2007a, p. 42)

Concluding Thoughts

Participants in our workshops almost universally acknowledge the benefits of a system of interventions and enrichment for students. They embrace the premise that a collective, coordinated, and systematic response to students is likely to be more effective and equitable than the individualistic and random response that occurs in their schools.

It is not uncommon, however, for those same participants to then explain why they should not be expected to create their own version of a pyramid of interventions in their schools or districts. "We don't have enough staff, we don't have enough money to hire staff," "The contract won't allow it," "The union won't support it," "Not everyone is on board," and the ubiquitous "The schedule won't let us" are among the predictable responses. The schools and districts that we have featured in this book have faced some or all of these obstacles. They chose to work their way through those obstacles rather than devoting their energy to explaining why they could not do what research, experience, and common sense say must be done in order to help all students learn at high levels. Every school that embarks on this journey will ultimately face the same choice. Educators must decide if they will work together collectively and collaboratively to overcome the inevitable barriers they will confront or if they will simply say the task is too hard and the challenges too great for them to do what they know must be done to support high levels of learning for all students. Will they expend their energy explaining why it cannot be done in their setting, or will they work together to do it?

16
CHANGING THE CULTURE OF SCHOOLING TO EMBRACE EFFORT-BASED ENRICHMENT

Give them the gift of the growth mindset. Create an environment that teaches the growth mindset to the adults and children in your life.

—CAROL DWECK, 2006

Probably the most important—and the most difficult—job of the school-based reformer is to change the prevailing culture of a school. . . . Ultimately, a school's culture has far more influence on life and learning in the schoolhouse than the state department of education, the superintendent, the school board, or even the principal can ever have.　　—ROLAND BARTH, 2001

Great schools "row as one"; they are quite clearly in the same boat, pulling in the same direction in unison. The best schools we visited were tightly aligned communities marked by a palpable sense of common purpose and shared identity among staff—a clear sense of "we."

—THOMAS LICKONA & MATTHEW DAVIDSON, 2005

Educators in search of the one new program that will transform their school may be tempted to view the development of systematic interventions and enrichment for students as the solution to their problems. Unfortunately, the effect of simply adding programs to traditional school practices is neither significant nor lasting. At the risk of redundancy, we repeat the message we have attempted to stress throughout this book: *attention to interventions and enrichment should not be viewed as a program or add-on, but rather should be considered as part of the larger process of creating the culture of a professional learning community.*

Structural changes such as changes in schedules to provide time for intervention and enrichment, creating new procedures for monitoring and reporting student progress, redefining roles, and providing time for teachers to work in teams can contribute to and support the essential cultural changes. If, however, structural changes are to have a lasting impact, they ultimately must become deeply rooted in the school's culture—the assumptions, beliefs, expectations, values, and habits that constitute the norm for that school. Once again, the culture of any organization shapes how people think, feel, and act. It explains their view of the world, reinforces their interpretation of events, and instructs them in appropriate conduct.

If organizational culture is found in "the stories we tell ourselves" (James, 1995) and "the assumptions we don't see" (Schein, 1992), the challenge facing those who hope to create PLCs in their schools and districts is the task of creating new stories based on new explicitly stated assumptions. In *Revisiting Professional Learning Communities at Work* (DuFour, DuFour, & Eaker, 2008, pp. 93–95), we articulate the cultural shifts—the moves to new stories based on new assumptions—that accompany the work of a PLC. We reiterate those assumptions here in table 16.1.

Table 16.1: Cultural Shifts in a Professional Learning Community

A Shift in Fundamental Purpose	
From a focus on teaching . . .	to a focus on learning
From emphasis on what was taught . . .	to a fixation on what students learned
From coverage of content . . .	to demonstration of proficiency
From learning for *some* students through processes of sorting and selecting . . .	to learning for *all* students through processes of intervention and enrichment
A Shift in Use of Assessments	
From infrequent summative assessments . . .	to frequent common formative assessments
From assessments to determine which students failed to learn by the deadline . . .	to assessments to identify students who need additional time and support
From assessments used to reward and punish students . . .	to assessments used to inform and motivate students
From assessing many things infrequently . . .	to assessing a few things frequently
From individual teacher assessments . . .	to assessments developed jointly by collaborative teams
From each teacher determining the criteria to be used in assessing student work . . .	to collaborative teams clarifying the criteria and ensuring consistency among team members when assessing student work
From an over-reliance on one kind of assessment . . .	to balanced assessments
From focusing on average scores . . .	to monitoring each student's proficiency in every essential skill

A Shift in the Response When Students Don't Learn	
From individual teachers determining the appropriate response . . .	to a systematic response that ensures support for every student
From fixed time and support for learning . . .	to time and support for learning as variables
From remediation . . .	to intervention
From invitational support outside of the school day . . .	to directed (that is, required) support occurring during the school day
From one opportunity to demonstrate learning . . .	to multiple opportunities to demonstrate learning
A Shift in the Work of Teachers	
From isolation . . .	to collaboration
From each teacher clarifying what students must learn . . .	to collaborative teams building shared knowledge and understanding about essential learning
From each teacher assigning priority to different learning standards . . .	to collaborative teams establishing the priority of respective learning standards
From each teacher determining the pacing of the curriculum . . .	to collaborative teams of teachers agreeing on common pacing
From individual teachers attempting to discover ways to improve results . . .	to collaborative teams of teachers helping each other improve
From privatization of practice . . .	to open sharing of practice
From decisions made on the basis of individual preferences . . .	to decisions made collectively by building shared knowledge of best practice
From "collaboration lite" on matters unrelated to student achievement . . .	to collaboration explicitly focused on issues and questions that most impact student achievement
From an assumption that these are "my kids, those are your kids" . . .	to an assumption that these are "our kids"
A Shift in Focus	
From an external focus on issues outside of the school . . .	to an internal focus on steps the staff can take to improve the school
From a focus on inputs . . .	to a focus on results
From goals related to completion of projects and activities . . .	to SMART goals demanding evidence of student learning
From teachers gathering data from their individually constructed tests in order to assign grades . . .	to collaborative teams acquiring information from common assessments in order to (1) inform their individual and collective practice, and (2) respond to students who need additional time and support

continued on next page →

A Shift in Focus (continued)	
From independence . . .	to interdependence
From a language of complaint . . .	to a language of commitment
From long-term strategic planning . . .	to planning for short-term wins
From infrequent generic recognition . . .	to frequent specific recognition and a culture of celebration that creates many winners
A Shift in Professional Development	
From external training (workshops and courses) . . .	to job-embedded learning
From the expectation that learning occurs infrequently (on the few days devoted to professional development) . . .	to an expectation that learning is ongoing and occurs as part of routine work practice
From presentations to entire faculties . . .	to team-based action research
From learning by listening . . .	to learning by doing
From learning individually through courses and workshops . . .	to learning collectively by working together
From assessing impact on the basis of teacher satisfaction ("Did you like it?") . . .	to assessing impact on the basis of evidence of improved student learning
From short-term exposure to multiple concepts and practices . . .	to sustained commitment to limited, focused initiatives

The Growth Mindset

As we have stressed throughout this book, the traditional culture of public schools has been based on the premise that students would learn if they were smart and that the purpose of schooling was to identify those with the innate gift of intelligence and educate them to high levels. Thus, the extent of a student's learning was almost exclusively a function of his or her ability. Psychologist Carol Dweck (2006) refers to this assumption—that our abilities are carved in stone—as a *fixed mindset*. Her research has demonstrated that this mindset actually discourages student learning. When students believe academic success is a function of personal ability that is predetermined, inherent, and fixed, they are likely to shut down when they confront an academic challenge. After all, if they were "smart," learning should be easy. Furthermore, they are not inclined to seek help because they are afraid it will signal to the teacher that they are not smart. Unfortunately, Dweck's research has also demonstrated that the traditional culture of schools reinforces this fixed mindset in teachers and students alike.

There is, however, an alternative. Dweck explains that a *growth mindset* is based on the belief that individuals can cultivate their abilities and talents through effort, and that this belief, in turn, generates a passion for learning. The willingness and desire to stretch oneself, to seek out challenge, and to "stick to it even (or especially) when it is not going well is the hallmark of the growth mindset" (Dweck, 2006, p. 7).

As educators develop their capacity to function as a PLC, they must create a culture that fosters the growth mindset, a culture that stretches the hopes, aspirations, and performance levels of students and adults alike. Students are encouraged to stretch beyond their comfort zone and perform high-quality work within a more challenging curriculum. Teachers are stretched to develop and implement more effective teaching strategies in their classrooms. Administrators and support staff are asked to seek out and implement best practices and rise to higher levels of performance. As we have seen throughout many of the chapters in this book, this commitment to raising the aspirations and performance levels of everyone can stretch even the highest-performing schools to improve continually.

The framework for developing a stretch culture rests upon recognizing the significance of expectations, which Good (1987) defined as the inferences teachers make about the future academic achievement of their students based on what they know about their students now. For over a quarter of a century, a climate of *high* expectations for student achievement has been cited as a critical aspect of effective schools.

Many schools, however, continue to misinterpret and misapply the research findings on high expectations. A commitment to high expectations requires more than expressing positive affirmations about the ability of students. Chanting, "We believe all our kids can learn" will have little impact on student achievement unless specific steps are taken to support that learning. Even teachers who have high expectations for student achievement and act on those expectations are likely to find that at the end of their instruction, some students did not learn.

Merely raising the bar higher and demanding more of students without providing them with additional time and support and expanding the skills of their teachers will not increase their achievement. As Dweck (2006) advises educators, "Remember that lowering standards doesn't raise students' self-esteem. But neither does raising standards without giving students ways to reach them. The growth mindset gives you a way to set high standards and have students reach them" (p. 212). The assumption that you have not learned *yet* is very different from the assumption that you cannot learn.

The assumption that you must keep working until you are successful is very different from the assumption that says you must learn within the time we have allotted. In a PLC, the entire culture of the school demands that students keep working and tempers that demand with additional time, increasing levels of support, and a nurturing environment that conveys the message that we care about and believe in the student.

As Larry Lezotte (1991) states, "High expectations for success will be judged, not only by the staff's initial beliefs and behaviors, but also by the organization's response when some students do not learn" (p. 2). The schools and districts we have studied demonstrate the powerful impact the organization's response can have on staff beliefs and expectations. Teachers left to their own devices to resolve the ongoing challenge of intervention and enrichment for their students are far more prone to a sense of resignation and helplessness. Teachers in schools with effective systems of interventions and enrichment have a stronger sense of both self-efficacy and collective efficacy. It is not so much their perception of their students' abilities that creates a culture of high expectations in these schools, but their conviction regarding their own collective abilities to impact student achievement in a positive way. In this stretch culture, teachers can advise their students: "This unit will be challenging, but we can do this. We have learned how to help students just like you be successful in accomplishing things they never thought were possible. We believe in you, and we will not give up on you. If you believe in us and do what we ask of you, together we can meet this challenge."

Enrichment in a Professional Learning Community: Beyond Proficiency

There are many students in schools across North America who demonstrate proficiency on test scores who are still "underlearning." There are large numbers of students who make very good grades in a culture of low expectations. One of the consistent messages students convey in surveys of their schooling experience is that their schools fail to challenge them. A school committed to high levels of learning for all students acknowledges this problem and intentionally pushes students beyond their comfort zone. Such schools constantly convey the message, "You have the potential to do more than you have ever thought possible, and we are here to help and support you as you work to realize that potential."

Plans for enriching and extending the learning of students must, however, provide additional support to help students be successful as they take on greater challenges. The work of Carol Ann Tomlinson offers great insights into how individual teachers can differentiate their instruction to enrich and enhance the learning of students of all abilities, but some strategies for interventions go beyond what an individual teacher can do. Some require collaboration and coordination among the members of a team of teachers who share not only strategies and materials, but also students. And, as we have stressed throughout this book, some practices, especially those that impact the school schedule, require a schoolwide effort.

Planning for enrichment follows the same process or way of thinking as developing plans for time and support for students who are struggling. Schools should build shared knowledge regarding best practice and move quickly to act on that knowledge. Formal plans that include multiple layers should be developed. The impact of those plans on student learning should be monitored, adjusted, and improved upon incrementally over time as part of the process of continuous improvement.

When schools are attentive to a systematic approach to enrichment, the results can be extraordinary. Throughout this book we have shown that schools and districts that have been successful in implementing the PLC process not only have helped low-performing students become proficient, but also have helped significantly more of their students achieve at the highest levels on state and national assessments.

- One of the three annual goals pursued by Adlai Stevenson High School is to provide more students with access to the most rigorous curriculum in each department. Since beginning the PLC process, Stevenson has increased the percentage of its graduating class scoring honor grades on the advanced placement exams by over 900 percent. No comprehensive high school in North America writes more AP exams than Stevenson, but providing all students with access to a program that was once reserved for the academic elite has not adversely impacted the performance of the most capable students. The mode, or most frequent score, earned by Stevenson students from 2002 through 2009 has been five—the highest possible score—and no school has produced the single top AP scholar in Illinois more frequently than Stevenson. The fact that the school is committed to the success of every student has not made it less effective in meeting the needs of high-performing students.

- The staff members of Boones Mill explicitly state their intent to increase the percentage of students who achieve at the highest level on state assessments in their annual school improvement plans. In 2008, 70 percent of the state exams written by Boones Mill's students earned Virginia's highest rating.

- The percentage of Cinco Ranch High School students earning commended status on the Texas Assessment of Knowledge and Skills has increased in all subject areas since the school began its PLC journey (see table 9.2 on page 127).

- Highland Elementary students, 73 percent of whom live in poverty and 60 percent of whom do not use English as their primary language, are far more likely to demonstrate advanced proficiency in reading at all grade levels than the students across Maryland. The comparison of percentages of advanced proficient students between Highland students and Maryland students as a whole in 2005 and 2008 is presented in table 16.2.

Table 16.2: Highland Students Advanced Proficient in Reading Versus All Maryland Students

	Highland 2005 Versus 2008	Percent Increase	Maryland 2005 Versus 2008	Percent Increase
Grade 3	3% to 31%	28%	15% to 17%	2%
Grade 4	8% to 43%	35%	23% to 28%	5%
Grade 5	7% to 80%	73%	34% to 51%	17%

- The percentage of Highland students achieving advanced proficiency in math is comparable to or better than the state averages for that category and has increased 10 percent, 34 percent, and 19 percent in third, fourth, and fifth grades, respectively between 2005 and 2008. The percentage of all Maryland students achieving advanced proficiency in math has increased 1 percent, 15 percent, and 8 percent for those grades.

- Kansas includes both exceeds standard and exemplary categories on its state assessments. Figures 6.2 and 6.3 on pages 97–98 demonstrate that since beginning its PLC journey, the percentage of Prairie Star Middle School students who qualified for those two categories in mathematics increased from 40 percent to 79 percent, while the percentage of students in the exemplary category jumped from 15 percent to 45 percent. In reading, the percentages increased from 45 percent to 81 percent in the top two categories and from 9 percent to 55 percent in exemplary.

- From 2004 to 2008, the percentage of Lakeridge Junior High School students who achieved the highest distinction on their state assessment in reading and math increased at every grade level and for all subgroups of students. The increase has been in double digits in seven of the eight subgroup categories. In 2008, over 60 percent of

Lakeridge students achieved at the highest level in English and over 50 percent achieved at that level in mathematics.

It is no accident that the six schools and three districts featured in this book have all helped more students achieve at the highest levels at the same time they committed to providing struggling students with additional time and support. Both collaborative teams and systems of interventions support a culture that stretches all students. When teachers work together to become so skillful in teaching a particular concept that even students who typically have difficulty can understand that concept, all students benefit. When students of all abilities and levels of performance have a place to turn for extra time and support if they experience initial difficulty in learning, all students benefit. A school culture that both stretches *and* supports students is a good place for all kids.

How Many Schools Would It Take?

More than three decades ago, Ron Edmonds (1979) asked how many highly effective schools it would take to convince skeptics that the professional practices of educators and the way in which their schools operate can overcome the effects of poverty. Edmonds argued that a single school should be persuasive. The stories we have presented are drawn from thirty-five different schools in nine different districts throughout the United States that have demonstrated the tremendous positive impact educators can have on the students they serve. Those schools are at all levels, spread from coast to coast, and serve students whose ethnicity and poverty levels are extremely diverse; nevertheless, *all* of the schools we have featured have not only helped low-performing students become proficient, but they have also helped significantly more of their students achieve at the highest levels on state and national assessments. For those who remain unconvinced by the evidence from thirty-five schools, but might find results from thirty-eight schools compelling, we conclude this chapter by offering three more schools whose purposeful attempts to create systematic interventions for their students have led to dramatic improvement in the achievement of students at *all* levels.

Stults Road Elementary School, Dallas, Texas

The Richardson Independent School District, located in northern Dallas County, Texas, includes forty-one elementary schools, eight junior high schools, four high schools (one with a separate freshman campus), and an alternative learning center. Approximately 35 percent of the district's 34,000 students are white, 31 percent are Hispanic, 26 percent are African American, and 8 percent are Asian/Pacific Islanders. Fifty percent of the district's students are classified as economically disadvantaged, and 22 percent are limited English proficient.

The student population at one of Richardson's elementary schools, Stults Road Elementary School, does not, however, reflect this distribution. The 450 students in this K–6 school are 5 percent white, 46 percent Hispanic, 39 percent African American, and 10 percent Asian. Three of every four students are classified as economically disadvantaged, and 43 percent are limited English proficient. Yet Stults Road Elementary, whose motto is "Whatever It Takes," and whose mission statement asserts, "We are committed to high expectations," consistently performs well above district and state averages and is recognized among the most exemplary schools in Texas.

The work of the staff at Stults Road revolves around the four critical questions of a learning community, and the school day has been structured to provide students with additional time for intervention and enrichment. The master schedule provides daily intervention times for all grades, and support personnel are assigned to assist the grade-level teams during that time. This additional support allows teams to establish small group learning opportunities and provide individual attention to students who require it. The materials used during intervention and enrichment time are aligned with the core program and student assessment results.

As a result of this collaboration, coordination, and systematic intervention, student achievement at Stults has moved steadily upward. In 2008, 95 percent of Stults students demonstrated proficiency on the state assessment in reading, 97 percent were proficient in math, and 98 percent were proficient in writing and science. The percentage of students achieving at the commended level on the state test has risen dramatically as demonstrated by table 16.3.

Table 16.3: Percentages of Commended Students on the Texas Assessment of Knowledge and Skills: Stults Road Elementary Students Versus Elementary Students Statewide

	Stults Road Elementary Results	State Elementary Results
2004	8%	8%
2005	10%	10%
2006	14%	11%
2007	23%	12%
2008	28%	15%

While the increase in the percentage of commended performance at the state level has been 88 percent, the percentage increase at Stults Road has been 350 percent. Considered another way, this increase means the number of students achieving at the commended level in a school of 450 students increased from 36 to 126. Furthermore, in 2008, there was virtually no discrepancy among the different groups in the school in terms of achieving commended status. Every group, including economically disadvantaged and limited English proficient students, outperformed the comprehensive state results.

Stults Road Elementary was recognized by the Texas Department of Education as an Exemplary School in 2007 and in 2008 and has been designated as a Title I Distinguished School. It was also among the fifty schools in the nation cited by Senator Ted Kennedy for its sustained academic excellence and effective professional development. A commitment to helping *all* students learn at Stults Road has clearly benefited not only low-performing students, but has greatly increased the number of students performing at the highest levels.

Pioneer Middle School, Tustin, California

Pioneer Middle School in Tustin, California, is another school that has been very purposeful in designing a curriculum and creating a culture that challenges all students to achieve at the highest levels. Through collaboration with high schools within the district, Pioneer teachers review the sequence of advanced high school offerings and list the prerequisite skills and knowledge needed for each course. With this information, department teams develop a college-prep course of study in each discipline, including language arts, social studies, mathematics, science, and electives. These courses are a minimum course of study at Pioneer. The school will not replace any student's college-prep class with a remedial, below-grade-level course of study.

Once students have demonstrated mastery of grade-level standards in a particular subject, they are transitioned into an honors class in that discipline. These classes are designed to move beyond grade-level standards and prerequisite skills and, instead, focus on the essential standards for the next grade-level course in that discipline. Honors coursework is offered in language arts, social studies, math, science, art, band, orchestra, chorus, video production, computers, and culinary arts.

At the midpoint of each semester students are identified who are ready to transition to advanced/honors courses. To prepare these students for the increased rigor, students are assigned to a preparatory tutorial class in the targeted subject. This tutorial period is offered during the school day as part of Pioneer's schoolwide pyramid of interventions.

While most schools may not consider helping students move into accelerated coursework as an intervention, Principal Mike Mattos and the faculty at Pioneer Middle School believe the purpose of their intervention program is to maximize *every* student's academic potential. Thus, their interventions do not solely target students below grade level, nor do they stop providing additional time and support once a student meets grade-level proficiency. Instead, these same resources are used to move students from proficient to advanced.

Pioneer Middle School has developed a true culture of high expectations for *all* students, and the staff views advanced coursework as the goal for all of their students. How they get each student to this end varies based upon the needs of the student, but the ultimate goal is the same for every child. As a result, Pioneer has increased the percentage of students achieving at the highest level on the state test in every grade level, for every subject, and for every subgroup in the school's population. Pioneer almost doubled the percentage of its eighth-grade students meeting the advanced-proficiency standard in language arts between 2003 and 2007, and now almost half of the students in the school meet that highest standard for that subject area. Math results are even more impressive, with the number of students in seventh and eighth grade taking advanced math classes increasing from 144 in 2004 to 346 in 2007. In 2003 only eighth-grade students completed the state algebra exam in California, and only 3 percent of Pioneer's students achieved the highly proficient standard on the state test. By 2007, one-third of the *seventh* graders were enrolled in algebra, 99 percent of them scored proficient or higher, and 46 percent achieved the advanced proficiency level on the state exam. In 2003, one-fourth of the eighth graders enrolled in geometry, and 48 percent achieved advanced proficiency. In 2007, one-third of eighth graders were enrolled in geometry, and 72 percent of those students scored at the advanced proficiency level. Clearly, this staff's attention to helping all students learn has resulted in more students learning at the highest levels. In 2008 the school was presented the No Child Left Behind National Blue Ribbon Award from the United States Department of Education. In 2009, Pioneer was named the best of the eighty-three middle schools in Orange County, California, by the *Orange County Register.*

Bernice MacNaughton High School, New Brunswick, Canada

Bernice MacNaughton High School, which serves about 900 students in the town of Moncton, New Brunswick, began its PLC journey in the spring of

2006. Teachers worked together to create "skills binders" that clarified exactly what students were to learn in each course, specified the instructional and assessment strategies to be used to help students acquire the essential skills, and included five formative assessments for each summative assessment created by the team.

The staff created a new placement test for entering students, and the school provided students who failed to demonstrate proficiency on that assessment in eighth grade with a supplemental period of math and English each day. Math and science lunch labs were created to assist any student who needed support. Teaching teams designated days after common assessments as RED days (remediation/enrichment days) to provide additional time and support for intervention and enrichment. A thirty-minute directed learning period was established at the end of each school day to provide students with time to complete homework, study for tests, or receive extra help from their teachers. The school became the first in the province to hire a full-time study hall teacher to help oversee the work of students who were not completing their assignments. A learning strategies class was created to support any student who failed the English Language Provincial Assessment, which is required for graduation in New Brunswick.

The school provided incentives for students to achieve at high levels, and then used upperclassmen as part of their support efforts. A reading tutorial course was created to train interested twelfth-grade students in the Great Leaps Reading program. Those students were then paired with struggling ninth-grade students to assist them in learning to read. Twelfth-grade honor students can reduce their course load by one class in their final semester if they agree to devote two periods each week to assisting the study hall teacher in providing support to struggling students. The school also instituted an advanced placement program to provide high-performing students with a challenging curriculum.

The results have benefited students at all levels. The grade distribution has improved in every course, and the school's failure rate has been cut from 11 percent to 2 percent. Even classes with traditionally high failure rates have experienced dramatic improvements. For example, the failure in the tenth-grade science class, which had hovered between 30 percent and 40 percent for years, plummeted to 3 percent in 2008. The number of students required to attend summer school has been cut in half. The improvement has not, however, been limited to students who had traditionally struggled to pass their courses. The percentage of students earning honor grades on advanced placement exams has increased in every course. Perhaps most tellingly, whereas only about one of every one hundred New Brunswick students achieved at the highest level on the provincial exams, *one of every four students* was able to earn that distinction at MacNaughton.

Concluding Thoughts

One key to becoming a PLC is a willingness to honestly assess the current reality of the school. An honest assessment of the data of each of the schools and districts highlighted in this book can only lead to one conclusion: a commitment to the success of every student stretches and benefits all students. A rising tide does indeed raise all boats.

17
MOVING FORWARD: PLANNING FOR EFFECTIVE INTERVENTION

Planning is an essential process of leadership. We define planning as articulating shared direction and coherent policies, practices, and procedures for realizing high standards of student performance.

—Ellen Goldring, Andrew Porter, Joseph Murphy, Stephen Elliott, & Xiu Cravens, 2007

When Gayle Karhanek works with schools and districts to assist in the creation of their systems of interventions, she begins by asking them to regard students who are struggling as "undersupported" rather than "at risk." She then leads them through a series of questions to guide their planning.

Questions to Guide Planning

Consider the following issues as you begin building your version of a pyramid of interventions.

1   **Do we accept the responsibility to help all students learn?**

    If educators in the school believe that some students deserve to fail or do not have the potential to succeed, the staff needs to address that issue. Assumptions should be explicitly stated and thoughtfully examined. Presenting evidence of teachers within the organization who are helping students achieve at high levels and/or schools with similar student populations that are outperforming the students in your school can help create the cognitive dissonance that challenges the assumption, "These kids cannot learn." Intervention works best when people in schools regard themselves as a community of shared responsibility in which members are willing to make collective commitments to be a part of and party to the success of each student.

2   **What interventions are currently in place in our school? What happens now when students are not learning?**

    Develop a list of what is currently available to assist students when they experience difficulty. Ask what is in place to *prevent* a student from experiencing difficulty, and what is in place to *intervene* after the difficulties emerge. Assess the effectiveness of those strategies.

What evidence do you have that they are resolving the issues confronting undersupported students? Which of the strategies should be kept, which should be modified, and which should be eliminated?

3   **Who will be responsible for identifying students who need additional time and support and ensuring those students are placed in the appropriate intervention?**

There should be no confusion regarding roles and responsibilities. Specific people should be designated to oversee the process, and everyone on the staff should be aware of who those people are. Staff members who play this vital role should be provided with time to collaborate on a regular basis. This team will be responsible for 1) identifying which students need intervention according to the criteria established by the school, 2) ensuring appropriate intervention takes place for any student who requires it, and 3) monitoring the impact of the intervention on an *ongoing* basis to determine when students need the next step in the intervention plan and when students no longer require intervention.

4   **What is the trigger point for initiating a specific intervention for specific students?**

Interventions should be based on the needs of students, and the needs of students must be based on evidence and data. There must be clear criteria for determining when a student warrants a specific intervention. If every student is to have equal and equitable access to the system of interventions, the question of when students qualify for support cannot be left to the discretion of individual staff members. Think in terms of "nondiscretionaries." For example, teachers *must* provide progress reports on each student every three weeks. No teacher can elect to ignore that requirement. The student support team *must* meet on a weekly basis to monitor the progress of students. Counselors *must* assign any student who is failing two or more classes after six weeks to a guided study hall.

5   **How will the school ensure that students assigned to intervention report to intervention?**

Just as intervention cannot be left to the discretion of individual teachers if it is to be effective, neither can it be left to the discretion of individual students as to whether or not they will utilize the services provided for them. Students must be directed, not invited, to attend, and failure to report to intervention should be treated the same as failure to report to a class. Student participation must be monitored closely. Once students recognize that they do not have the option of avoiding this service, they will begin to focus on what they need to do. Remember Sanger Middle School, which saw the number of students assigned to a lunchtime study hall for failure to complete homework drop from 300 students to 25 students in one month.

6   **Are the elements of each step of the intervention clearly defined and understood?**

Intervention works best when a staff is clear on the following:

- The desired outcome for the student

- The specific elements of the service the school will provide

- The staff member who will provide the service

- The frequency of the service

- The method for monitoring the student's progress

- The standard the student must achieve to no longer require the service

7   **What layers are included in the system of interventions?**

The system of interventions should be designed with multiple layers so that if the current level of time and support is not helping the student be successful, there is a next step that provides more time and support. Educators who create the system must constantly return to the question, if this does not work, what will we do next?

8   **How timely is the intervention?**

Schools cannot allow students to be in a downward spiral of failure for months before they respond to those students. Effective intervention must be proactive. Schools must create partnerships with their sending schools (middle schools with elementary schools and high schools with middle schools) to identify students who need additional time and support even before they arrive at the receiving school. Schools must create processes for assessing the knowledge and skills of all entering students to determine if they will need more intensive support. Schools must monitor each student's learning on a *timely* basis so that every few weeks, in every classroom, each teacher can say with confidence, "This student is doing fine, but that student needs additional time and support to learn this specific skill."

9   **Most importantly, does the plan ensure interventions take place systematically?**

When something is done systematically, it happens according to a defined plan that is arranged in an organized, methodical, step-by-step process. Thus, the systematic interventions we advocate represent the antithesis of the random, discretionary, haphazard way in which schools have traditionally responded to students who experience difficulty. The analogy for an effective pyramid of interventions is the process we described in an earlier chapter to monitor safety in nuclear power plants. The process is well defined, with very precise and specific steps that *must* be taken. Staff are neither invited nor encouraged to utilize the process; they understand it is nondiscretionary and that failure to adhere to the process puts people at risk. Redundancy is built into the process so that if one step fails to solve the problem, there is a second step, a third step, and a fourth step to ensure a successful outcome.

When a school creates a systematic pyramid of interventions, it is able to *guarantee* students that they will be given additional time and support if they struggle, to *guarantee* parents that their children will receive this support in a timely and directive way regardless of the teacher to whom their child is assigned, and to *guarantee* individual teachers that they are not alone when it comes to resolving the problems their students may experience. The entire staff realizes that there is a collective and coordinated effort to assist students.

Of course, guarantees are useless unless people are aware of them. So an important final step in creating systematic interventions is to communicate those guarantees to all stakeholders. Students, staff, and parents need to understand the rationale behind the interventions, the way the system works, how it can benefit them, and how they can contribute to it.

Building Momentum by Planning for Short-Term Wins

Another key strategy in planning for successful implementation of the professional learning community concept is translating the PLC journey into small steps and celebrating the attainment of each step. The process of becoming a PLC does not occur as a single, dramatic breakthrough or miracle moment. Instead, the process requires sustaining a consistent, coherent effort for an extended period of time. Jim Collins' (2001) description of organizations that made the leap from "good to great" also applies to schools that are able to make significant advancements on the PLC continuum:

> Good to great transformations never happened in one fell swoop. There was no single defining action, no grand program, no one killer innovation, no solitary lucky break, and no wrenching revolution. Good to great comes by a cumulative

process—step by step, action by action, decision by decision, turn by turn of the flywheel—that adds up to sustained and spectacular results. (p. 165)

Thus, while leaders need a few key big ideas to provide the conceptual framework and coherence essential to successful school improvement, it is equally imperative that they recognize the need for specific, short-term implementation steps to advance those ideas. They can paint an attractive picture of the desired future state of the school, but they must balance this futuristic vision of what the school is working toward with steps that can be taken today.

The implementation and celebration of small steps generate both the sense of self-efficacy for staff and the momentum essential for improvement initiatives. While it takes time to drive PLC concepts deep into the culture of a school, the effort will lose momentum if there is nothing to celebrate in the short term. Jim Kouzes and Barry Posner (1987) advise leaders to "break down big problems into small, doable steps . . . plan for small wins. Small wins form the basis for a consistent pattern of winning that appeals to people's desire to belong to a successful venture" (p. 218). Ken Blanchard (2007) cites small wins as an essential element for building the momentum of any change effort, providing evidence the change is working, and reinforcing vital behaviors. John Kotter and Dan Cohen (2002) contend small wins are essential to an improvement process because they "nourish faith in the change effort, emotionally reward the hard workers, keep the critics at bay, and build momentum" (p. 125). Rosabeth Moss Kanter (2004) found that the celebration of small wins energizes people by giving them a taste of victory. Kerry Patterson and colleagues (Patterson, Grenny, Maxfield, McMillan, & Switzler, 2008) caution leaders against waiting for phenomenal results and, instead, urge them to recognize and reward small improvements. Gary Hamel's advice to leaders is succinct: "Win small, win early, win often" (2002, p. 202).

The leaders who built the powerful PLCs presented in this book were effective in articulating the conceptual framework and the key guiding ideas for their schools and districts. They were equally masterful in translating those big concepts into incremental steps. They did more than hope for short-term wins; they *planned* for short-term wins to sustain momentum. They established calendars that called for the completion of projects in weeks and months rather than years, and they helped teams establish interim goals as stepping stones to more ambitious stretch goals.

Completion of tasks and achievement of objectives will not, however, fuel momentum unless people in the school are made aware of the progress that is being made. The leaders of the schools and districts recognized this fact, and each set out to make celebration a significant part of the culture of the school. They viewed every meeting—from large-group faculty meetings to small-group dialogues, parent programs to public assemblies—as a forum for preaching the message, "We are achieving great things. We are becoming the school or district we set out to become because of our collective efforts." They bombarded staff members with consistent stories reminding them of their common purpose, the importance of their work, and their collective commitments. But they went beyond simple cheerleading. They constantly sought and publicly celebrated evidence of short-term wins and indicators of improving student achievement. They solicited and reported student and parent testimonials regarding teachers who made a significant difference in the lives of students. They publicly acknowledged individuals and teams whose efforts brought the vision and collective commitments of the school or district to life in compelling stories.

It becomes very difficult to claim that educators have no impact on student learning when teachers are immersed in stories of goals not only met, but exceeded, of the extraordinary accomplishments and commitments of their colleagues, of steadily rising student achievement, and anecdotal evidence that students and parents recognize teachers who have inspired a child. These leaders promoted a palpable sense of self-efficacy among their entire staff because they were attentive to creating conditions for short-term wins and immersing educators in a culture that celebrated those wins as evidence of the school's success. Our advice here is simple: do not forget the importance of *planning* for short-term wins.

From Planning to Doing

One of the most powerful lessons we have learned in working with schools and districts as they attempt to implement the PLC concept is that those who make the most progress are those who take action. Many educators have a tendency to procrastinate. They contend that before they can take the first steps on the journey to becoming a PLC they need more time to study, or more training, or the conversion of the last few resisters. We have seen no evidence that spending excessive time in preparation to become a PLC leads to greater success. In fact, we concur with Mike Schmoker (2004), who found a negative correlation between the time spent preparing and developing strategic plans and actual school improvement. Teachers and principals who do the best job in learning what it takes to build a PLC are those who immerse themselves in the process. They act, they make mistakes, they learn from their mistakes, and then they begin again more intelligently.

In his study of the functioning of the brain, Jonah Lehrer (2009) found that learning by doing, including making mistakes, is "the most powerful kind of learning" (p. 54). As he wrote, "The brain always works the same way, accumulating wisdom through error. There are no shortcuts to this painstaking process; becoming an expert just takes time and patience" (p. 249).

Think of your own experience in preparing to enter the field of education. Most teachers spend four or five years taking courses in their subject areas, in methodology, and in the foundations of the profession. Yet virtually every teacher would acknowledge that they learned more about the real work of education in their first semester of actually *teaching* than in all their years of *preparing* to teach. People learn by doing, and schools that learn what it takes to become PLCs are those that are doing the work of PLCs. Don't wait for the stars to align perfectly, for just the right conditions, or for the support of the last staff members. No school ever completed this process flawlessly, and you are unlikely to be the first. *Just do it!* As Stephen Covey (2002) admonishes, "To *know* and not to *do* is really not to know" (p. xiv).

A Final Analogy

We conclude with the analogy that we presented in *Whatever It Takes* because it remains an effective way to summarize the issues facing any school or district that hopes to become a professional learning community.

The 1995 movie *Apollo 13* tells the story of how the men and women of NASA responded to the crisis of a crippled spacecraft that threatened the lives of its three astronauts. Problems emerged that NASA engineers had never anticipated or simulated. They were being called upon to do things that had never been done before in the space program. Time was short, as the oxygen in the spacecraft was rapidly depleting. Resources were few. In one powerful scene an engineer empties a box of varied materials on a table and announces that those materials are all that is available to the astronauts to correct the problem in their spacecraft. The world watched and waited to see how this drama would unfold.

How did NASA respond to this difficult, desperate situation? First, the leader of the NASA team called upon its members to recommit to the fundamental purpose of NASA—to send men into space *and return them safely to earth*. He then called upon them to build greater collective knowledge than they ever had before regarding the capacity of the spacecraft. He insisted they contact every designer, technician, and engineer who had played a role in developing every component of the spacecraft to come to deeper understanding of its capabilities. Most importantly, the scientists and engineers of the NASA team did not retreat to their individual cubicles to search for solutions. They worked together, collaboratively, and built upon each other's insights and strengths. They did so because lives hung in the balance.

It is unlikely that Hollywood will make a movie about the efforts a school makes to meet the challenges confronting it, but in many ways those challenges are similar to the *Apollo 13* scenario. Educators are also being called upon to do something that has never been done before. They, too, face a difficult, even desperate situation. They, too, feel the pressure of not enough time to complete what they are asked to accomplish. They, too, are frustrated by a lack of adequate resources. So how will they respond?

Will educators recommit to their fundamental mission—to ensure high levels of learning for each student? Will they do more than chant the empty phrase, "All kids can learn," and, instead, begin to align all of their practices to promote that mission? Will they build shared knowledge and come to a deeper understanding of their professional craft? Will they work together collaboratively to address their problems and challenges because they know there is no hope of success if they work in isolation? Will they recognize that, in a very real sense, lives are hanging in the balance? Will they acknowledge that they cannot be indifferent to the success of our students in light of the overwhelming evidence that adult behaviors contribute enormously to that success? We urge them to do so, not for the sake of improved test scores, but for the sake of the dreams and aspirations of the children whose lives they touch.

Concluding Thoughts

We believe it is possible for educators to embrace a new story of the purpose of schooling and the way in which they must work to fulfill that purpose. That change cannot be brought about by legislation, but will instead require an ever-growing chorus of voices challenging the assumptions of the past and presenting a new narrative until we reach the tipping point at which schools that function as Professional Learning Communities at Work will represent the norm rather than the exception. As Abraham Lincoln (1862) once said, "We can succeed only by concert. It is not, 'can *any* of us do better?' but 'can we *all* do better?' The dogmas of the quiet past are inadequate to the stormy present. The occasion is piled high with difficulty, and we must rise with the occasion. As our case is new, so we must think anew and act anew" (p. 537). We urge all those who read this book, whatever their position or role, to become the persistent champions of a new and powerful story that will help members of this wonderful profession think and act anew.

RESOURCES

www.allthingsplc.info

Adlai E. Stevenson High School: www.d125.org/

Boones Mill Elementary School: http://bmill.frco.k12.va.us/

Cinco Ranch High School: http://kisdwebs.katyisd.org/campuses/crhs/
Pages/Default.aspx

Highland Elementary School: www.montgomeryschoolsmd.org/schools/
highlandes

Kildeer Countryside Community Consolidated School District 96:
www.district96.k12.il.us

Lakeridge Junior High School: http://lakeridge.alpinedistrict.org/

Prairie Star Middle School: www.bluevalleyk12.org/education/school/
school.php?sectionid=269

Sanger Unified School District: www.sanger.k12.ca.us/education/district/
district.php?sectionid=1

Whittier Union High School District: www.wuhsd.k12.ca.us/whittieruhsd/
site/default.asp

REFERENCES

ACT. (2008). *Summary table: National persistence to degree rates by institutional type.* Accessed at www.act.org/research/policymakers/pdf/retain_2008 .pdf on August 19, 2009.

ACT. (2009). *Fewer students returning to same school for second year of college.* Accessed at www.act.org/news/releases/2009/1-22-09.html on August 19, 2009.

Alliance for Excellent Education. (2006). *Issue brief: Paying double-inadequate high schools and community college remediation.* Accessed at www.all4ed.org/ files/archive/publications/remediation.pdf on August 19, 2009.

Axelrod, R. (2002). *Terms of engagement: Changing the way we change organizations.* San Francisco: Berrett-Koehler Publishers.

Barth, R. (2001). *Learning by heart.* San Francisco: Jossey-Bass.

Best of State. (2008). *Best of state: The premier recognition and awards program.* Accessed at www.bestofstate.org/about_us.php?bestofstatesess=1c2369 af70526b229736d589d8e042a4 on May 25, 2009.

Black, P., & Wiliam, D. (1998). The formative purpose: Assessment must first promote learning. In M. Wilson (Ed.), *Towards coherence between classroom assessment and accountability* (pp. 20–50). *103rd yearbook of the National Society for the Study of Education.* Chicago: University of Chicago Press.

Blanchard, K. (2007). *Leading at a higher level: Blanchard on leadership and creating high performing organizations.* Upper Saddle River, NJ: Prentice Hall.

Bossidy, L., & Charan, R. (2002). *Execution: The discipline of getting things done.* New York: Crown Business.

Bottoms, G. (1998). *Things that matter most in improving student learning.* Atlanta: Southern Regional Education Board.

Brookover, W. (1979). *School social systems and student achievement: Schools can make a difference.* Santa Barbara, CA: Praeger.

Brooks, D. (2006, October 6). Pillars of cultural capital. *New York Times.*

Bryk, A., & Schneider, B. (2004). *Trust in schools: A core resource for improvement.* New York: Russell Sage Foundation Publications.

Buckingham, M. (2005). *The one thing you need to know . . . about great managing, great leading and sustained individual success.* New York: Free Press.

Buffum, A., Mattos, M., & Weber, C. (2009). *Pyramid response to intervention: RTI, professional learning communities, and how to respond when kids don't learn.* Bloomington, IN: Solution Tree Press.

Bureau of Labor Statistics. (2008). *College enrollment and work activity of 2007 high school graduates.* Accessed at www.bls.gov/news.release/pdf/hsgec. pdf on August 19, 2009.

Burkett, H. (2006, May). Six don'ts of school improvement. *Center for Comprehensive School Reform Newsletter.* Accessed at www.centerforcsri.org/ index.php?option=com_content&task=view&id=325&Itemid=5 on March 14, 2008.

Bush, G. H. W. (1991, April 18). *Address to the nation on the National Education Strategy.* Accessed at http://bushlibrary.tamu.edu/research/public_papers .php?id=2895&year=&month= on March 29, 2008.

Champy, J. (1995). *Reengineering management: The mandate for new leadership.* New York: HarperCollins.

Chenoweth, K. (2009). It can be done, it's being done, and here is how. *Phi Delta Kappan, 91*(1), 38–43.

Coleman, J., Campbell, E., Hobson, C., McPartland, J., Mood, A., Weinfield, F., & York, R. (1966). *Equality of educational opportunity.* Washington, DC: U.S. Government Printing Office.

Collins, J. (2001). *Good to great: Why some companies make the leap . . . and others don't.* New York: Harper Business.

Collins, J., & Porras, J. (1997). *Built to last: Successful habits of visionary companies.* New York: Harper Business.

Commission on No Child Left Behind. (2007). *Beyond NCLB: Fulfilling the promise to our nation's children.* Washington, DC: The Aspen Institute.

Consortium on Productivity in the Schools. (1995). *Using what we have to get the schools we need.* New York: Teachers College Press.

Covey, S. (2002). Foreword. In K. Patterson, J. Grenny, R. McMillan, & A. Switzler (Eds.), *Crucial conversations: Tools for talking when stakes are high* (pp. xi–xiv). New York: McGraw-Hill.

Cox, K. (2008). What's working in Whittier. *Educational Leadership Online, 65*(8). Accessed at www.ascd.org/publications/educational_leadership/may08/vol65/num08/what's_working_in_whittier.aspx on May 25, 2009.

de Vise, D. (2008, December 19). School turns English learners into top achievers. *Washington Post.*

DuFour, R. (2002). *Through new eyes: Examining the culture of your school.* Bloomington, IN: Solution Tree Press (formerly National Educational Service).

DuFour, R. (2003). Central office support for learning communities. *The School Administrator, 60*(5), 15–16.

DuFour, R. (2007a). In praise of top-down leadership. *The School Administrator,* November, 38–42.

DuFour, R. (2007b). Once upon a time: A tale of excellence in assessment. In D. Reeves (Ed.), *Ahead of the curve: The power of assessment to transform teaching and learning* (pp. 253–267). Bloomington, IN: Solution Tree Press.

DuFour, R., DuFour, R., & Eaker, R. (2008). *Revisiting professional learning communities at work: New insights for improving schools.* Bloomington, IN: Solution Tree Press.

DuFour, R., DuFour, R., Eaker, R., & Karhanek, G. (2004). *Whatever it takes: How professional learning communities respond when kids don't learn.* Bloomington, IN: Solution Tree Press (formerly National Educational Service).

DuFour, R., DuFour, R., Eaker, R., & Many, T. (2006). *Learning by doing: A handbook for professional learning communities at work.* Bloomington, IN: Solution Tree Press.

DuFour, R., & Eaker, R. (1998). *Professional learning communities at work: Best practices for enhancing student achievement.* Bloomington, IN: Solution Tree Press (formerly National Educational Service).

Dweck, C. (2006). *Mindset: The new psychology of success.* New York: Ballantine Books.

Eaker, R., DuFour, R., & DuFour, R. (2002). *Getting started: Reculturing schools to become professional learning communities.* Bloomington, IN: Solution Tree Press (formerly National Educational Service).

Edmonds, R. (1979). Effective schools for the urban poor. *Educational Leadership,* *37*(1), 15–18, 20–24.

Edmonds, R. (1982). Programs of school improvement: An overview. *Educational Leadership, 40*(3), 4–11.

Elmore, R. (2006). *School reform from the inside out: Policy, practice, and performance.* Cambridge, MA: Harvard Education Press.

Fullan, M. (1997). Emotion and hope: Constructive concepts for complex times. In A. Hargreaves (Ed.), *Rethinking educational change with heart and mind* (pp. 216–233). Alexandria, VA: Association for Supervision and Curriculum Development.

Fullan, M. (2001). *Leading in a culture of change.* San Francisco: Jossey-Bass.

Fullan, M. (2006). *Turnaround leadership.* San Francisco: Jossey-Bass.

Fullan, M. (2007). *The new meaning of educational change* (4th ed.). New York: Teachers College Press.

Fullan, M. (2008). *The six secrets of change: What the best organizations do to help their organizations survive and thrive.* San Francisco: Jossey-Bass.

Gardner, H. (1990). *Leading minds.* New York: Basic Books.

Gardner, H., & Laskin, E. (1996). *Leading minds: An anatomy of leadership.* New York: HarperCollins.

Goldring, E., Porter, A., Murphy, J., Elliott, S., & Cravens, X. (2007). *Assessing learning-centered leadership: Connections to research, professional standards, and current practices.* Accessed at www.wallacefoundation.org/ SiteCollectionDocuments/WF/Knowledge%20Center/Attachments/PDF/ Assessing%20Learning-Centered%20Leadership.pdf on August 18, 2009.

Good, T. L. (1987). Two decades of research on teacher expectations: Findings and future directions. *Journal of Teacher Education, 38*(4), 32–47.

Hamel, G. (2002). *Leading the revolution: How to thrive in turbulent times by making innovation a way of life* (Rev. ed.) Cambridge, MA: Harvard Business Press.

Hargrove, T., & Stempel, G. (2007). *Scripps Howard News Service.* Accessed at www .scrippsnews.com/node/23421 on May 30, 2007.

Hattie, J. (2009). *Visible learning: A synthesis of over 800 meta-analyses relating to achievement.* New York: Routledge.

Hernez-Broome, G., Hughes, R., & Center for Creative Leadership. (2004). Leadership development: Past, present, and future. *Human Resource Planning, 27*(1), 24–32.

James, J. (1995, December). Thinking in the future tense. Keynote address presented at the 1995 Annual Conference of the National Staff Development Council, Vancouver, Canada.

James, J. (2008). *Telling a new story.* Accessed at www.jenniferjames.com/forum/ telling.htm on May 25, 2009.

Jenks, C., Smith, M., Ackland, H., Bane, M., Cohen, D., Grintlis, H., Heynes, B., & Michelson, S. (1972). *Inequality: A reassessment of the effects of family and schooling in America.* New York: Basic Books.

Kaine, T. (2008). *Press release on VIP awards.* Accessed at www.doe.virginia.gov/VDOE/newhome/pressreleases/2008/jan10.htm on May 25, 2009.

Kanter, R. (2004). *Confidence: How winning streaks and losing streaks begin and end.* New York: Three Rivers Press.

Kanter, R., IBM, Council of Chief State School Officers, & National Association of Elementary School Principals. (2002). *The IBM reinventing education change toolkit.* Accessed at www.reinventingeducation.org/re3web/ctk?browsetools&action=open_resourcelink&topicid=118&type=overview on May 25, 2009.

Kolta, G. (2007, January 3). A surprising secret to a longer life: Stay in school. *New York Times.* Accessed at www.nytimes.com/2007/01/03/health/03aging.html?ex=1325480400&en=b8ffe64abf1b1466&ei=5088&partner=rssnyt&emc=rss on March 17, 2008.

Kotter, J. (1996). *Leading change.* Boston: Harvard Business School.

Kotter, J., & Cohen, D. (2002). *Leading change.* Boston: Harvard Business School.

Kouzes, J., & Posner, B. (1987). *The leadership challenge: How to get extraordinary things done in organizations.* San Francisco: Jossey-Bass.

Lehrer, J. (2009). *How we decide.* Boston: Houghton-Mifflin Harcourt.

Lezotte, L. (1991). *Correlates of effective schools: The first and second generation.* Okemos, MI: Effective Schools Products. Accessed at www.effectiveschools.com/Correlates.pdf on May 25, 2009.

Lezotte, L. (2004). *Revolutionary and evolutionary: The effective schools movement.* Okemos, MI: Effective Schools Products. Accessed at www.effectiveschools.com/images/stories/RevEv.pdf on May 25, 2009.

Lickona, T. (2004). *Character matters: How to help our children develop good judgment, integrity, and other essential values.* New York: Touchstone Books.

Lickona, T., & Davidson, M. (2005). *Smart and good high schools: Integrating excellence and ethics for success in school, work, and beyond.* Cortland, New York: Center for the 4th and 5th Rs (Respect and Responsibility), and Washington, DC: Character Education Partnership.

Lincoln, A. (1862). Annual message to Congress. In R. Basler (Ed.), *The collected works of Abraham Lincoln, Vol. 5* (pp. 518–537). New Brunswick, NJ: Rutgers University Press.

Little, J. (2006). *Professional community and professional development in the learning-centered school.* Washington, DC: National Education Association.

Louis, K., Kruse, S., & Marks, H. (1996). Schoolwide professional community. In F. Newmann (Ed.), *Authentic achievement: Restructuring schools for intellectual quality* (pp. 179–204). San Francisco: Jossey-Bass.

Marzano, R. (2003). *What works in schools: Translating research into action.* Alexandria, VA: Association for Supervision and Curriculum Development.

Maslow, A. (1966). *The psychology of science: A reconnaissance.* New York: Harper.

McKinney, M. (2005, Fall). *The persistence of vision.* Accessed at www.leadershipnow.com/Persistence_of_Vision.html on May 23, 2009.

McLaughlin, M., & Talbert, J. (2001). *Professional communities and the work of high school teaching.* Chicago: University of Chicago Press.

McLaughlin, M., & Talbert, J. (2006). *Building school-based teacher learning communities: Professional strategies to improve student achievement.* New York: Teachers College Press.

National Association of Elementary School Principals. (2002). *Leading learning communities: Standards for what principals should know and be able to do.* Alexandria, VA: National Association of Elementary School Principals.

National Center for Education Statistics (NCES). (2007). *Percentages of degree-granting institutions offering remedial services.* Accessed at nces.ed.gov/programs/digets/d07/tables/dt07_317asp on May 25, 2009.

National Center on Response to Intervention. (2006). *What is response to intervention?* Accessed at www.rti4success.org/index.php?option=com_content&task=blogcategory&id=22&itemid=79 on May 25, 2009.

National Commission on Excellence in Education. (1983, April). *A nation at risk.* Accessed at www.ed.gov/pubs/NatAtRisk/risk.html on March 17, 2008.

National Commission on Teaching and America's Future. (2003). *No dream denied: A pledge to America's children.* Washington, DC: Author.

Newmann, F., Smith, B., Allensworth, E., & Bryk, A. (2001). Instructional program coherence: What it is and why it should guide school improvement policy. *Educational Evaluation and Policy Analysis, 23*(4), 297–321.

O'Neil, J. (1995, April). On schools becoming learning organizations: A conversation with Peter Senge. *Educational Leadership, 52*(7), 20–23.

Oraibi Elders, Arizona Hopi Nation. (2001). The Hopi elders speak: We are the ones we've been waiting for. *The Spirit of Maat,* 2. Accessed at www.spiritofmaat.com/messages/oct28/hopi.htm on August 19, 2009.

Patterson, K., Grenny, J., Maxfield, D., McMillan, R., & Switzler, A. (2008). *Influencer: The power to change anything.* New York: McGraw-Hill.

Patterson, K., Grenny, J., McMillan, R., & Switzler, A. (2002). *Crucial conversations: Tools for talking when stakes are high.* New York: McGraw-Hill.

Peters, T., & Austin, N. (1985). *A passion for excellence: The leadership difference.* New York: Warner Books.

Pfeffer, J., & Sutton, R. (2000). *The knowing-doing gap: How smart companies turn knowledge into action.* Boston: Harvard Business School.

Pfeffer, J., & Sutton, R. (2006). *Hard facts, dangerous half-truths and total nonsense: Profiting from evidence-based management.* Boston: Harvard Business School.

President's Commission on Excellence in Special Education. (2002). *A new era: Revitalizing special education for children and their families.* Washington, DC: U.S. Department of Education Office of Special Education and Rehabilitative Services. Accessed at www.ed.gov/inits/commissionsboards/whspecialeducation/reports/info.html on May 25, 2009.

Ravitch, D. (2007). *The future of NCLB.* Accessed at www.huffingtonpost.com/diane-ravitch/the-future-of-nclb_b_44227.html on March 24, 2008.

Reeves, D. (2000). *Accountability in action: A blueprint for learning organizations.* Denver: Advanced Learning Press.

Reeves, D. (2002). *The leader's guide to standards: A blueprint for educational equity and excellence.* San Francisco: John Wiley & Sons.

Reeves, D. (2004). *Accountability for learning: How teachers and school leaders can take charge.* Alexandria, VA: Association for Supervision and Curriculum Development.

Richardson, J. (2004). *From the inside out: Learning from the positive deviance in your organization.* Oxford, OH: National Staff Development Council.

Rose, L., & Gallup, A. (2006). The 38th Annual Phi Delta Kappa Gallup Poll of the public's attitudes toward the public schools. *Phi Delta Kappan, 88*(1), 41–56.

Rutter, M. (1979). *Fifteen thousand hours.* Cambridge, MA: Harvard University Press.

Saphier, J. (2005). *John Adams' promise: How to have good schools for all our children, not just for some.* Acton, MA: Research for Better Teaching.

Schein, E. (1992). *Organizational culture and leadership.* San Francisco: Jossey-Bass.

Schmoker, M. (2001). *Results fieldbook: Practical strategies for dramatically improved schools.* Alexandria, VA: Association for Supervision and Curriculum Development.

Schmoker, M. (2003). First things first: Demystifying data analysis. *Educational Leadership, 60*(5), 22–24.

Schmoker, M. (2004). Tipping point: From feckless reform to substantive instructional improvement. *Phi Delta Kappan, 85*(6), 424–432.

Schools to Watch. (2004). *Organizational structures and processes.* Accessed at www.schoolstowatch.org/OurCriteria/OrganizationalStructure/tabid/123/Default.aspx on August 19, 2009.

Senge, P., Kleiner, A., Roberts, C., Ross, R., & Smith, B. (1994). *The fifth discipline fieldbook: Strategies and tools for building a learning organization.* New York: Currency Doubleday.

Sergiovanni, T. (2005). *Strengthening the heartbeat: Leading and learning together in schools.* San Francisco: Jossey-Bass.

Snyder, C. R. (1991). The will and the ways: Development and validation of an individual-differences measure of hope. *Journal of Personality and Social Psychology, 60*(4), 570–585.

Stiggins, R. (2007). Assessment *for* learning: An essential foundation of productive instruction. In D. Reeves (Ed.), *Ahead of the curve: The power of assessment to transform teaching and learning* (pp. 59–76). Bloomington, IN: Solution Tree Press.

Stiggins, R., & DuFour, R. (2009). Maximizing the power of formative assessments. *Phi Delta Kappan, 90*(9), 640–644.

Swanson, C. (2008). Cities in crisis: A special analytical report on high school graduation. Bethesda, MD: Editorial Projects in Education Research Center. Accessed at www.americaspromise.org/~/media/Files/Our%20 Work/Dropout%20Prevention/Cities%20in%20Crisis/Cities_In_ Crisis_Report_2008.ashx on April 4, 2009.

Thaler, R., & Sunstein, C. (2008). *Nudge: Improving decisions about health, wealth, and happiness.* New Haven, CT: Yale University Press.

Tichy, N. (1997). *The leadership engine: How winning companies build leaders at every level.* New York: Harper Business.

Tilly, W. D. (2006). Response to intervention: An overview. What is it? Why do it? Is it worth it? *The Special Edge, 19*(2), 1–3.

Tyack, D., & Cuban, L. (1995). *Tinkering toward utopia: A century of public school reform.* Cambridge, MA: Harvard University Press.

United States Census Bureau. (2008a). *Historical income tables—households.* Accessed at www.census.gov/hhes/www/income/histinc/h13.html on August 18, 2009.

United States Census Bureau. (2008b). *Public schools spent $9138 per student in 2006.* Accessed at www.census.gov/press-release/www/releases/archiveseducation/011747.html on May 25, 2009.

Weast, J. (2008). *Highland elementary named Maryland blue ribbon school.* Accessed at www.montgomeryschoolsmd.org/press/index.aspx?pagetype=showrelease&id=2442 on May 25, 2009.

Whittier Union High School District. (2008). *USC researchers confirm Whittier Union to be a "district of excellence."* Accessed at www.wuhsd.k12.ca.us/whittieruhsd/lib/whittieruhsd/usc_wuhsd_dist_excellence.pdf on August 19, 2009.

Wiliam, D., & Thompson, M. (2007). Integrating assessment with learning: What will it take to make it work? In C. A. Dwyer (Ed.), *The future of assessment: Shaping teaching and learning* (pp. 53–82). Mahwah, NJ: Lawrence Erlbaum Associates.

INDEX

A

action orientation, 182–183

Adlai E. Stevenson High School. *See* Stevenson High School, Adlai E.

Ainsworth, L., 30

Alexrod, R., 9

Allensworth, E., 182

Apollo 13 analogy, 227–228

assessments. *See* common formative assessments

attained curriculum, 34

B

balanced assessment processes, 34

Barth, R., 43, 207

Blanchard, K., 225

Boones Mill Elementary School, 4, 67, 175

   background, 67–68

   building shared knowledge of current reality, 68–70

   challenges, response to, 196–198

   collaborative teams for identifying students who need work, 71

   communication systems, creating, 79–80

   connecting special and general education, 77–78

   current situation at, 80–83

   leadership at, 187

   parent workshops, 75–76

   peer tutoring/buddy programs, 76

   resources and purposes, aligning, 71–77

   resources on, 86

   results and conclusions, 83–86, 213

   Save One Student program, 77

   tutor, use of floating, 72, 74–75

Brasic, B., 121–128, 202

Brookover, W., 14

Bryk, A., 182

Buckingham, M., 190

Buffum, A., 7, 19–21

Built to Last: Successful Habits of Visionary Companies (Collins and Porras), 172–173

Burkett, H., 193

Bush, G. H. W., 13

Bush, G. W., 15, 17

C

capacity building, 186

Cinco Ranch High School

   background, 121

   freshman and Fish Camp, 121–122

   groundwork for intervention, 122–123

   intervention at, 123–124

   Katy Management of Automated Curriculum, 122

   Katy Online Learning Academy, 124

   leadership at, 186–187

   resources on, 128

   results and conclusions, 126–128, 214

   technology, use of, 124–126

clarity of purpose, 180

Cobbs, B., 67, 80–81

Cohen, D., 225

coherence, 182

collaborative culture, 181

collaborative teams

    prerequisites, 25, 33–35

    resources for, 30

    role of, 8, 24

collaborative teams, learning process steps

    common formative assessments, administration of and analysis of results, 31–32

    common formative assessments, developing, 28–31

    curriculum maps/guides, creating, 27–28

    identify essential outcomes, 26–27

    proficiency target scores, establishing, 31

    strengths and weaknesses, identifying, 32–33

collective study of best practices, 181–182

Collins, J., 7, 124–125, 172–173, 224–225

Commission on Excellence in Special Education, 17–19

common formative assessments, 8–9

    administration of and analysis of results, 31–32

    balanced, 34

    defined, 28–29

    developing, 29–31

    prerequisites, 25

    summative versus, 28–29

Consortium on Productivity in the Schools, 182

continuous improvement, commitment to, 183–184

Covey, S., 227

Cravens, X., 221

Crucial Conversations (Patterson, Grenny, McMillan, and Switzler), 204

Cuban, L., 22

cultural shifts, 208–210

culture of compliance, 17

curriculum levels, 34–35

curriculum maps/guides

    creating, 27–28

    prerequisites, 25

D

Davidson, M., 173, 207

default option, 169–170

De Vise, D., 109

differentiated instruction, 40

discrepancy model, 17–18, 19

District 96. *See* Kildeer Countryside Community Consolidated School District 96,

DuFour, R., 3, 14, 16, 20, 24, 29, 142, 173, 205–206, 208

Dweck, C., 207, 210, 211

E

Eaker, R., 3, 14, 16, 20, 24, 29, 35, 142, 173, 208

Edmonds, R., 14, 215

education

    "all students can learn" versus "all students must learn," 14–16

    historical development, 13–14

Education for All Handicapped Children Act (Public Law 94-142) (1975), 17

Elliott, S., 221

Elmore, R., 151

endurance, 27

enrichment, 212–215

"Equality in Educational Opportunity," 13

essential outcomes, identifying, 26–27

F

fixed mindset, 210
formative assessments. *See* common
  formative assessments
Freeport Intermediate, 3–4
Fullan, M., 1, 3, 16, 141, 177, 179, 181,
  185, 186, 193

G

Gardner, J., 188
Goldring, E., 221
Good,T. L., 211
Grenny, J., 142, 168, 204
growth mindset, 210–212

H

Hamel, G., 225
Hattie, J., 8–9, 33, 184
Highland Elementary School
    background, 109–112
    Lindamood Phoneme Sequenc-
      ing Program, 115
    reading intervention, 114–117
    resources on, 119
    results and conclusions, 117–119,
      214
    scheduling intervention, 112–114
    SOAR to Success program, 115
    Wilson Reading System, 115

I

implemented curriculum, 34
implementing PLC in small steps,
  224–226
Individuals with Disabilities Education Act (IDEA), 19
Individuals with Disabilities Education Improvement Act (IDEIA)
  (2004), 7, 19, 176
*Influencer: The Power to Change Any-
  thing* (Patterson, Grenny, Maxfield,
  McMillan, and Switzler), 168
intended curriculum, 34

interventions, planning questions,
  221–224
IQ tests, 18

J

James, J., 10
Johnson, M., 151–162

K

Kanter, R. M., 11, 163, 225
Karhanek, G., 3, 20 , 142
Kildeer Countryside Community
  Consolidated School, District 96
    ASAP (After School Assistance
      Program), 134
    assessments and attention, 136
    background, 129–132
    challenges, response to, 199–200
    Double Dose program, 135
    leadership at, 189–190
    PACE (Providing Academic
      Challenge for Excellence) pro-
      gram, 135
    resources on, 139
    results and conclusions, 137–139
    SPEED Intervention Criteria, 133,
      134, 190
    systematic interventions, 132–135
knowledge, prerequisites, 25
Kotter, J., 225
Kouzes, J., 225

L

Lakeridge Junior High School
    background, 99–100
    challenges, response to, 198–199
    intervention at, 100–102
    intervention pyramid, 105
    leadership at, 187
    nonlearners, reaching, 103–104
    resources on, 108
    results and conclusions, 106–108,
      214–215

scheduling intervention, 102–103

students, support for, 106

teachers, support for, 104

leadership

autonomy within parameters, 188–190

positive assumptions about others, 186

role of, 185–190

situational, 187–188

support for, 188

widely dispersed, 186–188

Leadership Now, 9–10

learning

emphasis on, 7–8

intentions, 33–34

levels, 34–35

outcomes, determining if they are being met, 34

proficient students, working with, 35

student versus teacher responsibility for, 165–170

Learning by Doing (DuFour, DuFour, Eaker, and Many), 24

legislation/policies

Education for All Handicapped Children Act (Public Law 94-142) (1975), 17

Individuals with Disabilities Education Act (IDEA), 19

Individuals with Disabilities Education Improvement Act (IDEIA) (2004), 7, 19

No Child Left Behind (NCLB) Act, 6–7, 15–16

special education reform, need for, 17–19

Lehrer, J., 37, 227

leverage, 27

Lezotte, L., 14, 33–34, 212

Lickona, T., 173, 207

Lincoln, A., 228

Los Peñasquitos, 3

M

MacNaughton High School, Bernice, 218–220

Many, T., 24, 129–139

Marzano, R., 14, 34–35

Maslow, A., 175

Mattos, M., 7, 19–21, 218

Maxfield, D., 142, 168

McKinney, M., 9–10

McLaughlin, M., 23, 38, 121, 129, 181

McMillan, R., 142, 168, 204

mindset

fixed, 210

growth, 210–212

Murphy, J., 221

Myrtle, R., 110–118, 204–205

N

National Assessment of Educational Progress, 30

National Association of Elementary School Principals, 67, 109

National Center on Response to Intervention, 19

National Commission on Teaching and America's Future, 23

Nation at Risk, A, 15, 22

Newmann, F., 182

No Child Left Behind (NCLB) Act, 6–7, 15–16

O

Obama, B., 16

P

Patterson, K., 142, 168, 203, 204, 225

Peterson, G., 101–108, 199, 202, 203

Pfeffer, J., 12, 202

Pioneer Middle School, 217–218

planning questions, 221–224

Popham, W. J., 30

Porras, J., 172–173

Porter, A., 221

Posner, B., 225

Prairie Star Middle School
background, 87–88
assessments, use of, 93–96
challenges, response to, 198
collaboration, providing, 93
groundwork for PLC, 88–89
guided study periods, 90–91
intervention and enrichment at, 89–90
Learning Lab, 91, 198
leadership at, 187
PACE, 92
resources on, 98
results and conclusions, 96–98, 214
Scholastic READ, 92
Study Island, 92
support, methods of, 91–92
teacher practice, changing methods, 92–96
vision statement example, 94

prerequisites for systemic intervention, 6, 23–24, 25

President's Commission on Excellence in Special Education, 175, 176

professional learning communities (PLCs)
action, taking, 226–227
benefits to all students, 6
central/district offices, role of, 5
creating conditions for success, 11–12
cultural shifts, 208–210
defined, 7–9
enrichment, 212–215
implementing, in small steps, 224–226
legislation/policies, role of, 6–7
list of districts recognized as models for, 5
list of schools recognized as models for, 4–5
planning questions, 221–224
prerequisites, 6, 23–24, 25, 33–35
questions to ask about, 1–7
resistance to, 201–206
sustainability, 3–4
transferable issues, 4–5

Professional Learning Communities at Work: Best Practices for Enhancing Student Achievement (DuFour and Eaker), 173

proficiency standards
establishing target scores, 31
prerequisites, 25

purpose, clarity of, 180

pyramid of interventions, Stevenson's, 57

pyramid, strengthening the, 61–62

Pyramid Response to Intervention (Buffum, Mattos, and Weber), 7, 19–20

R

Rantz, L., 87–98, 198, 203, 205

Ravitch, D., 11

readiness, 27

Reeves, D., 27, 29, 30, 184

response to intervention (RTI), 7,
defined, 19–21
determinants of success for, 21
levels in, 19

results, focus on, 184–185

Revisiting Professional Learning Communities at Work (DuFour, DuFour, and Eaker), 14, 16, 24, 29, 43–44, 208

Richardson, J., 45, 65

Rutter, M., 14

S

Sanger Unified School District, 175
  administrative retreats, 158–159
  background, 151–153
  challenges, response to, 200–201
  interventions at, 153–155
  leadership skills of principals,
    developing, 155–156, 158, 189
  ongoing support and focus,
    159–160
  rectification, 154
  resources on, 162
  results and conclusions, 160–162
  Summits 2008–2009, 156–157
Saphier, J., 99, 179
Schmoker, M., 1, 33, 45, 181, 226
Senge, P., 37
Sergiovanni, T., 168
SMART goals, 24, 93
Smith, B., 182
Snyder, C. R., 11
special education
  reform, need for, 17–19
  role of, 175–176
  separated from general educa-
    tion, 18
specific learning disabilities (SLD), 17
  overidentification of students
    with, 18
Stevenson High School, Adlai E., 4, 45,
    168, 181, 184
  ACT exam, 63
  advanced placement exams, 63
  advisory program, 50–51
  challenges, response to, 193–196
  cocurricular programs, 51–52
  conferencing, 54
  Counselor Check-In program, 49
  Counselor Watch program, 47
  credits earned, 63
  enrichment at, 56–59
  freshman mentor program, 51

Good Friend program, 49
grade distribution, 62
Guided Study program, 55
interventions pyramid, 57
leadership at, 186, 187
a look back, 45–46
mentoring, 55–56
monitoring student progress,
    52–53
orientation day, 50
pre-enrollment initiatives, 46–49
proactive student registration, 47
pyramid of interventions, 57
pyramid, strengthening the,
    61–62
resources on, 66
results and conclusions, 64–66,
    213
state assessment, 62–63
support for students, 49, 53–54,
    60–61
Survival Skills for High School,
    summer course, 48–49
sustainability, 62–63
transition to high school, 50–53
tutoring, 54
Stiggins, R., 30
stories, power of, 9–11
student performance
  "all students can learn" versus "all
    students must learn," 14–16
  enrichment, 212–215
  historical look at, 13–14
  student versus teacher responsi-
    bility for, 165–170
students who do not learn
  time and support, need for,
    40–43
  traditional responses to, 37–40
Stults Road Elementary School,
    215–217
summative assessments, 28–29
Sunstein, C., 13, 168–169

Sutton, R., 12, 202

Switzer, A., 142, 168, 204

systematic interventions, challenges
to

confronting, 177

impact on higher levels of education, 170–172

neglect of the gifted and high-
achieving students, 174–175

philosophical concerns, 165–176

pragmatic concerns, 163–165

scheduling problems, 164–165

special education, role of,
175–176

staffing concerns, 163–164

student versus teacher responsibility for learning, 165–170

whole child needs, 172–174

systematic interventions, prerequisites,
6, 23–24, 25

T

Talbert, J., 23, 38, 121, 129, 181

teachers, ranking, 32

teamwork. *See* collaborative teams

Thaler, R., 13, 168–169

Thorstenson, S., 141–150

*Through New Eyes: Examining the Cul-
ture of Your School,* 37–39

Tichy, N., 7

Tilly, D., 20

time and support, need for, 40–43

time for intervention, prerequisites, 25

Tomlinson, C. A., 212–213

tutoring, 35–36

Tyack, D., 22

V

vertical articulation, 27

W

Weast, J., 110, 119

Weber, C., 7, 19–21

*Whatever It Takes: How Professional.
Learning Communities Respond
When Kids Don't Learn* (DuFour,
DuDour, Eaker, and Karhanek), 3,
20, 142

Whittier Union High School District

background, 141–143

challenges, response to, 200

leadership, dispersing, 143–146,
189

promoting prevention, 146

resources on, 150

results and conclusion, 148–150

systematic interventions, 147–148

Wiliam, D., 30

Revisiting Professional Learning Communities at Work™: New Insights for Improving Schools
Richard DuFour, Rebecca DuFour, and Robert Eaker
This 10th-anniversary sequel to *Professional Learning Communities at Work™* offers advanced insights on deep implementation, the commitment/consensus issue, and the human side of PLC. **BKF252**

Learning by Doing: A Handbook for Professional Learning Communities at Work™
Richard DuFour, Rebecca DuFour, Robert Eaker, and Thomas Many
The second edition of this pivotal action guide includes seven major additions that equip educators with essential tools for confronting challenges. **BKF416**

On Common Ground: The Power of Professional Learning Communities
Edited by Richard DuFour, Robert Eaker, and Rebecca DuFour
Examine a colorful cross-section of educators' experiences with PLC. This collection of insights from practitioners throughout North America highlights the benefits of PLC. **BKF180**

Collaborative Teams in Professional Learning Communities at Work: Learning by Doing
Richard DuFour, Rebecca DuFour, Robert Eaker, and Thomas Many
This video shows exactly what collaborative teams do. Aligned with the best-selling book *Learning by Doing*, it features unscripted footage of collaboration in action. **DVF023**

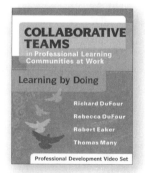